Infidel Poetics

Infidel Poetics

Riddles, Nightlife, Substance

DANIEL TIFFANY

The University of Chicago Press   Chicago and London

DANIEL TIFFANY is professor of English and comparative literature at the University of Southern California. His most recent critical study is *Toy Medium: Materialism and Modern Lyric* (2000), and his most recent book of poems is *Puppet Wardrobe* (2006).

The University of Chicago Press, Chicago 60637
The University of Chicago Press, Ltd., London

Printed in the United States of America
18 17 16 15 14 13 12 11 10 09   1 2 3 4 5
ISBN-13: 978-0-226-80309-8 (cloth)
ISBN-13: 978-0-226-80310-4 (paper)
ISBN-10: 0-226-80309-0 (cloth)
ISBN-10: 0-226-80310-4 (paper)

Library of Congress Cataloging-in-Publication Data
Tiffany, Daniel
Infidel poetics : riddles, nightlife, substance / Daniel Tiffany.
p. cm.
Includes bibliographical references and index.
ISBN-13: 978-0-226-80309-8 (cloth : alk. paper)
ISBN-10: 0-226-80309-0 (cloth : alk. paper)
ISBN-13: 978-0-226-80310-4 (pbk. : alk. paper)
ISBN-10: 0-226-80310-4 (pbk. : alk. paper)
1. Poetry—History and criticism. 2. Poetry—Social aspects. 3. Riddles in literature. 4. Nightlife in literature. 5. Cant. 6. Slang. I. Title.
PN1126.T54 2009
809′.93355—dc22   2009001339

♾ The paper used in this publication meets the minimum requirements of the American National Standard for Information Sciences—Permanence of Paper for Printed Library Materials, ANSI Z39.48-1992.

This book is dedicated to Nancy Worth Tiffany

Φύσις κρύπτεσθαι φιλεῖ

HERACLITUS

Contents

Introduction: Lyric Substance and Social Being

In popular music today, there is a flourishing market in poetic obscurity—in lyrics composed in various kinds of slang, jargon, or patois, which make little or no sense to most listeners. Animated by the inscrutable or garbled refrain, eclectic communities take root in the urban chatter of hip-hop, the Haitian creole of Wyclef Jean, the cockney slang of British punk, the Jamaican argot of reggae. No longer does the distribution of music recordings—whether CD or download—require translation of the lyric vernacular. The practice of including song lyrics and occasionally even glossaries in liner notes appears to have fallen from favor, precisely because the task of deciphering lyrics defies the latest poetic and cultural ethos of obscurity. At the same time, lyric obscurity in this context appears to function as a potent ingredient of publicity and celebrity, as the inevitable condition (and the indelible object) of exposure.

This kind of transaction, or seduction, has been going on for a very long time: in 1536, Robert Copland published the first treatise on "cant" (the jargon of the criminal underworld) in English. Among the canting lyrics he offered to the cultivated reader are the following lines:

Enow, enow. With bousy cove maund nase,
  Tour the patrico in the darkman case,
Docked the dell for a copper make:
  His watch shall feng a prounce's nab-cheat.
Cyarum, by Solomon, thou shalt peck my jere

In thy gan; for my watch it is nace gear;
Or the ben bouse my watch hath a wyn.[1]

Though Copland's reader might have been tantalized by the obscenity and sordid events depicted in this passage, Copland supplied no immediate translation of these lines, thereby leaving in suspense their exact meaning. By not glossing these "quire whids" (queer words), Copland exposed the tastes of a sentimental reader who, though unfamiliar with the "thieves' latin" in which these lines were composed, nevertheless found pleasure in "reading" such lyrics—without understanding them. In this respect, the reader of these lines in the twenty-first century, like his sixteenth-century counterpart, finds himself in the dark—a verbal darkness—and indeed is willing to pay for the pleasure of cruising the unknown in a text, to sample the tongue of the cultural "infidel" (a term first used in this sense in the eighteenth century and referring to a persona shaped at once by the criminal underworld and by political radicalism). Furthermore, the phenomenology of lyric obscurity (and perhaps its political economy as well) remains relatively constant across the conventionally formidable boundaries between literary and vernacular poetries—even as vernacular obscurity vividly and alluringly marks the horizons of class identity.

Lyric obscurity's possible role in the formation of expressive communities, or subcultures, of identification does not, one must emphasize, depend on the elimination of perplexity or incomprehension in the experience of poetry. On the contrary, if verbal obscurity in general presents an obstacle to communication, and obscurity in literature therefore leads to solipsism and hermeticism, then poetry—the genre of literature most commonly associated with obscurity—exercises a mode of linguistic being, so to speak, that involves only the most tenuous sorts of external relations. A poem that defies comprehension is windowless, one might say, at once inviolate and inscrutable. Yet poetry somehow *displays* the inwardness of language, practicing a kind of naked hermeticism.

I want to emphasize that my analysis of the poetics of obscurity should not be viewed as a defense of obscurantism or an apology for "difficult" poetry (in contrast to the plain style). Obscurity in poetry is a matter disclosed upon reception—what G. W. Leibniz calls "perception"—not something intrinsic to particular properties of the verbal artifact. All verbal phenomena are simultaneously obscure and transparent, taking into

1. Robert Copland, *The Highway to the Spital-House,* reprinted in A. V. Judges, ed., *The Elizabethan Underworld* (1930; New York: Octagon Books, 1965), 24.

account the range of possible responses—or the variability within a single response. Obscurity, from this perspective, is native to the ontology of poetry. More specifically, despite a recent "bubble" in the accreditation of poetry, the art of poetry persists today—as perhaps it always has—in cultural obscurity. Poetry, it's true, sustains a *visible* subculture, yet common resistance to poetry cannot be isolated from poetry's perceived resistance to communication. Most readers, including many literate and scholarly readers, find poetry to be perplexing or annoying. Indeed, even ordinary language in a poem strikes many readers as confusing, at once alienated and alienating. By contrast, a small coterie of readers (mostly poets and students of poetry) is so thoroughly habituated to lyric obscurity that all poetry—from this perspective—appears to be immune to the conditions of obscurity. Another segment of readers (and poets) advances a poetics of transparency, forgetting that even the most accessible poetry will be considered obscure by many readers.

Given the fact of lyric obscurity—perhaps the only fact a poem yields to its readers—one wonders what sort of bond, if any, a poem establishes with its readers, with the sensory realm evoked by its words, or with the society in which it appears (if indeed it makes an appearance). More to the point, after a century of programmatic obscurity, a great deal of serious poetry appears to have abandoned the task of communication, the will to directly influence common, public discourse and evolving conceptions of community. Must we therefore presume that the obscurity of poetry, in comparison with other genres and media, bars it from overt social engagement and, even more radically, that no viable model of relational being can be deduced from the conditions of lyric obscurity?

Historical attempts to make poetry more directly meaningful to social and political realities—that is, to resolve the tension between obscurity and social relevance—have generally called, at least implicitly, for poetry to become more transparent and accessible.[2] Even the most programmatic and highly politicized campaigns have made little progress, however, in establishing the social relevance of poetry or in revising the tastes of the dominant literary tradition (even advocates of the plain style), which still presumes a measure of obscurity in poetic composition. These failures are

2. Dana Gioia's essay "Can Poetry Matter?" may be the most visible recent effort to address what he calls the "divorce of poetry from the educated reader." One should note his emphasis on "the educated reader," yet he also seeks to address the interests of the "common reader": "To regain poetry's readership one must begin by meeting Williams's challenge to find what 'concerns many men,' not simply poets." Ultimately, for Gioia—citing Ezra Pound—recovering a larger audience for poetry must coincide with recognition of poetry's role in "keeping the nation's language clear and honest." Gioia, "Can Poetry Matter?" (1992), reprinted in Dana Gioia, *Can Poetry Matter? Essays on Poetry and American Culture* (Saint Paul, MN: Graywolf Press, 2002), 9, 17, 18.

not surprising, since lyric obscurity has been identified either as a problem, or as a virtue, at least since the modern revival of the category of the sublime by Boileau and Leibniz in the late seventeenth century. For lyric obscurity has traditionally been theorized during the modern period as a symptom—as the epitome—of the aesthetic experience of the sublime.[3] To insist periodically that poetry become more prosaic or more theatrical to expand its social horizons, its relational aptitude, seems therefore not only dubious as a political strategy but unsatisfactory as an aesthetic—and philosophical—program. Yet to admit defeat on these terms, to view poetry's relational character as inherently limited in scope, ignores the possibility that the solution to the problem of lyric sociability may lie in the principle of obscurity itself. From this perspective, obscurity, rather than being the principal impediment to poetry's social relevance, would provide the key to models of community derived specifically from the nature of lyric expression.

Even if a discussion of lyric expression were to remain focused strictly on the term "obscurity," one would have ample grounds for developing a *sociology* of incomprehension from certain rudimentary forms of lyric poetry. The deliberate obscurity of riddles, for example (a poetic genre with ancient roots, including the earliest secular poems in English), does not imply the absence of disclosure or sociability. A riddle, after all, is posed in the form of a question—a kind of secret, a literary secret—to be deciphered by the listener or reader. The lengthy Anglo-Saxon riddles of the Exeter Book manuscript serve as the impetus and object of a guessing game—a social configuration which converts the sound bite of the oracle into a literary toy, improvised in contests of wit on convivial occasions.

The relations implicit in the phenomenon of lyric obscurity, which extend far beyond the social configuration of the enigma, can be drawn out more fully with reference to the concepts of *privacy* and *secrecy*—terms oriented more explicitly toward the *sociality* of hermetic phenomena. In his essay "The Sociology of Secrecy," Georg Simmel argues that "secrecy is a universal sociological form," an orientation toward secrecy which treats it as a communicative event.[4] Simmel emphasizes "the formal attractiveness of secrecy" (466), viewing it as a "relation mysterious in form, regard-

3. In the preface to his translation of Longinus's *On the Sublime* (1674), Nicolas Boileau makes a distinction between sublime experience and the "sublime *style*" (which he illustrates with a passage of verse from the Old Testament). Leibniz wrote "On the Secrets of the Sublime" two years later, in 1676, a text that would leave its mark on Edmund Burke's discussion of poetry and the sublime in his *Philosophical Enquiry into the Origin of our Ideas of the Sublime and the Beautiful* (1757).

4. Georg Simmel, "The Sociology of Secrecy and of Secret Societies," trans. Albion W. Small, *American Journal of Sociology* 11, no. 4 (January 1906): 463. Hereafter, page numbers are given in the text for further references to this source.

less of its accidental content" (464). Thus, "the secret element in societies is a primary sociological fact, a definite mode and shading of association" (483). Simmel stresses "the usefulness of secrecy" (462) and regards its application as a "sociological technique" (464), an orientation which leads to a heightened awareness of the material *means* of secrecy. Though secrecy may require practicing "the art of silence" (474), language—especially poetry—remains the principal medium of secrecy.[5]

Every social relation possesses a "quantum of secrecy" (463), and one may therefore assess the "ratio of secrecy" in any relational structure (467). Thus, every relation is secretive to some degree, yet every secret forms a relation—a dialectic evident in the formation of secret societies and social underworlds. Because of its sociological properties, secrecy implies exposure, yet one could go further, following Simmel's argument, and say that every secret is an open secret. From this perspective, a secret, as Diderot defines it in the *Encyclopédie,* is "everything that we have confided to someone, or that someone has confided to us, with the intention that it not be revealed."[6] A secret, according to this view, is always engendered by an act of communication; no phenomenon characterized by secrecy, privacy, or obscurity can therefore be entirely closed or inscrutable.

Returning to the scene of poetry's appropriation of cant, we find that a basic anatomy of obscurity's social configuration must then acknowledge from the start two basic orientations to the phenomenon: the first—a position of dramatic communal responsibilities—is that of the initiate, the one who speaks or understands "cant," the secret tongue; the second position is that of the stranger, the outsider, for whom the secret tongue sounds like gibberish—like cant. Although the outsider's relation to cant appears to be characterized by an absence of communication, it is not a position, as the historical appeal and social phenomenology of lyric obscurity suggest, that is without social or expressive relations. Indeed, both the initiate (who understands cant) and the stranger (who does not) may participate in powerful social and expressive networks based on the secret tongue.

Typically, in the wake of modernist practice, literary critics frame the

5. Mary Mulvey Roberts notes the central paradox of secrecy as a communicative event: "If it can be assumed that the primary function of language is communication, then the notion of a private or even secret language is paradoxical. But in practice the public and private may not be diametrically opposed." Roberts, "Masonics, Metaphor, and Misogyny: A Discourse of Marginality," in *Languages and Jargons: Contributions to a Social History of Language,* ed. Peter Burke and Ray Porter (Cambridge, UK: Polity Press, 1995), 133.

6. Denis Diderot, *Encyclopédie; ou Dictionnaire raisonnée des sciences, des arts et des métiers* (Neufchatel: Faulché, 1765), 14:562–563. The passage occurs in the first entry under the heading "Secrets."

question of lyric obscurity in terms of "difficulty," a condition always susceptible, in principle, to the restoration of meaning.[7] Obscurity then becomes a problem that may be resolved through interpretation or, for those critics who wish to avoid the stigma of hermeneutics, through experimental strategies of *reading,* extending beyond annotation to more critical and disruptive procedures, such as appropriation, reformulation, and deletion.[8] Psychoanalytic critics have refined and, let us say, reenchanted formalist strategies to develop intricate models of cryptonymy or cryptography, which proceed under the assumption as well that meaning and reference may be produced by deciphering, by the act of reading.[9] Hermeneutical or cryptographic approaches to lyric obscurity (preoccupied with extracting meaning from texts whose meaning is strategically or incidentally impaired) fail therefore to come to terms with the phenomenology of unknowing, of unresolvable obscurity. At the core of these methodologies, blind faith in the efficacy—or the desirability—of "reading" precludes understanding of the manifold tasks of obscurity, per se, and indeed ignores altogether the spectacle of its pragmatic, aesthetic, and social effects.

Most accounts of lyric obscurity preserve as a default position (even

7. George Steiner breaks down the possible "difficulty" encountered by readers of poetry (the essay focuses solely on poetry) into four categories: contingent, modal, tactical, and ontological. While all four categories of difficulty require of the reader "the reconstructive acquaintance achieved by virtue of knowledge and archaeology of feeling," Steiner limits his use of the term "obscurity" to the latter two categories (tactical and ontological). Steiner, *On Difficulty and Other Essays* (Oxford: Oxford University Press, 1978), 32. James Longenbach astutely identifies the correlation between "the resistance to poetry" in literate society (on account of its "difficulty") and poetry's resistance to *itself*—to language and its own lyric devices. Longenbach, *The Resistance to Poetry* (Chicago: University of Chicago Press, 2005), 1.

8. In a recent critical study addressing examples of "poetic illegibility," Craig Dworkin contrasts "modernism's hermeneutic concern for 'interpretation'" with his own adversarial method of "paragrammatic 'misreading.'" In the end, however (as the term "illegibility" implies), strategies of "misreading" cannot escape the aspirations of reading (and perhaps of understanding), as Dworkin acknowledges: "If I have, at times, abjured interpretation in the following pages, it has only been to give onto *reading*." Dworkin, *Reading the Illegible* (Evanston, IL: Northwestern University Press, 2003), xx, xxiv.

9. It would probably be more accurate to say that neoformalist critics such as Dworkin have sought to disenchant the earlier psychoanalytic models of obscurity. Nicolas Abraham and Maria Torok, for example, developed a psychoanalytic theory of secrecy—what they call a "cryptonymy"—focusing on the phenomenon of verbal crypts and the methods necessary for "deciphering" these occluded signs. Attempting to characterize the extreme obscurity of the particular class of symbols they are investigating, Abraham and Torok write: "it is as if the sense of the words were shrouded by an enigma too dense to be deciphered by known forms of listening." Abraham and Torok, *The Wolf Man's Magic Word: A Cryptonymy,* trans. Nicholas Rand (Minneapolis: University of Minnesota Press, 1986), 79. Despite the avowed "hieroglyphical" nature of Abraham and Torok's orientation, Jacques Derrida, in his foreword to *Wolf Man's Magic Word,* suggests: "let us set aside the name *hermetics* to designate the science of cryptological interpretation. It is not a form of hermeneutics." Derrida, "*Fors:* The Anglish Words of Nicolas Abraham and Maria Torok," in Abraham and Torok, *Wolf Man's Magic Word,* xiv–xv.

when it is acknowledged as failing on its own terms) the implicit orientation of hermeneutical or cryptographic models of reading. John Hamilton, for example, in his thoughtful study of Pindar's obscurity and its reception, writes: "Clarification, then, is not to be renounced, but upheld. Still, instead of explicating a dark passage as something that is in fact clear, my readings often reveal that an obscurity in the text should be clearly acknowledged as obscure."[10] Instead of compelling Hamilton to search for an alternative paradigm apart from the question of meaning, however, the unresolvable obscurity of Pindar's poetry simply becomes a mirror reflecting back the "truth" of the hapless reader: "recognition of infinite veiling has the effect of finding the truth, not of a discoverable Greece, but of us, the interpreters."[11] Hamilton's inability to relinquish the paradigm of communication, even when it fails completely, robs the poem of any possible expressive or pragmatic effects resulting from its obscurity—precisely those effects which might help us to account for obscurity, not simply as a failure of meaning, but as a productive phenomenon in its own right.

To his credit, George Steiner reserves a place in his anatomy of "difficulty" (tied inescapably to lyric poetry) for what he calls "ontological difficulty," which "puts in question the existential suppositions that lie behind poetry as we have known it."[12] Given the erudition of Steiner's treatment of obscurity, one is surprised to find no reference to the long history of theorizing lyric obscurity as a central feature of the aesthetic experience of the sublime, which in its most extreme forms produces the catastrophic effects (in language) associated with ontological difficulty. Nevertheless, to begin to understand the "ontological" aspect of obscurity (with the implication of its relation to metaphysics), one might activate the problem of the sublime, first, by suspending hermeneutical and cryptographic approaches to lyric obscurity and, second, by pursuing a critique of obscurity rooted in concepts of action, expression, and aesthetic captivation. By its very nature, the problematic of lyric obscurity requires that one isolate the moment of exchange or enactment, focusing not so much on a poem's composition or construction—and this point is implicit in Steiner's category of ontological difficulty—as on its *reception* by the reader, on poetic readership, and on the social configuration of poetry.

Furthermore, in questioning the "existential suppositions" of lyric

10. John Hamilton, *Soliciting Darkness: Pindar, Obscurity, and the Classical Tradition* (Cambridge, MA: Harvard University Press, 2003), 9.

11. Hamilton, *Soliciting Darkness,* 9–10.

12. Steiner, *On Difficulty,* 41.

obscurity, one must reject as well the common presumption, associated with models of textual difficulty, that obscurity is principally a feature of works considered to be arcane, virtuosic, or deliberately experimental. On the contrary, taking into account the social implications of the term "obscure," one must consider the possibility that literary conceptions of obscurity may be rooted in the social *misunderstanding* of demotic speech, thereby shifting the phenomenology of obscurity away from its conventional association with elite culture and toward the lyric vernacular—especially poems composed in slang, jargon, or dialect. From the perspective of the educated elite, therefore, lyric obscurity, by its ability to evoke the dangerous speech of various social underworlds, produces a kind of *sociological* sublime—a significant revision of theories linking poetry and the sublime. Instead of reinforcing the traditional association of sublimity and elevation, lyric obscurity may trigger a variation of the sublime associated with the abject: a vernacular sublime (a disposition inherent in the etymological—and dialectical—correspondence between the terms "sublime" and "subliminal"). Focusing on the pragmatic and expressive correspondences integral to lyric obscurity furthermore compels attention to vernacular *culture*—to the history of nightlife, in particular—especially as it pertains to class identity. It is no accident, with regard to correspondences between lyric and sociological modes of obscurity, that the words "slang" and "slum" both originate in canting speech and appear to be related etymologically.[13] Indeed, the word "slum" was used for a time as a synonym for "cant" or "jargon."[14]

If semantic intelligibility (or meaningfulness) is to be rejected as the principal framework for assessing the function of lyric obscurity, then one must necessarily ask: what sort of linguistic, or literary, models would be useful in examining the phenomenon of obscurity? Setting aside the question of meaning, lyric obscurity might be regarded principally as an *event* or deed, as a way of *doing things with words* (in J. L. Austin's memorable phrase).[15] This pragmatic orientation has the advantage of aligning obscurity with certain existing, if anachronistic, poetic forms: charms,

13. Mike Davis cites the earliest published definition of the word "slum" (a "racket" or "criminal trade"), which is found in J. H. Vaux's 1812 *Vocabulary of the Flash Language*. Davis, *Planet of Slums* (London: Verso, 2006), 21. The word "slang," as I explain more fully in chapter 5, is a verb meaning "to display stolen goods, or some kind of anomaly, in a marketplace."

14. The *Oxford English Dictionary* records the cant word "slum" as meaning "nonsensical talk or writing" but also "gypsy jargon or cant." The word's association with verbal obscurity may be related to the fact that "slum" as a verb can also mean "to hide, to avoid observation."

15. J. L. Austin, *How to Do Things with Words* (Cambridge, MA: Harvard University Press, 1962). Austin, however, would have rebelled at the idea of viewing obscurity as the basis of a "felicitous" speech act.

spells, curses, oaths, and other performative models. In this guise, the binding properties of lyric obscurity would also be implicated in the social and economic apparatus of the "society of the spectacle," realizing in the most sinister fashion a dialectic of verbal fetishism.

A pragmatic consideration of obscurity—including its allure as a literary commodity—would seem to ignore, however, the natural phenomenon anchoring the *trope* of verbal obscurity: the material dark (a physical condition or substance, appearing to possess properties of an incorporeal entity). Yet Marx's theory of commodity fetishism presumes and indeed articulates a theory of *substance*—a phantasmagorical substance capable of blinding us to the palpable and useful qualities of things. More fundamentally, the curious ontology of the fetish, which expresses the social and economic implications of obscurity, accords as well with the incorporeal properties of *metaphysical* substance—that is to say, with the insensible and inscrutable substance of *Being* in the broadest sense.

The innate obscurity of metaphysical substance (which the philosopher makes manifest, paradoxically, by seeking to define it) therefore possesses the curious immunity—and the telling secrecy—of vernacular speech. Yet theorizing the transitivity, or sociability, of obscurity, which presumes an array of pragmatic "obscurity effects" generated by the hermetic phenomenon, risks ignoring, in a more rigorous sense, the absolute conditions of lyric obscurity: solipsism, inscrutability, meaninglessness. Two distinct models of social being therefore arise from the conditions of lyric obscurity: the first, a matrix of counterfeit relations contingent on various obscurity effects (at once social, economic, and aesthetic) generated by the poetic enigma; the second, a constellation, or mass, of expressive relations between entities which are essentially solipsistic.

What sorts of relations obtain between entities whose relational being is inherently limited, or proscribed altogether? The significance of metaphysics, or the history of metaphysics, for a theory of lyric obscurity pertains precisely to the problem of solipsistic relations, to transactions occurring in the absence of ostensible relations. For a theory of metaphysics seeks to explain relations between domains which appear to be incommensurable: Being and beings, substance and phenomenon. In addition, more specifically, the most powerful and enduring theories of metaphysical substance posit the existence of discontinuous elements, ranging from the concept of the atom (as a framework for metaphysical materialism) to the monads, or "immaterial atoms," of Leibniz's "Monadology." Metaphysics, from this perspective, can offer critical insights into the relational powers of hermetic forms.

A philosophy of metaphysics is judged by its simplicity, universality, and comprehensiveness—that is, by its capacity to explain not only the nature of Being, or substance, but also the nature of mere phenomena—such as physical bodies—which certain conceptions of Being may not, in the strictest sense, encompass. A good metaphysics must therefore furnish a theory of the unreal, in addition to leaving room for what Leibniz calls "courtesy substances" and "semi-beings." In this regard, to view lyric obscurity as a "courtesy substance"—the very substance of poetry—allows one to treat the verbal artifact as a "semi-being" straddling the divide between sensible and insensible orders of existence.

If metaphysics requires one to think about *Being* as a substance distinct from the sensory appearance of things yet also secretly gathering all things into a single order of existence, then metaphysics may be said to provide an erotic dimension to our perception of the discontinuity of things. Lyric obscurity, by analogy, serves as an expressive medium, or substance, harmonizing disparate phenomena, just as sociological obscurity defines the basic condition of countless subcultures and historical underworlds. The obscurity of Being, it may be said, permeates our knowledge of sensible things, though Being itself may, as Heidegger claimed, be forgotten.

The momentous—and seemingly anachronistic—turn toward the concept of Being associated with Heidegger's thinking (which was in fact anticipated by renewed interest in Leibniz's "Monadology" around the turn of the century) required that Heidegger redefine the idealist orientation of metaphysics. He undertook this task by approaching the question of Being (*Dasein*) from, paradoxically, a phenomenological perspective—that is, he sought to define Being (substance) in terms of what it is *not* (phenomenon)—a model possessing the accidental earthliness of Plato's theorization of beauty. More importantly, he identified language as the phenomenological ground of Being, declaring famously: "language is the house of Being."[16] By asserting that Being dwells in language, Heidegger nevertheless sustained the main line of Western metaphysics, beginning with the equation of *logos* and substance in Parmenides and continuing through the linguistic fundamentalism of Leibniz's theory of monads.

The verbal phenomenology of Heidegger's metaphysics rests on a bold reconsideration of philosophy's general orientation, marked by a controversial appraisal of poetry's significance for philosophy: "Philosophy never arises out of science or through science," Heidegger declared; "only poetry stands in the same order as philosophy and its thinking."[17] By

16. Martin Heidegger, "Letter on Humanism," in *Basic Writings,* by Martin Heidegger, ed. David Farrell Krell (San Francisco: HarperCollins, 1993), 217.

17. Martin Heidegger, *An Introduction to Metaphysics,* trans. Ralph Manheim (New Haven, CT: Yale University Press, 1959), 26.

adopting this position, by turning metaphysics away from science and idealist speculation toward poetry and phenomenology, Heidegger implicated metaphysics in a kind of philosophical *vernacular,* in what is still seen in certain quarters as a matrix of frivolous reflection. One could even claim that he *vulgarized*—quite literally, if we understand the linguistic connotations of that term—the conventional equation of *logos* and Being by focusing on the lyric vernacular, by asserting that one could understand Being (*Dasein*) only by thinking poetically (*denkend-dichtend*). Conversely, his extraordinary essays on the nature of poetry and poets—surely among the most important thinking about poetry in the twentieth century—came about through his efforts to understand poetry's role in disclosing the nature of metaphysical substance. Indeed, his eccentric readings of Hölderlin, Trakl, and Rilke suggest that Being must be located, not simply in "the house of language," but in the house of *poetry*.

Although Heidegger remained notoriously silent about the political implications of his theory of *Dasein,* his alignment of poetry and metaphysics reminds us that certain conceptions of lyric substance (associated, for example, with the poetics of the riddle or the canting song) combine obscurity and transmissibility in ways that have distinct implications for social being. In the history of thinking about metaphysics, Leibniz's theory of "perceptive" monads, which relies on certain basic principles derived from his thinking about language, holds that substance is nothing other than "perception," a thesis (essential to Romantic poetics) which becomes the basis for a manifold doctrine of "clear but confused perception." Leibniz thus posits a mode of obscurity integral to the nature of Being itself, a foundational obscurity replicated in our understanding of the phenomenal world, in forms of sociability, and (of course) in language itself. The phenomenological obscurity of poetry therefore offers a genetic model of the essential obscurity of Being, fashioned by Leibniz in the image of language itself (in the image, that is, of its capacity for "clear but confused perception"). Leibniz thus conceives of the aesthetic category of the sublime, for example, as an expression of the metaphysical obscurity of monadic perception (the substance of Being). The sublime properties of language, inextricably linked to its reception and transmission, constitute as well the basis of "obscure" forms of sociability.

Lyric substance, refracted through the essential discontinuity of monadological Being, allows for the existence of certain kinds of hermetic yet expressive communities, certain social underworlds, within the global fabric. In other words, the transitivity of the verbal enigma—its conjoining of destruction and revelation, its *apocalyptic* nature—reminds us of the possibility of communities that defy the seemingly inexorable logic of transparency and continuity implicit in the social imaginary of the Internet. In contrast to the new ethos of instant accessibility and universality (i.e., the dogma of translation), the poetics of obscurity offers a blueprint for monadic communities which are at once inscrutable and reflective, discontinuous and harmonious, solipsistic and expressive. Lyric obscurity therefore needs to be regarded, not as an impediment to social being—if that term may encompass a productive negation of its general significance—but rather as the very ground, or medium, of negative sociability: a splintering of mass experience into "sleeper cells," the fragmentation of a posthuman world into countless underworlds.

The monadic constellation is not so much a community (since that word implies communication) as a *mass* of elements unified by expressive correspondences. Noam Chomsky's early writing on the philosophical foundations of his theory of the "deep structure" of language (a deterministic model) emphasizes the expressive and poetic, rather than the communicative, functions of language—and he points to Leibniz's thought as a precursor to his own model of linguistic fundamentalism.[18] The sociology implicit in a monadic, or Chomskian, theory of language manifests itself in historical constellations of individuals whose relations are radically mediated, or dispossessed—that is, who have no direct relations with one another as individuals or with other monadic subcultures.

Although monadic "communities" (whose elements never engage in any form of direct communication with one another) are essentially linguistic in nature, language need not play any pragmatic role in the phenomenology of the monadic constellation. In other words, it is not the appearance, or use, of language but its *substance* that determines the monadic character of the "community." At the same time, since Leibniz indicated that monadic perception is akin to *reading,* one could consider readership itself—though not because of its literal or phenomenological dependence on language—as an expressive model of monadic relations. To activate effectively the analogy of monadic readership, one must presume that a set of readers reads but a single text and, indeed, that this text constitutes the only knowledge they possess of an external world. All readers of that text know in common—from diverse perspectives—the world produced by that text. Yet the "reality" they "perceive" together depends on a text consumed in complete isolation from one another. So, the fact that this text is *common* knowledge depends solely on expressive and reciprocal correspondences among the solipsistic renders. All who

18. Noam Chomsky, *Cartesian Linguistics: A Chapter in the History of Rationalist Thought* (New York: Harper and Row, 1966), 107–108 nn. 110–111.

are privy to the world of that text thus share expressive knowledge of that world, and insofar as "reality" is restricted to that text, they have knowledge of one another's "perceptions"—though they remain unknown to one another, nameless, and without any direct form of interaction. The obscurity of their expressive relations with one another—nothing more than the act of reading the same text—constitutes for them, as readers, their social being, indeed, the very substance of Being itself.

A more palpable model (though still anonymous, sublime, dispossessed) of the monadic constellation may be found in what Leo Bersani has called the "anticommunal model of connectedness" intrinsic to the homosexual underworld of the bathhouse: a "model for intimacies devoid of intimacy."[19] Further, exposing a sociological sublime magnetized by abjection, these singular transactions take place in a larger topology—a genuine monadology—of asocial relations: "the aversion of inverts to the society of inverts may be the necessary basis for a new community of inversion."[20] Advancing Bersani's thesis, Lee Edelman has theorized what he calls "queer negativity" and "its figural status as resistance to the viability of the social."[21] Edelman's emphasis on the "figural status" of the monadology of the bathhouse is furthermore critical to his understanding of the interdependence between queer negativity and linguistic obscurity: "queer theory must always insist on its connection to the vicissitudes of the sign, to the tension of the signifier's collapse into the letter's cadaverous materiality and its participation in a system of reference wherein it generates meaning itself."[22] Edelman's implication of queer theory in the "cadaverous materiality" of language—a verbal underworld—reminds us that the monadology of the bathhouse, like the "privacy effects" of the closet, is a structure of social and lyrical obscurity whose significance extends well beyond the trick vocabulary and the invisible sites of homosexuality. From this perspective, the monadologies of the bathhouse and of the shrinking domain of modern readership become available as general models of social hermeticism compounding the substance of lyric obscurity.

19. Leo Bersani, *Homos* (Cambridge, MA: Harvard University Press, 1995), 127–128.

20. Bersani, *Homos,* 131.

21. Lee Edelman, *No Future: Queer Theory and the Death Drive* (Durham, NC: Duke University Press, 2005), 6, 3.

22. Edelman, *No Future,* 7.

ONE

The Spectacle of Obscurity

Hark! hark! the dogs do bark,
The Beggars are coming to town.
Some in rags & some in jags,
And some in velvet gowns.
MOTHER GOOSE RHYME

When one of the warriors in *The Iliad* finds himself in mortal danger on the battlefield, a god will sometimes rescue him by making him invisible. Homer describes these disappearances by saying that the god "hides" (κάλύπτω) the warrior in "thick mist" (ἠέρι πολλῇ) or "darkness" (νυκτὶ).[1] The German critic and philosopher G. E. Lessing identifies these tropes as examples of the special effects of which poetry alone—in contrast to painting—is capable: "concealment by cloud or night is, for the poet, nothing more than a poetic expression for rendering a thing invisible."[2] Further, he explains, "it was not because a cloud appeared in the place of the abducted body, but because we think of that which is wrapped in mist as being invisible" (69). Hence, the reader comprehends the *effects* of the verbal emblem of darkness.

1. One episode with Aphrodite and Paris occurs in book 3, line 381, where the hero is said to "be wrapped in thick mist." The same verbal formula recurs in the description of Hector's abduction by Apollo, in book 20, line 444. A variation of this formula, "enshrouded by darkness," characterizes Idaeus's abduction by Hephaistus in book 5, line 23. Homer, *The Iliad,* trans. Richmond Lattimore (Chicago: University of Chicago Press, 1973). The Greek term for "mist" or "cloud," αήρ, is the root of the English word "air."

2. Gotthold Ephraim Lessing, *Laocoön: An Essay on the Limits of Painting and Poetry,* trans. Edward Allen McCormick (Baltimore, MD: Johns Hopkins University Press, 1984), 68. Hereafter, page numbers are given in the text for further references to this source.

Lessing, for this reason, declares, "the cloud is a true hieroglyphic" (68): the dark mist becomes an index of disappearance. Since the substances—air and obscurity—enveloping the endangered mortal in the trope of disappearance may be understood as figures for the meteoric phenomenon of the poem itself—for the rhapsodic "air" and its rhetorical darkness—one must conclude that the obscurity of poetry in general is likewise a "hieroglyphic," a substance, to be deciphered (not for its content, but for its expressive and pragmatic effects). Further, the device of the Homeric mist, a luxurious accessory of the gods, offers a thesis concerning the task of poetic obscurity, an image of its aesthetic function: obscurity is a way of making things disappear with words. At the same time, disappearance becomes a legible, material event through the verbal craft of obscurity. Indeed, crafting obscurity in a poem perfects the palpable art of disappearance.

Every secret, however deep or dark, produces what Eve Sedgwick, for example, in her study of the homosexual closet, calls "privacy effects," a revelation of "unknowing *as* unknowing, not as a vacuum or as the blank it can pretend to be but as a weighty and occupied and consequential epistemological space."[3] Thus, the figurative absence characterizing secrecy, privacy, or obscurity presents itself as a *spectacle* to be consumed, deciphered, judged: "'Closetedness' itself is a performance," she contends, "initiated as such by the speech act of a silence—not a particular silence, but a silence that accrues particularity by fits and starts" (3). The "clear but confused perception" attributed by Leibniz to monadic substance may be regarded as a metaphysical analogue for the clear signature of the unknowable, for the spectacle of obscurity, for the transitivity of the sublime. Every phenomenon characterized by secrecy, privacy, or obscurity makes an appearance in the world and can therefore be comprehended by the unmistakable features of its putative absence.

Surveying what she calls "topologies of privacy," Sedgwick (like Simmel) analyzes "the projective potency of the open secret" (145) principally as a *formal* structure. Thus, because the secrecy of the closet, which Sedgwick describes as a "riddle," can be reduced to a purely formal operation, she understands that "the establishment of *the spectacle of the homosexual closet* as a presiding guarantor of rhetorical community . . . extends vastly beyond the ostensible question of the homosexual" (250). That is to say, the dialectic of "privacy effects" pertains to a variety of commu-

3. Eve Kosofky Sedgwick, *Epistemology of the Closet* (Berkeley and Los Angeles: University of California Press, 1990), 77. Hereafter, page numbers are given in the text for further references to this source.

nities structured along the axes of secrecy/disclosure, obscurity/transparency, privacy/publicity. Any type of hermetic phenomenon thus produces an array of privacy effects.

Poetry, by analogy, may be said to produce certain *obscurity effects*. One could also contend that these "obscurity effects" betray a model of expression mirroring the inexplicit relations among individuals forming a secret society—a world apart from the world—but also the occult relations between discontinuous worlds. The anonymity and anarchic relations of such communities would help to explain Simmel's contention that "secrecy is thus, so to speak, a transitional structure between being and not being"—between identity and namelessness, order and anarchy.[4]

Strictly speaking, however, the "obscurity effects" generated by poetry must be distinguished from obscurity, per se, a verbal "substance" defined by a lack of understanding, communication, and external relations. Though not unrelated to the phenomenon of obscurity effects, the problem of lyric hermeticism requires more careful consideration of the solipsistic nature of verbal substance, as a precondition of lyric sociability. A model of negative sociability, a lyric monadology distinct from the obscurity effects—the verbal fetishism—generated by the poetic enigma, therefore arises from the conditions of lyric discontinuity and solipsism. For the nature of metaphysical substance presumes, by analogy, an absence of sensory relations between "being-in-language" and the physical world, between substance and phenomenon, Being and "not being" (to invoke Simmel's hypothesis about secrecy).

The hypothesis of obscurity effects nevertheless raises the question of whether secrecy, privacy, or obscurity is possible in any rigorous, or authentic, sense. Accordingly, the permeability of the secret must be assessed directly in relation to lyric poetry, especially as it pertains to the riddle, which openly stages the problematic of obscurity. One must bear in mind the riddle's double origin in antiquity as oracular utterance and as a congenial form of *wit*. For the puzzling words of the oracle, which neither hide nor reveal, are at once genial and congenial. The riddle reminds us of the abysmal nature of words by displaying its obscurity, by turning secrecy into an event and making a spectacle of incomprehension. Indeed, what is remarkable about the structure of the riddle—about any closed structure—is its inherent openness, its presupposition of exposure, its apocalyptic nature. The privacy of the closet, as Sedgwick reminds us, is only its most obvious—and misleading—feature; its permeability and

4. Georg Simmel, "The Sociology of Secrecy and of Secret Societies," trans. Albion W. Small, *American Journal of Sociology* 11, no. 4 (January 1906): 472.

expressiveness remain concealed, unacknowledged. The common secret, never more than an open secret, nevertheless maintains the illusion of absolute secrecy.

In the Vernacular

Lyric obscurity, like any commodity, is a volatile substance. Historically, the cultivation of literacy, inconceivable without the binding measures of poetry, spells out the affinities of grammar, glamour, and *grimoire*, yet grade-school teachers do not ordinarily give writing assignments with the prescription "Be obscure!" (Diderot's notorious exhortation to poets—perhaps the earliest programmatic call for obscurity in poetry).[5] Nursery rhymes are cherished at once for their pedagogical value and their nonsensical charm, while modern poetry—catching up with Diderot's advice—is simply condemned for its obscurity. These fluctuations in the prestige and the allure, not to mention the usefulness, of obscurity help to sustain the perceived gulf between the ode and the nursery rhyme, between literary and vernacular poetries.

Lyric obscurity may also serve, however, as a medium linking vernacular poetry to its literary counterpart. Stéphane Mallarmé, for example, whose verse represents a kind of gold standard, one might say, of lyric obscurity, toiled as a young writer in one of poetry's frivolous underworlds, the topsy-turvy realm of Mother Goose, converting 141 English nursery rhymes into veritable prose poems.[6] One would want to mention that Mallarmé was sampling Mother Goose at about the same time he first began translating the verse of Edgar Allan Poe, but it is more important to stress that he produced these nursery rhymes for his day job as an English teacher, as grammatical exercises for a classroom of chattering ten-year-olds. Mallarmé discovered in the verbal prosthetics of the classroom, comprising mnemonic phrases, philological jargon, and antiquarian kitsch, a sort of glamour akin to the netherworld of his own poetry.

Indeed, one of Mallarmé's songs from the nursery discloses the contagious effect of the rhyme's illogic on the translator. Mallarmé adopted the practice of presenting the English song followed by his prose rendering of it in French (which I translate below):

5. Denis Diderot, *Salon de 1767*, in *Diderot et l'art de Boucher à David: Les salons, 1759–1781* (Paris: Editions de la Réunion des Musées nationaux, 1984), 44.

6. Mallarmé's nursery rhymes remained in obscurity, so to speak, until they were published for the first time in 1964. Stéphane Mallarmé, *Recueil de nursery rhymes*, ed. Carl Paul Barbier (Paris: Gallimard, 1964).

Hey! diddle, diddle,
The cat and the fiddle,
The cow jumped over the moon;
The little dog laughed
To see such sport
While the dish ran after the spoon.

What a strange scene! Look at the cat with his violin—and that's not all: there's the moon, and a cow jumping right over it! I act like the little dog, laughing hard to see such foolishness. And then it seemed to me, as I contemplated this spectacle, that my ideas ran away with themselves, one after another, just as—in the words of the song—the dish runs after the spoon. Hey! diddle, diddle.[7]

Mallarmé alters the original verse considerably, identifying the speaker of the poem with the laughing dog, while acknowledging that the "spectacle" of illogic he is witnessing replicates itself in his head, in the realm of ideas. We might also regard the strange scene (*curieux tableau*) he contemplates as the verbal "spectacle" of the nursery rhyme itself, so that the poet finds reproduced in his head a spectacle of obscurity made of words. Mallarmé does indeed repeat the nonsensical invocation, "Hey! diddle, diddle" at the end of his prose poem (which does not occur in the English verse), suggesting that the poet has adopted the magical phrase for his own purposes, intending perhaps to reprise the "spectacle" of the nursery rhyme.

Mallarmé's transactions in lyric obscurity—between the illogic of Mother Goose and his own, evolving Symbolist doctrine—demonstrate a particular orientation between literary verse and vernacular poetry, which may be deduced from the etymology of the term itself. The Latin root, *vernaculus,* of the English word "vernacular" means "pertaining to slaves," yet the Latin term *verna* designates more precisely a *domestic,* or *house, slave.*[8] Thus, the speaker of vernacular language occupies an ambiguous position that is at once within the master's house—or the "house of poetry," to refashion a concept of Heidegger's—and fundamentally alien to the dwelling of the dominant tradition.[9] One could argue, with Hugo

7. Mallarmé, *Recueil de nursery rhymes,* 99.

8. *Cassell's Concise Latin-English, English-Latin Dictionary* (New York: Macmillan, 1977), 235. The linguistic connotation of the word "vernacular" in English incorporates Varro's phrase *vernacula vocabula* (language of slaves), according to *The Compact Edition of the Oxford English Dictionary* (Oxford: Oxford University Press, 1971).

9. Heidegger, as I mentioned in my introduction, uses a variation of this trope in several essays, including the "Letter on Humanism": "Language is the house of Being. In its home man dwells. Thinkers and poets are the guardians of this house." Martin Heidegger, *Basic Writings,* ed. David Farrell Krell (San Francisco: HarperCollins, 1993), 217.

Friedrich, that modern poetry (of the literary sort) develops a programmatic rationale for obscurity consistent with a genealogy of literary precedents; yet Mallarmé's dalliance with Mother Goose suggests that vernacular poetry as well, with its diverse repertoire of masking techniques and deliberate obfuscation, might be viewed as an inscrutable model, or catalyst, for certain kinds of obscurity commonly associated with literary modernity.[10] More boldly, as the etymology of the term suggests, one should perhaps regard the vernacular (to paraphrase Hermann Broch's definition of "kitsch") as a foreign body lodged in the system of literary poetry.[11]

Anon

According to the *Oxford English Dictionary,* the term "obscurity" refers not only to "lack of perspicuity in language, uncertainty of meaning," in a verbal sense, but to certain modes of social identity. In reference to social being, the term "obscure" means "of persons, their station, descent, etc.: Not illustrious or noted; unknown to fame; humble, lowly, mean." This definition suggests that being enveloped by obscurity in a social sense—a kind of social death, one might say—resembles the act of erasure, the partial disappearance, produced by verbal obscurity. Indeed, the general "uncertainty of meaning" associated with verbal obscurity may well be derived originally, not from certain kinds of texts, but from the speech habits of commoners or marginal social classes—viewed from the vantage point of the dominant, or literate, social class. Thus, the general notion of literary obscurity would be contingent on a social *misunderstanding* of the material and historical features of demotic speech: dialect, jargon, pidgin, slang. The principle of lyric obscurity, in the abstract, would therefore always refer obliquely to the impression made on the uninitiated listener by the siren song of the vernacular. From this perspective, the atavistic trait of lyric obscurity would be traceable to a dark repertoire of infidel forms: riddles, thieves' carols, beggars' chants.

The social definition of "obscurity" yields other nuances pertaining to

10. In modern poetry, according to Hugo Friedrich, "obscurity has become the predominant aesthetic principle, outlawing the customary communicative function of language"; hence, "it speaks in enigmas." Friedrich, *The Structure of Modern Poetry*, trans. Joachim Neugroschel (Evanston, IL: Northwestern University Press, 1974), 140, 3.

11. Hermann Broch declares that kitsch is "lodged like a foreign body in the overall system of art." Broch, "Notes on the Problem of Kitsch," in *Kitsch: The World of Bad Taste,* ed. Gillo Dorfles (New York: Bell Publishing, 1969), 62.

a verbal and social underworld of lyric obscurity. Persons of "obscure" origin who are "humble, lowly, or mean" are at the same time "not illustrious or noted; unknown to fame." That is to say, in the eyes of the dominant, literate class, the "obscure" strata of society are—or should be—inconspicuous, all but invisible. "Obscure" in this sense is therefore essentially a synonym for "anonymous," a form of identity with a direct bearing on the sources of vernacular literature and—more specifically, as it pertains to poetry—on the historical construction of authorship and publication.

For lyric poems have historically been published, from the poetry miscellanies of the early seventeenth century until the late nineteenth century, under the nameless signature of "Anon."[12] While the practice of anonymous publication was common with prose texts as well, it began earlier, lasted longer, and was generally more prevalent with poetry. Most poetry in literary history has indeed been published anonymously or under a pseudonym, and the adjective "anonymous" (abbreviated to Anon) was used solely in relation to nameless, or unnamed, authors until the appearance of the noun "anonymity" in the middle of the nineteenth century. Thus, the formulations of modern subjectivity and social identity associated with the term "anonymity" are inescapably linked to the curious signature of "Anon," a kind of accessory to poetry for centuries, marking the ambiguous act of publication. "Anonymity," like "obscurity," is therefore a mode of social identity directly linked to lyric poetry: a form of social obscurity modeled on the uncertain and epiphanic appearance of poetic language. Furthermore, just as lyric obscurity is a verbal property alternately prized and shunned in various contexts, so anonymity is, as Virginia Woolf observes, a kind of "possession" used strategically by authors for centuries to diverse effect.[13]

Kryptonite

While lyric obscurity may owe its general disposition to the vernacular parlance of various social underworlds, the history of the term's usage

12. My knowledge of the history of the term "anonymous" (or Anon) and its usage in the publication of poetry derives from Anne Ferry's excellent essay "*Anonymous:* The Literary History of a Word," published in a special issue of *New Literary History* devoted to the topic of anonymity: *New Literary History* 3, no. 2 (2002): 193–214.

13. In her posthumously published essay "Anon," Virginia Woolf declares, "Anonymity was a great possession" (397). The essay appeared for the first time in *Twentieth Century Literature* 25, no. 4 (1979): 382–398. On the various aesthetic, social, and economic motivations for the uses of the signature Anon, see Robert J. Griffin, *The Faces of Anonymity: Anonymous and Pseudonymous Publication from the Sixteenth to the Twentieth Century* (London: Palgrove, 2003), 1–17.

reveals that it gains broader significance by its lexical and figurative correlation with the epistemological status of *metaphysical substance.* Philosophy's rendering of the inscrutable substance of Being thus provides a coherent and distinctive component of the greater spectacle of obscurity. Turning to metaphysics to help define the *substance* of lyric obscurity—an extravagant idea, on the face of it—would seem only to exacerbate, one might presume, the stubborn abstraction of both concepts. Yet by disclosing the common ground of obscurity and substance (in a technical sense), and by examining them in light of one another, one inevitably confronts their entwined historical construction, thereby lending greater definition—and greater practical significance—to both concepts.

Remote from perception and often from understanding as well, the nature of metaphysical substance would appear to exemplify the basic topology of lyric obscurity: the substance of Being and the substance of obscurity in language both appear to lie beneath the threshold of verisimilitude, even if they permeate unavoidably the manifest features of an intelligible world. Whether it is conceived in material or ideal terms, the substance of Being is, from a philosophical perspective, incommensurable with the world it constitutes and hence innately obscure. In the case of atomism, for example, the foundational doctrine of Western materialism, atoms (or subnuclear "particles") are said to constitute the basic substance of all material bodies, yet these corporeal elements remain beyond the reach of the senses. The epistemological status of atomic substance—a paradox—therefore constitutes one of the basic paradigms of obscurity.

One of the definitions for the term "obscure" in the *Oxford English Dictionary* pertains in this respect to categories of insensible, material phenomena, such as "*obscure rays,* the dark or invisible heat-rays of the solar spectrum." From this perspective, lyric obscurity corresponds to the visible darkness of metaphysical materialism (i.e., atomism), which holds that only material bodies exist but that all material bodies consist of insensible elements. Thus, according to the doctrine of atomism, *all* matter is dark matter: hidden, inconspicuous, unknown to the senses. All metaphysical systems, by seeking to relate the innate obscurity of Being to the phenomenal world, offer critical insights into the puzzling relations formed by lyric obscurity—into the very substance of poetry.

The relevance of metaphysics to definitions of poetic obscurity lies partly in the historical revision of the very concept of obscurity which occurred with the development of seventeenth-century materialism and its metaphysical claims. Obscurity became, inadvertently, an ornament of "mechanical philosophy": it became less subtle and more procedural, less discursive and more calculable. That is to say, obscurity became less scholastic and more modern, once it could be grasped, not as a symptom of the unknowable, but as a basic condition of certain kinds of knowledge, as a residue of logical procedures (a condition that later permitted Novalis, for example, to postulate a "poetic logic"). Modern obscurity, including the poetic kind, must therefore be reconciled with the premises of rationalism. To be more precise, questions concerning the hermeticism of poetry, or the harmonies of the sublime, yield in surprising ways to modern formulations of logic—first developed by Leibniz—which are at once rooted in speculation about verbal signification and integral to advances in metaphysics.

In the development of modern metaphysics, logic and obscurity are not, contrary to what one might expect, antithetical conditions. Indeed, by applying the premises of modern logic—his own invention—to metaphysical speculation, Leibniz converts obscurity from a discursive problem (or a problematic object) in metaphysical thinking to a logical condition integral to his conception of monadic substance. Beyond the technical details of its elaboration, the significance of logical obscurity for Leibniz's metaphysical system is immediately evident in the curious rhetoric of the monadology: "monads have no windows through which something can enter or leave."[14] That is to say, monads, which represent a kind of pure interiority—an inside without an outside—have no openings that might admit the data of the physical world: monads exist in conditions of phenomenological darkness. Furthermore, Being itself, which consists of nothing other than monadic "perception," is fundamentally obscure; for the "perceptions" of "bare monads" (the substance constituting all inert phenomena) are infinitesimally small, folded, and hence unconscious: "petite perceptions," Leibniz calls them.[15] (The elemental and unconscious perceptions of monadic substance may be compared, in this respect, to the imperceptible atoms of materialism or to "the infinity of small, hidden springs" feeding the experience of the sublime.) All monads express the world darkly—even those capable of "apperception" or reflection, whose "perceptions" (their substance) are "clear but confused."[16] Thus, in Leibniz's theory of monads, obscurity is intrinsic to the Being of all things, since Being consists solely of monadic perception, and perception (like the roar of the sea, according to Leibniz) is founded upon

14. G. W. Leibniz, "The Principles of Philosophy, or, the Monadology," in *Philosophical Essays*, by G. W. Leibniz, ed. and trans. Roger Ariew and Daniel Garber (Indianapolis: Hackett, 1989), 214.

15. Leibniz, "Monadology," 216. Leibniz's theory of "*petites perceptions*" constitutes the earliest explicit conception of the unconscious mind—an unconscious without the mechanism of repression.

16. Leibniz, "Monadology," 214, 215, 220–221.

the obscurity of countless, indistinguishable elements. And the intrinsic obscurity of Being replicates itself in every aspect of the phenomenal world.

The expressive correspondence between lyric obscurity and ontological substance does not, of course, depend solely on philosophical doctrine or on the lexical configuration of the term "obscure." Beginning with the groundbreaking, poetological "research" of the Jena Circle in German Romanticism, whose poetic principles owe a significant debt to Leibniz's metaphysical system, modern poetry succumbs to the "cult of infinity," expanding to become what Friedrich Schlegel calls "transcendental poetry"—a totalizing concept encompassing all things.[17] The infinitizing of poetry recurs in Mallarmé's unrealized project of *Le Livre*, a monadological form of innumerable "folds," guided by the precept that "all earthly existence must ultimately be contained in a book."[18] For Mallarmé, the poetic obscurity resulting from the verbal annihilation of the objective world possesses a genetic relation to the metaphysical substance of obscurity: "My work was created only by *elimination*, and each newly acquired truth was born only at the expense of an impression which flamed up and burned itself out, so that its particular darkness could be isolated and I could venture ever more deeply into the sensation of Darkness Absolute."[19] As a result, according to Hugo Friedrich, "the progress of the poem turns into an ontological event," a disposition emphasized by Steiner as well in his reading of Mallarmé and "ontological difficulty."[20] For Mallarmé, then, "obscurity is not poetical arbitrariness, but an ontological necessity."[21] The gesture of negation upon which Mallarmé's ontological poetics depends is, in fact, essential to any conception of obscurity, including sociological obscurity, in which anonymity and the unintelligibility of vernacular parlance serve to defy and resist the poetry and social order of the dominant tradition.

In addition, with modern poetry's deliberate cultivation and rationalization of obscurity (starting with Romanticism), the spectacle of lyric obscurity projects itself more broadly as a symptom of social alienation and therefore as an element in the social economy. That is to say, lyric obscurity becomes a verbal commodity or fetish—a counterfeit substance.

17. *Friedrich Schlegel's "Lucinde" and the Fragments*, trans. Peter Firchow (Minneapolis: University of Minnesota Press, 1971), Athenaeum frag. 238.

18. Stéphane Mallarmé, "As for the Book" (1895), in *Selected Poetry and Prose*, by Stéphane Mallarmé, ed. Mary Ann Caws (New York: New Directions, 1982), 80.

19. Mallarmé, letter to Eugène Lefébure, in *Selected Poetry and Prose*, 88.

20. Friedrich, *Structure of Modern Poetry*, 91; George Steiner, *On Difficulty and Other Essays* (Oxford: Oxford University Press, 1978), 41–43.

21. Friedrich, *Structure of Modern Poetry*, 89.

Yet the fetish, according to Marx, is "a very strange thing, abounding in metaphysical subtleties," hence the equivocation between substance and phantasm, between obscurity and its effects.[22] Understood solely as an effect, a commodity, the appeal of lyric obscurity waxes and wanes in different contexts, often in a polarizing fashion: witness, for example, the reception of contemporary hip-hop lyrics, where obscurity is a genuine mass ornament, in contrast to post-avant-garde poetry, where obscurity is little more than a cottage industry (economically speaking).

As an ornament of social and economic alienation, the obscurity effects of modern lyric may therefore be assessed in part within the framework of Guy Debord's conception of "the society of the spectacle"—though Debord virtually ignores the possible role of language, or poetry, in composing the logic of "spectacle."[23] Analyzing the role of "obscurity" in securing the "spectacle"—that is, in advancing the metaphysical purchase of social being—would seem to be a dialectical necessity, especially in regard to the increasing prestige of vernacular obscurity in pop culture.

Def Rhapsody

The principle of poetic obscurity must be understood as a historical construction—a spectacle—owing its general properties to numerous correspondences between three primary modes of obscurity: verbal, sociological, and metaphysical. Alternatively, one could say that a shared conception of obscurity discloses a kinship between poetic language, metaphysics, and negative sociability. Either way, the qualities one asso-

22. Karl Marx, *A Critique of Political Economy*, introduction by Ernest Mandel, trans. Ben Fowkes (Harmondsworth: Penguin, 1976), 1:163. Regarding the phenomenon of verbal fetishism, one should bear in mind that Freud's foundational essay on sexual fetishism—a discourse usually associated with object relations—revolves around an episode of *verbal* fetishism in the Wolf Man case. Sigmund Freud, "Fetishism," in *Standard Edition of the Complete Psychological Works of Sigmund Freud,* ed. James Strachey, 24 vols. (London: Hogarth Press, 1953–1974), 22:152–157. For a more detailed account of verbal fetishism, see Nicolas Abraham and Maria Torok, *The Wolf Man's Magic Word: A Cryptonymy,* trans. Nicholas Rand (Minneapolis: University of Minnesota Press, 1986).

23. Although the term "spectacle" suggests a critical focus on visual culture and technology in Guy Debord's analysis of "the society of the spectacle," he is careful to undermine this assumption: "The spectacle is not a collection of images, but a social relation among people. . . . The spectacle cannot be understood as an abuse of the world of vision, as a product of the techniques of mass dissemination of images." Debord, *Society of the Spectacle* (Detroit: Black and Red, 1983), paragraphs 4 and 5. Debord even goes so far, at moments, to characterize the "spectacle" in linguistic terms (e.g., "The language of the spectacle consists of signs of the ruling production"), yet the role of language, or literature, in securing "spectacle" is touched upon only briefly by Debord: "When *analyzing* the spectacle one speaks, to some extent, the language of the spectacle itself" (paragraph 11).

ciates most commonly with poetic obscurity—its literary properties—have been determined by a historical constellation of specific models of poetic composition, though not always the models one presumes to be relevant.

Strategically, to illustrate the indigenous character of lyric obscurity, I have chosen to examine types of poems that are deliberately, or idiomatically, obscure: riddles, nursery rhymes, and songs written in dialect, slang, or jargon. As these models suggest, the thesis that obscurity is intrinsic to *lyric* poetry per se, in contrast to other genres of poetry, must come under scrutiny in the effort to identify certain paradigms of poetic obscurity. For one discovers in vernacular poetry many types of poems (songs for healing, marching, or vending, for copycats, crybabies, and bullies) which bear little if any resemblance to models of lyric poetry associated with the dominant tradition. At the same time, lyric poetry has clearly inherited and become indelibly associated with the problem of obscurity, obliging one to address the conditions of lyric obscurity in particular. It may be, however, that our notions of *lyric* obscurity rest upon a matrix of lost, or submerged, genres of poetry.

Some surprising historical conjunctions link various elements in this constellation. For example, the first "rhapsody," or compilation, of canting songs (verse written in the jargon of the criminal underworld) and the first English riddle book (aside from the Anglo-Saxon riddles assembled in the Exeter Book manuscript) both emerged from the same historic—and indeed physical—site: the printshop of the English printer Wynkyn de Worde. *Demaundes Joyous,* a riddle book, was printed in 1511 by de Word; and *The Hye-way to the Spyttel-hous,* a cant "rhapsody," was printed by Robert Copland, de Worde's apprentice and frequent translator, in 1536.[24] To put things in perspective, only a handful of printers were active in England in the first quarter of the sixteenth century, and very little work by contemporary poets found its way on to the relatively short list of books printed in England during this period.[25] Wynkyn de Worde did, however, print John Skelton's satire *The Bowge of Court* circa 1509, which means that a riddle book and a cant "rhapsody" shared space on a very short shelf with the work of the poet laureate of England.

The term "rhapsody," referring originally to a mode of composition in

24. On the publication of *Demaundes Joyous,* see Mark Bryant, *Dictionary of Riddles* (London: Routledge, 1990), 33; and on the publication of Copland's *The Hye-way to the Spyttel-hous,* see John S. Farmer, ed., *Musa Pedestris: Three Centuries of Canting Songs and Slang Rhymes* (London: privately printed, 1896), 199–200. Farmer's title alludes to the "Walking Muse" of itinerant poets.

25. On the publications of early English printers, see E. Gordon Duff and W. W. Greg, *Hand-Lists of Books Printed by London Printers, 1501–1566* (London: Blades, East and Blades, 1913).

verse, holds together an intricate web of associations pertaining to lyric obscurity. The signature Anon, for example, first appeared in an anthology of poems published in 1602 under the title *A Poetical Rapsody*. Its title page bears a curious inscription preparing the reader, perhaps, for the "diverse power" of rhapsodic measures: "The bee and spider by a diverse power, sucke hony & poyson from the self same flower."[26] For the term "rhapsody," derived from "rhapsode" (the name for the anonymous, itinerant singer of Homeric epic), means both a medley of epic verses (a type of poetic composition) and, by analogy, a miscellaneous collection of things, persons, languages—hence a medley of poems. The gathering of the anonymous into a rhapsody therefore draws attention to the inscrutable figure of the nameless, itinerant poet of common parlance. Virginia Woolf reminds us that Anon is "a nameless wandering voice, a counterpart to the enigmatic rhapsode of antiquity."[27]

The submerged affinities of the rhapsode reach still further into the well of the anonymous and indigent poet, touching the most ancient artifact of poetic obscurity, the riddle: Sophocles called the Sphinx a *rhapsode,* while Euripides and other commentators called her deadly riddle a "song." The Sphinx, who has no proper name, is called a rhapsode because she was said to wander the streets of Thebes, homeless, reciting her queer "demaunde" to strangers—habits recalling the vocation of Presocratic thinkers such as Parmenides, who made his living as an itinerant philosopher and composed his baffling treatise on Being in epic hexameters, thereby adopting practices associated with the rhapsode.

Demotic, promiscuous, and enigmatic, the binding measures of the homeless rhapsode (singer, riddler, sage) may be found as well at the birth of English lyric, in the Anglo-Saxon riddles (nearly one hundred of them) collected in the tenth-century Exeter Book manuscript.[28] These lengthy and ingenious riddles (the first lyric poems written in the English vernacular) range widely in subject matter (religion, natural history, warfare, technology) and treat the nature of writing itself and, more speculatively, the relation between the "substance" of poetry and the substance of the material artifacts masked—and unmasked—by the riddles.

Some scholars have found similarities between the bold, sensuous, and virtuosic nature of the Anglo-Saxon riddles and the contrarian quali-

26. Francis Davison, ed., *A Poetical Rapsody* (London, 1602). The *Rapsody* includes an anonymous poem belonging to the canting tradition: "In Praise of a Beggar's Life" (later reprinted in Izaak Walton's *The Compleat Angler,* a seventeenth-century meditation on fly-fishing).

27. Woolf, "Anon," 390, 382.

28. Craig Williamson, ed. and trans., *A Feast of Creatures: Anglo-Saxon Riddle Songs* (Philadelphia: University of Pennsylvania Press, 1982).

ties of Metaphysical poetry.[29] There can be no doubt that seventeenth-century poets such as John Donne and Abraham Cowley took pleasure, like the anonymous Anglo-Saxon riddlers, in devising elaborate and incongruous conceits, some of which reflected on the nature of material substance. Indeed, Aristotle's definition of a riddle as "a putting together of impossible things" appears to be the occluded source of the *discordia concors* that Samuel Johnson and, later, T. S. Eliot identified as the touchstone of Metaphysical poetry.[30]

In addition to these canonical formulations, the rhapsodic paradigm encompasses as well various recurring waves of "indigent" poetry. Most provocatively, the songs of the canting tradition—infidel oaths, thieves' carols, beggars' chants—present a side of the rhapsodic tradition associated with profanity, malediction, and enchantment. At the same time, the siren song of cant is explicitly agitational with regard to social conduct and often self-conscious in its garbling of standard English and the lyric tradition.

The poetics of dissolution, thievery, and homelessness formulated in the canting tradition found its way as well into rhapsodic subversion that was more explicitly political in nature. Songs of indigence became songs of radical "infidelity." The so-called shoemaker poets and working-class *philosophes*—the "Rousseaus of the gutter"—active in London during the decades immediately following the French Revolution helped to make poetry a critical component in the political praxis of "infidel" culture. Appropriating the gothic intimations of sympathizers like Byron and Percy Shelley, the manifestos and rude songs of the ultraradical "tavern underworld" anticipated the convergence of avant-garde practice and modern nightlife in the early part of the twentieth century. Yet one could argue that poetic rhapsody has always been *modern,* in the sense that the rhapsodic measures I have described are symptoms of modernity, if modernity is viewed not as a historical concept but as a theoretical category designating certain literary, sociological, and even metaphysical dispositions.[31]

Traveling through the inner and outer chambers of rhapsodic "his-

29. See W. P. Ker, *The Dark Ages* (London: Blackwell, 1904); and Northrup Frye, *Anatomy of Criticism* (Princeton, NJ: Princeton University Press, 1971).

30. Aristotle, *Poetics*, trans. James Hutton (New York: Norton, 1982), 69 (1458a); Samuel Johnson, "Lives of the Poets," in *Selected Poetry and Prose,* ed. Frank Brady and W. K. Wimsatt (Berkeley and Los Angeles: University of California Press, 1977), 348–349; and T. S. Eliot, "The Metaphysical Poets" (1921), in *Selected Prose of T. S. Eliot,* ed. Frank Kermode (New York: Harcourt Brace, 1975), 64.

31. For a reading of lyric modernity as a theoretical, rather than historical, concept, see Paul de Man's essay "Lyric and Modernity," in *Blindness and Insight,* by Paul de Man (Minneapolis: University of Minnesota Press, 1983).

tory," then, the dissolute forms and sociality of infidel poetry in postrevolutionary London echo from afar the unfinished symposia and swarms of poetic fragments issuing from the "vortex" (to use Ezra Pound's term) of early German Romanticism (*Frühromantik*). Among the writers and thinkers of the so-called Jena Circle, associated with the journal *Athenaeum* (published between 1798 and 1800), were Friedrich Schlegel and Novalis.[32] Committed to the integration of poetic, philosophic, and social experiment, the Athenaeum group was, essentially, the first European avant-garde—though it has not escaped a reputation for unrealized projects and failed aspirations, all characterized by "a certain attention to (and taste for) the phenomenon of decadence (Alexandrianism) and a great precision in the analysis of movements of dissolution and transition."[33] Ultimately, the twin strains of dissolution and infidelity become fully activated—and superrationalized—in the modernist movement of the twentieth century. Reflexive, experimental, heterogeneous in its materials, and deliberately obscure, the poetry of the modern avant-garde betrays many of the features of the rhapsodic paradigm.

Thick as Thieves

Soon after making its earliest appearance in European legal records in the fifteenth century, canting speech became a literary property through an elaborate process of cultural mediation involving spies, "grammarians," anthologists, printers, dramatists, and poets—all eager to sample and exploit the obscurity, at once verbal and sociological, of canting speech. Thomas Dekker, the Jacobean dramatist whose work most fully inhabits this verbal underworld, goes so far as to call the jargon of the demimonde a "canting commodity": the medium of a sociological sublime procuring the abject.[34] He and Thomas Middleton wrote a comedy together called *The Roaring Girl* (about the historical figure Mary Frith, a notorious criminal and transvestite), in which the appropriation of cant as a verbal commodity is openly and satirically staged.

In one scene of *The Roaring Girl,* a quartet of gullible gentry—Sir Thomas, Lord Noland, Sir Beauteous Ganymede, and Jack Dapper—seeks

32. Other members of the group included Friedrich's brother, August Wilhelm Schlegel; his wife, Caroline; F. W. Schelling; Ludwig Tieck; and F. D. E. Schleiermacher.

33. Phillip Lacoue-Labarthe and Jean-Luc Nancy, *The Literary Absolute,* trans. Philip Barnard and Cheryl Lester (Albany: State University of New York Press, 1988), 10.

34. Thomas Dekker, *"The Guls Hornbook" and "The Belman of London" in Two Parts* (1608), Temple Classics (London: J. M. Dent, 1926), 186.

out, as part of a night of slumming among the "dangerous classes," some exposure to "pedlar's French," the canting language of the demimonde. Sailing in "amorous weather" to the "World's End" (a tavern), they meet up with three rogues—Tearcat, Trapdoor, and Moll Cutpurse (the Mary Frith character)—who flamboyantly demonstrate their underworld "credentials" by trading an oath or two in cant.[35] A second round of signifying—gauging the authenticity of the "thieves' latin" spoken by the rogues—occupies the gentry before the wallets come out and the canting crew is paid for its performance of bona fide gibberish. In a deliberate display of street credibility, Tearcat defends his rank in the hierarchy of rogues to Moll, within earshot of the gentry:

Moll: So, sir, no churl of you.
Tearcat: No, but a ben cove, a brave cove, a gentry cuffin.
Lord Noland: Call you this canting?
Jack Dapper: Zounds, I'll give a schoolmaster half a crown a week and teach me this Pedlar's French.
Trapdoor: Do but stroll, sir, half a harvest with us, sir, and you shall gabble your bellyful.
Moll [to Trapdoor]: Come you rogue, cant with me.
Sir Thomas: Well said, Moll.—[to Trapdoor] Cant with her, sirrah, and you shall have money—else not a penny.[36]

As the rogues "gabble" songs in cant—for a price—the swells are continually asking for translations: "Moll, what was in that canting song?" "What was his gibberish?" etc.[37]

The remarkable thing about this scene—and its many variations in the canting literature—is the way in which it dramatizes the complex social and economic "market" for vernacular speech, revealing the inevitable rationalization of cant's poetic and sociological obscurities. In these sorts of verbal transactions, which always take place in the streets, the tavern, or the "spyttel-hous" (the hospice for the indigent), lyric obscurity becomes a verbal and sociological fetish, a literal commodity. And insofar as poetic obscurity becomes a fetish, a medium of sentimentality, infused with reflections of itself, it also becomes, in Marxian terms, a kind of "metaphysical" substance: neither here nor there, sensible nor insensible, yet all the more valuable for its mercurial properties, which serve as

35. Thomas Dekker and Thomas Middleton, *The Roaring Girl* (1608), ed. Paul A. Mulholland (Manchester, UK: Manchester University Press, 1987), 212 (act 5, scene 1).
36. Dekker and Middleton, *Roaring Girl*, 220–221 (act 5, scene 1).
37. Dekker and Middleton, *Roaring Girl*, 224, 221 (act 5, scene 1).

a medium of social cohesion between the ruling class and the citizens of the demimonde. Indeed, the fatuous scene of procurement depicted in *The Roaring Girl* reproduces itself in our own world: in the consumption of contemporary hip-hop culture, for example, or in the teaching of literary obscurity in the schools. Obscurity is expensive. At the heart of the spectacle, one finds the logic of the open secret, the apocalyptic mode of the riddle: obscurity is converted into its effects; the enigma becomes the object of a guessing game; the inwardness of language—its incommensurability—finds expression in social being.

The same principle functions, as we saw earlier, in the signature of Anon, which has historically marked the ghostly event of poetic *publication,* the polarized apparition of the poet in the world: namelessness becomes a means of exposure. Disappearance submits to the laws of appearance under the sign of Anon. In a similar fashion, the topology of lyric obscurity—its *stanzas,* its web of placeless places—finds expression, as we found in *The Roaring Girl,* in the *topography* of infidel culture. The obscurity of canting speech models the inaccessibility of the tavern at "World's End": the locus of the infidel sublime.

The word "slang," which was originally a canting term, and the word "cant" itself in fact refer to social activities, as well as to linguistic phenomena. Before it entered modern usage, "slang" meant, in canting jargon, "to exhibit anything in a fair or market, such as a tall man, or a cow with two heads."[38] Hence, "slang" originally referred to the exhibition of freakish things—a kind of social and economic profanity. The word "cant," too, as Dekker reveals when citing an oath of initiation, can refer to the obscure *trade* of "Beggerie": "so that henceforth it shall be lawfull for thée to *Cant,* (that is to say) to be a *Vagabond* and *Beg.*"[39] The verbal obscurity of cant or slang cannot be isolated then from the social obscurity of the trades these words name.

Tavern talk thus captures in words the orphic subculture of nightlife. A public place providing cover for illicit and sometimes illegal activities, for the mingling of otherwise-stratified classes of persons (rich and poor, lawful and unlawful), the reality of the tavern, like its ragged speech, is fundamentally dissolute. Indeed, the actual existence of the tavern is called into question by the obscurity of its material conditions: its derelict address and graveyard hours; its nameless (or nicknamed) and promiscuous society. In this respect, the nightspot, like the figure of Anon, appears

38. George Parker cited in Eric Partridge, *Slang, Today and Yesterday* (New York: Macmillan, 1960), 75.

39. Dekker, *"The Guls Hornbook" and "The Belman of London,"* 83 (emphasis in original).

in the world under erasure, its disappearance betrayed by its own apparition. Nightlife, in the words of Siegfried Kracauer, may be understood as "the appearance of lost inwardness."[40]

The tavern has always been an important locus for speakers of cant and slang, and for the appropriation of cant by ostensibly lawful and literate classes. Hence, poetry and nightlife have sustained—principally through song—a lengthy, productive, and profane relationship. As the praxis of nightlife became more deliberately politicized (as a laboratory for radical culture following the French Revolution) and more highly mediated (by its association with the underground press), the manifold obscurity of nightlife became increasingly susceptible to commodification—just like the fetishizing of cant, appealing to classes well beyond the subculture of the demimonde. The territory of nightlife thus yielded historically to rationalization and to sentimentality, as Schiller understood the category of the sentimental: an object, event, or place infused with verbal reflection—with reflections of itself—and with rational feeling.[41] These developments indeed became the distinguishing feature of *modern* nightlife, of the spectacular topos of the nightclub. Obscurity became a mode of publicity. Quite remarkably, the sentimentality of modern nightlife made it available as a staging ground—a counterfeit underworld—for the incipient avant-garde, which deliberately cast itself in the mold of the cultural infidel. Indeed, the first modern nightclubs in Paris, Berlin, and London, which opened in the late nineteenth century, provided a theater of indigence and infidelity for launching the historical avant-garde.

The Riddle of Being

Fetishizing the obscurity of the demimonde—in a variety of registers—produces the visible underworld of modern nightlife, a sociological sublime. Extrapolating Marx's understanding of fetishism, we could say that the composition of social obscurity—understood as the substance of infidel culture—evokes, as I suggested earlier, the philosophical construction of metaphysical substance. Even more germane to the problematic of *lyric* obscurity is Marx's repeated description of the commodity fetish as a "riddle" or "enigma," a claim that could be made about meta-

40. Siegfried Kracauer, "The Blue Angel" (1930), reprinted in Anton Kaes, Martin Jay, and Edward Dimendberg, eds., *The Weimar Sourcebook* (Berkeley and Los Angeles: University of California Press, 1994), 631.

41. Friedrich Schiller, *On the Naïve and the Sentimental in Literature,* trans. Helen Watanabe-O'Kelly (Manchester, UK: Manchester University Press, 1981), 42.

physical substance as well, given its insensible nature.[42] The inscrutability of Being thus produces the inevitable riddle of metaphysics: what kind of material body is composed of immaterial substance? Parmenides, the founder of Western rationalism and the first philosopher of metaphysics, answers this riddle by suggesting that material bodies are composed of a substance determined by the character of *logos*—of *language*—hence the verbal aspect of metaphysical substance and its potential obscurity.

Like Parmenides' theory of Being, Leibniz's monadology—after atomism, the most powerful and comprehensive system of Western metaphysics—posits, it could be argued, a vision of linguistic fundamentalism, shaped by Leibniz's alignment of etymology and logic. Monadic substance, as I summarized earlier, unfolds along an increasingly rationalized spectrum of "perception"; it offers a solution, moreover, to the riddle of metaphysics by adapting the structure of atomism to a vision of incorporeal substance: monadological Being is "clear but confused" in precisely the same way that material bodies, according to the premises of atomism, are at once manifest and obscure, occupying the gulf between sensible appearance and inscrutable substance. With this model in mind, emphasizing the indelible obscurity underlying all manifest appearance—which merely replicates the structure of monadic substance—Leibniz declares that "*sensible qualities* are in fact *occult qualities*," a paradigm he recognized as well in the aesthetic category of the sublime.[43]

Leibniz's definition of metaphysical obscurity, coupled with the essential discontinuity of monadic substance, provides as well a conceptual vocabulary for modeling the organization of *mass phenomena*—of communities and artifacts—from elements that are otherwise innately hermetic. More specifically, when understood according to a metaphysics of obscurity, the world expressed by each monad may be compared to the historical *underworld* of the demimonde, the estranged sociological substance of society itself. Furthermore, the term "infidel" must then refer to the social implications of a secular monadology (robbed of the harmony between monads preestablished by God); that is, "infidel" refers not only to the absolute isolation of monads from one another (and from the phenomenal world whose substance they constitute) but also to the nonfidelity of monadic underworlds in general (their faithlessness and their insoluble estrangement from society). At the same time, Walter Benjamin

42. Marx, *Critique of Political Economy,* 1:163, 167. On the phenomenon of verbal fetishism, see n. 22 above.

43. G. W. Leibniz, "On What Is Independent of Sense and Matter" (letter to Queen Sophia Charlotte of Prussia, 1702), in *Philosophical Papers and Letters,* by G. W. Leibniz, ed. and trans. Leroy E. Loemker (Dordrecht: Reidel, 1976), 547 (emphasis in original).

recognized that "the infinity of reflection" comprising monadic substance implies an "infinity of connectedness."[44] In other words, the faithless and solipsistic relations of monadic substance supply a critical model for expressive social constellations echoing the medium of lyric obscurity.

From a phenomenological perspective, the improbable correlation between modern nightlife and metaphysical substance begins with the intuitive resemblance between the hermetic forms of the nightclub and the monad, each constituting a place, a topos, that has disappeared from the map of the world. Yet this correspondence is more than intuitive, as Leibniz employs architectural analogies to characterize the formal—that is, nonintuitive—properties of the monad. In addition to the famous reference to windowless monads, Leibniz describes monads as "architectonic models" (*échantillons architectoniques*) of a physical universe from which each monad is nevertheless radically isolated by its incorporeal substance.[45] Further, he views architectural experience (the unconscious awareness of spatial proportions) as emblematic of the monadological structure of perception.[46]

Walter Benjamin later identified the windowless monad as the basic model for the lyrical structure of the Parisian Arcades. Describing the Arcades Project as a fragmentary vision of "the true city—the city indoors," Benjamin explains, "What obtains in the windowless house is the true. And the arcade, too, is a windowless house. The windows that look down on it are like loges from which one gazes inside, but one cannot look out from them."[47] The introverted vista of the windowless arcade corresponds in remarkable ways to the "lost inwardness" of poetry and modern nightlife.

Concerning the essential lyricism of introverted structures, one must bear in mind that Benjamin's monadology of the Arcades always reverts to an understanding of language and its role in configuring the phenomenal world, a deductive sequence characteristic of Leibniz's formulation of monadic substance. Furthermore, Benjamin's appropriation of Leibniz's monadology, with its doctrine of metaphysical obscurity, betrays a significant debt to the poetics of early German Romanticism—especially to Novalis and Friedrich Schlegel, whose lyric monadologies remain the most significant literary engagement with Leibniz's philosophy.

44. Walter Benjamin, *The Concept of Criticism in German Romanticism* (1920), in *Selected Writings*, vol. 1, *1913–1926*, by Walter Benjamin, ed. Marcus Bullock and Michael W. Jennings (Cambridge, MA: Harvard University Press, 1996), 126. Benjamin cites a fragment of Novalis as the source of his observation: "An infinitely characterized individual is a member of an *infinitorium*" (166).

45. Leibniz, "Monadology," 223.

46. Leibniz, "Principles of Nature and Grace, Based on Reason," in *Philosophical Essays*, 212.

47. Walter Benjamin, *Arcades Project*, trans. Howard Eiland and Kevin McLaughlin (Cambridge, MA: Harvard University Press, 1999), 532.

TWO

Riddlecraft

In poetry a garment is not a garment; it conceals nothing.

G. E. LESSING, *LAOCOÖN*

Or if the air will not permit,
Some still removed place will fit,
Where glowing embers through the room
Teach light to counterfeit a gloom.

JOHN MILTON, "IL PENSEROSO"

In the Parlance of Things

The form of the earliest secular poetry in English—the riddle—descends, by most accounts, from the genre of the *aenigma,* first composed by English scholars (in Latin) in the seventh century.[1] Because the Latin clerical tradition of riddling was far less robust and inventive than its Anglo-Saxon descendant, however, this literary-historical account may be less significant for a genealogy of lyric than the cul-

1. W. P. Ker comments on Anglo-Saxon literature's affinity for the riddle: "Poetical riddles were produced in England more largely than anywhere else in the Dark Ages, both in Latin and the native tongue. . . . The difference is that the old English poetical fashions are much more favorable to this kind of treatment than anything in Latin. It is the proper business, one might say, of the old English poetry to call things out of their right names." Ker, *The Dark Ages* (London: Blackwell, 1904), 92. Northrop Frye makes a bolder claim, identifying the riddle as the primordial form of one of the two basic modes of lyric poetry: *melos* and—the mode proper to the riddle—*opsis*. Frye, *Anatomy of Criticism* (Princeton, NJ: Princeton University Press, 1971), 280. On the riddle as one of the essential roots of lyric poetry, see Andrew Walsh, *Roots of Lyric: Primitive Poetry and Modern Poetics* (Princeton, NJ: Princeton University Press, 1978), chapter 2.

tural associations of the riddle poem. Archaeological evidence reveals that the earliest poetry in English displays an affinity for objects whose rarity and eccentricity were signaled by a peculiar verbal disposition. Indeed, it may be possible to claim that lyric poetry first emerged in English as the enigmatic voice of certain highly wrought objects.

In the Anglo-Saxon world prior to the eleventh century, certain artifacts (crosses, weapons, bells, jewelry, sundials, chess pieces) bear inscriptions—in the first person—that refer to the object's maker or owner (or both), to the world at large, and to the object itself. For the most part, the scope of these inscriptions is quite limited, consisting of formulaic phrases such as "Godric made me" or "Aelfred ordered me to be made" or "Aenred owns me."[2] A smaller number of objects, however, bear more complex inscriptions betraying the form of a riddle. One object, for example, declares, "Cross is my name. Once, trembling and drenched with blood, I bore the mighty king."[3] Evoking the form of Anglo-Saxon riddles that end with an exhortation such as "Say who I am" or "Say what I am called," the first statement in this inscription ("Cross is my name") is the solution to the riddle posed by the second sentence. A riddle containing its own solution (in the title or embedded in the "enigma" itself) is a common feature of the Latin tradition, refined considerably by the Anglo-Saxon poet.

The incorporation of verbal identities by these objects reveals—even in the case of the meanest inscription—important details about their social and imaginative identities. Unlike the phenomenon of the modern commodity fetish, which comes to life only at the moment of exchange, these artifacts speak on the occasion of their manufacture or under the condition of ownership (as distinct from simple possession). Yet the grammatical construction of the owner/maker formulae undermines the peculiar agency of the artifact. For, although these objects speak and thus appear to occupy, at a linguistic level, the position of a subject, their grammatical position in these statements is usually in the accusative case ("Godric made me"), thereby preserving their status as objects that are acted upon. The incorporation of verbal identities thus secures for these artifacts a novel position suspended between subject and object, human and thing.

The scope of animation increases considerably when the object speaks in riddles, which coincides with its assumption of unambiguous agency. In the riddle inscription I cited earlier, for example, the "I" of the object

2. Elisabeth Okasha, *Hand-List of Anglo-Saxon Non-Runic Inscriptions* (Cambridge: Cambridge University Press, 1971), 106, 49, 89.

3. Okasha, *Hand-List*, 57.

exists in the nominative case, and it possesses a name (though its name, "Cross," blurs the distinction between ordinary nouns and proper names). In addition, the riddle endows things with a history, since the artifact, even as it presents itself to us, provides us with an image of itself in the past ("Once . . ."). The artifact, through its riddling form, is now capable of disappearing into the past—a past, moreover, that is false, since the cross bearing the inscription did not actually bear "the mighty king." Not only, then, does the riddle permit the object to tell lies about itself (and thus exist in an ambiguous state of not being present), but the moment of animation coincides with the object's transformation into what it is not: flesh. For the being whose name is "Cross" claims to have "trembled" under the weight of the king, suggesting that this particular cross (which is made of precious metals) possesses qualities of a living body—the king's body. The artifact, altered by its enigmatic voice, has become a kind of god.[4]

Now, before I proceed to comment further on the possible significance of lyric poetry's role in composing the "riddle creature," I want to make some observations about the terms of the analysis I have initiated here, in order to bring to light certain assumptions that are characteristic generally of the analysis of material culture. Nothing in my introductory remarks suggests any reason to doubt the coherence of these artifacts as *material* phenomena. That is to say, I do not call into question the material substance of the things I have been examining, nor do I believe most readers would hold me accountable were I not to do so in the course of an extended analysis. Nothing about these particular artifacts, as far as I have described them, appears to call for such scrutiny. Indeed, the evidence of material culture ordinarily possesses, insofar as it becomes the object of academic criticism, a similar immunity from critical reflection concerning its physical mass.

In the humanities, the material substance of ordinary things is judged to be either an intuitive certainty or an arcane possession of physics. Matter is no longer viewed as a problem relevant to humanistic criticism. These assumptions, which extend to the ostensibly critical study of material culture, are among the long-term effects of literature's (and philosophy's) withdrawal from serious debate over the nature of mate-

4. Because this particular object, a cross, involves the death of an individual, the ambiguity of its animate being (suspended between human and thing) may be compared to the principle of the "deodand" (accursed object) in English law. Rooted in Germanic and Anglo-Saxon common law, the deodand (meaning, literally, "that which must be given to god") pertains to "the liability of inanimate objects," to objects implicated in the death or injury of a human being. See William Pietz, "Death of the Deodand: Accursed Objects and the Money Value of Human Life," *Res* 31 (Spring 1997): 97–108.

rial substance. Science has long been regarded as the sole arbiter in the determination of matter or metaphysical substance. The result is that the authority and explanatory power of literary or cultural theory in relation to material culture is limited by its dependence on science not only to furnish a plausible account of material substance but to determine, in a fundamental sense, what sets material things apart from ideas or events.

In this chapter, I am concerned essentially with what lyric poetry may be able to tell us about the material substance of things, but also if what matters about the world in a poem holds any particular significance for a philosophy of metaphysics and, more specifically, for theories of metaphysical materialism, which hold that anything without a material body does not exist. Physical matter becomes metaphysical *substance* when it becomes the sole and insensible ground of all Being (a model exemplified by the doctrine of atomism). Metaphysical materialism (only bodies exist) envisions material bodies composed of a substance that lies beyond the reach of our senses. I want to know if our basic models of lyric obscurity—such as the innate obscurity of riddles—disclose anything about our construction of the hidden *substance* of things.

Science continues to be puzzled by distinctions between ponderable and imponderable bodies or, more precisely, by the coexistence of these properties in a single entity. What do the intuitive properties of an object (what we can perceive of it) have in common with the invisible foundation of material substance? Following the development of modern physics, this question has become more acute, since certain kinds of subatomic events do not appear to observe the laws of intuitive bodies—the very bodies that are ostensibly founded on these inscrutable events. Hence, real bodies appear to be composed of unreal substance. And the *substance* of things—the insensible foundation of material bodies—possesses intuitive reality solely in the form of equations, images, or tropes.

Substance, in this sense, is the solution to the conundrum posed by things that speak in riddles: the verbal identity of these objects, which is the source of their obscurity, corresponds to the role of analogy in the determination of material substance. More precisely, when an object speaks in riddles, it reveals its true "substance." That is to say, the innate obscurity of matter in the history of physics, like the inscrutability of things in lyric poetry, betrays the inescapable role of language in depicting the nonempirical qualities—the invisible aspect—of material phenomena. The production of verbal or lyric substance in poetry therefore corresponds to an essential aspect of the way science understands the nature of the material world.

My contention that metaphysical materialism betrays an affinity with lyric poetry in particular (rather than, say, with fiction or painting) depends in part on a conception of poetry formulated and reiterated by the leading figures of Western aesthetic philosophy. That is to say, I am interested not only in the aesthetic qualities of poetry as such but also in poetry as a discursive formation that has come to be defined in relation to other arts and other forms of knowledge. This historical formation relies in part on a fundamental correspondence between the heightened technicality of poetry (its craft) and its obscurity—including the attenuated substance of the lyric "air." Hence, the productive (or, to use Vico's term, "genetic") character of poetry has always raised important questions about the relation between *techne* (or technology) and material substance.

Metaphysical materialism, from antiquity to the present day, has sought to establish an authoritative account of physical reality by depicting a world of invisible and frequently unverifiable entities: the lawlessness of visible reality masks, it is said, the lawful—but invisible—realm of atoms. Correspondingly, poetry is to be distinguished from the other arts, according to Lessing, Kant, and Heidegger, by its freedom from intuition and its disavowal of imitation. In effect, poetry renders the world by making illusory and even impossible images of things—by rendering the world as what it is not. Kant, for example, states, "Poetry fortifies the mind: for it lets the mind feel its ability—free, spontaneous, and independent of natural determination—to contemplate and judge phenomenal nature as having aspects that nature does not on its own offer in experience either to sense or to the understanding."[5]

Metaphysical materialism has been plagued (and enabled) since its inception by its reliance on tropes and imaginary pictures (starting with the figure of the atom) to render the invisible foundation of matter. It is not therefore a question of a particular moment in the history of metaphysics when substance is captured by language and thus, suspended between materiality and immateriality, begins to lose its tangible, or even ponderable, qualities. Rather, metaphysics in its most rigorous forms descends unavoidably into language, to a place where matter is

5. Immanuel Kant, *Critique of Judgment,* trans. Werner S. Pluhar (Indianapolis: Hackett, 1987), 196–197. Kant's position echoes that of Lessing, who observes, regarding the impression conveyed by a poem, "I am a long way from seeing the object itself"—because, he says, "illusion" is "the principal object of poetry." G. E. Lessing, *Laocoön: An Essay on the Limits of Painting and Poetry,* trans. Edward Allen McCormick (Baltimore, MD: Johns Hopkins University Press, 1984), 88. Furthermore, Kant's position anticipates Heidegger's view that, in the language of poetry, "Everything ordinary and usual becomes nonbeing . . . everything is other than usual." Martin Heidegger, "The Origin of the Work of Art," in *Poetry, Language, Thought,* by Martin Heidegger, trans. Albert Hofstadter (New York: Harper and Row, 1971), 72.

mostly not matter, where matter cannot be distinguished from the tropes and analogies that make it intelligible (and hence secure the equation of materialism and realism). I am therefore interested in the problem of obscurity not only for what it can tell us about the improbable metaphysics of lyric poetry but also as an authentic model of the figurative aspect of metaphysical materialism. And I undertake this analysis in order to make available to literary and cultural studies a more productive sense of the ambiguity of material substance—a project that challenges the epistemological and ethical priority frequently assigned to materialist criticism.

I want to return now to the correspondence between riddles and things by invoking, with some trepidation, the Marxist premise of technological determinism, as a way of picking the lock that currently bars the literary critic from addressing the problem of material substance. Contributing to a collection of papers on the topic of "material evidence," Yves Bonnefoy (in an essay on the indexicality of photography and poetry) claims that Edgar Allan Poe and Stéphane Mallarmé were among the first writers "to announce that photography was going to change the world." Further, aligning Mallarmé's lyrical conception of "Nothingness" with the ontological effects of the "new look" of photography, Bonnefoy contends, "Mallarmé wants to accomplish consciously—wants to accomplish as an ultimate act of consciousness, at the threshold of a new age—what the photographic machine does outside any consciousness. . . . Mallarmé wants to look as photography looks."[6]

Now, this is an interesting (and debatable) point, but the principle of technological determinism, which serves for Bonnefoy (and for many others) to explain the "new age" precipitated by photography, appears—as far as Bonnefoy is concerned—to have no application to poetry. Is it not the case that the determinism governing the effects of the photographic machine might also be extended to lyric poetry, surely the most technical, and even mechanistic, of literary forms (given the requirements of meter, rhyme, and stanza)? As a veritable "machine" of literature—Paul Valéry, for example, called poetry "a kind of machine for producing the poetic state of mind by means of words"—the lyric poem appears to have a special affinity for the implications of a doctrine of technological determinism.[7] Bonnefoy's thesis of indexicality may be worth considering, but it seems likely that the apparatus of a lyric poem would yield a very

6. Yves Bonnefoy, "Igitur and the Photographer," trans. Mary Ann Caws, *PMLA* 114, no. 3 (May 1999): 333, 335.

7. Paul Valéry, "Poésie et pensée abstraite," quoted in the *Princeton Encyclopedia of Poetry and Poetics* (Princeton, NJ: Princeton University Press, 1993), 1124. I want to thank Barbara Bowen for referring me to this citation.

different kind of substance (as a Mallarmé lyric yields the peculiar "Nothingness" of objects) from the photographic machine. And it is therefore conceivable that the technics of poetry (by which I mean prosody and the craft of ordering words, but also the poem's image-making and rhetorical apparatus) might yield a consistent and coherent doctrine of lyric substance.

If we return to a discussion of riddles and artifacts with an explicit concern for material substance, it appears that the grammatical suspension between subject and object, the projection of things into the past, the assumed identities, and the transubstantiation from metal to human flesh to divine matter may all have distinct implications for what we regard as the substance of the "riddle creature." To gain a fuller sense of the riddling formation of objects, and of the significance of riddles for the origins of lyric poetry in English, we must turn to the Anglo-Saxon riddles collected in the Exeter Book in the late tenth century (though the riddles themselves date from the eighth century). One of the four great miscellanies of Old English literature, the Exeter Book contains, in addition to riddles, the source texts for "The Wanderer" and "The Seafarer." Though these two celebrated poems are typically granted, in contrast to the riddles, a privileged place in the genealogy of English lyric, the prosody of the riddles (the standard four-beat, alliterative line of Old English verse) is identical to that of "The Wanderer," "The Seafarer," and "Beowulf." The elevation of the riddling form is confirmed by "The Dream of the Rood," the greatest Christian poem in Old English, which was composed as a riddle.[8] These formal correspondences bear witness to the hermeneutical implications of the word "riddle," which is directly linked to the verb "to read."[9]

The formal sophistication and delicacy of the riddle poem, coupled with its inherent obscurity, points to an unresolvable—and productive—ambiguity in its literary character. For although the archaic aspect (and historical origin) of riddles derives in part from the tradition of prophetic and oracular speech, the Anglo-Saxon riddle no longer functions, quite obviously, in a prophetic mode—though it retains, in its construc-

8. W. P. Ker views the riddle in Old English literature as an important source of innovation in the history of lyric: "In some of the riddles the miracle takes place which is not unknown in literary history elsewhere: what seems at first the most conventional of devices is found to be a fresh channel of poetry." Ker, *Dark Ages*, 93.

9. According to the entries for "riddle" and the verb "to read" in the *Oxford English Dictionary*, the etymological root of "riddle" and "read" is the Old English verb *raedan*, meaning "to give or take counsel, to advise, to deliberate." Further, revealing the enigmatical disposition of "ordinary" writing, the entry for "read" notes: "The sense of considering or explaining something obscure or mysterious is common to the various languages, but the application of this to the interpretation of ordinary writing, and to the expression of this in speech, is confined to English."

tion, the inscrutability of the oracle. Thus, the riddle as a secular form is already, in its earliest manifestations, a disenchanted song, a literary toy, which invites us to regard the riddle not as an archaic mode of poetic speech but as a form of literary decadence.

The genealogy of lyric poetry in English therefore begins late in the life of an archaic form, the riddle, and this tension between archaism and decadence appears to stabilize the form and to remain integral to its endurance and mutability as poetic model. Indeed, as W. P. Ker suggests, the genealogy of the riddle can be drawn to encompass the seventeenth-century Metaphysical lyric, with its bold conceits, its obscurity, and its curious amalgam of analysis and sensibility.[10] From this perspective, what may appear in the present context to be a misguided attempt to extend the poetics of the riddle beyond its historical moment actually supplements T. S. Eliot's alignment of modernist and Metaphysical poetry, which he calls "the direct current of English poetry."[11] Thus, if we link Eliot's influential thesis to Ker's observation, modernist poetry, insofar as it follows the example of the Metaphysical lyric, might be viewed as preserving certain atavistic traits of the riddle.

Anglo-Saxon riddles display a high degree of artifice and formal sophistication, yet their basic design differs little from the two-sentence inscription on the cross I described above. In about half of the ninety-six riddles in the Exeter Book, the mystery object speaks directly to the reader, and the riddle ends (as I mentioned earlier) with a phrase such as "Say what I am called" or "Say who I am." The solutions to most of the riddles (not all of them have been solved) are familiar objects (and sometimes animals) of the house, hall, farmyard, monastery, or battlefield. One finds riddles, for example, about storms and wine cups, churn and key, rake and bagpipe, quill pen and gold. Thus, a riddle is essentially an allegory, though, unlike conventional allegory, the phenomenon veiled by the "dark" or enigmatical description is not a concept (e.g., justice) or a divinity but a physical object or phenomenon. A riddle is a *materialist* allegory (as well as an allegory of metaphysical materialism). The "weird creature" we encounter at the outset of the poem turns out to be a phenomenon common to most people's experience; the "dark speech" of the riddle veils, even as it describes precisely, a familiar object.

The riddle produces a complex object—a "riddle-creature"—that, by

10. Ker writes, "Though it is only a game, it [the riddle] carries the poetic mind out of the world: as not infrequently with the Metaphysical poets, the search for new conceits will land the artist on a coast beyond his clear artifices." Ker, *Dark Ages*, 93.

11. T. S. Eliot, "The Metaphysical Poets" (1921), in *Selected Prose of T. S. Eliot*, ed. Frank Kermode (New York: Harcourt, 1975), 66.

speaking, sheds its human qualities yet goes on speaking.[12] The thing becomes human and then performs a verbal striptease in the dark, before our eyes, divesting itself of its human attributes. The verbal gestures composing the striptease are, at the same time, the movement that obscures the thing and transforms it into what it is not. For that is what a riddle does: it withholds the name of a thing, so that the thing may appear as what it is not, in order to be revealed for what it is. Here's how it works:

My dress is silver, shimmering gray,
Spun with a blaze of garnets. I craze
Most men: rash fools I run on a road
Of rage, and cage quiet determined men.
Why they love me—lured from mind,
Stripped of strength—remains a riddle.
If they still praise my sinuous power
When they raise high the dearest treasure,
They will find through reckless habit
Dark woe in the dregs of pleasure.[13]

There is an element of burlesque both in the main persona of the riddle and in the teasing performance of the riddle itself. The inherently seductive quality of a riddle, which can be attributed in part to a manner of speaking that simultaneously illuminates and obscures its object, finds itself embodied in the dangerous yet irresistible object evoked by the riddle: a wine cup. Thus, the object itself resembles the form of its dark speech: the source of its fascination, according to the speaker, remains a "riddle" to its suitors. What's more, like the inherent obscurity of the riddle, a darkness associated with pleasure lies at the bottom of things—and of this thing in particular. It is the darkness that remains after the thing has disrobed, after the wine cup has been emptied, after the object has reverted, but for the darkness of speech, to its inhuman origin.

Black Wonder

What can a riddle, a word trick that allows an object to speak directly to us, even as its identity remains a mystery, tell us about the material sub-

12. See Craig Williamson, *A Feast of Creatures: Anglo-Saxon Riddle Songs* (Philadelphia: University of Pennsylvania Press, 1982), 41.

13. Williamson, *Feast of Creatures*, riddle 9, 69.

stance of things and about the substance of the riddle itself? The riddle I cited above, along with a number of others in the Exeter Book, turns upon a moment of reflexivity, which reveals the object, aside from its verbal identity, to be inherently puzzling or mysterious. In one riddle, for example, the mystery object declares:

My race is old, my seasons many,
My sorrows deep. . . . .
. . . .
My craft and course, power and rich passage,
I must hide from men. Say who I am.[14]

Here, the persona of the riddle creature—that of a wanderer or fugitive—thematizes not only the veiled course of the object through the riddle but also its inherently cryptic nature: "I must hide from men. Say who I am." The object—gold—thus reflects by its enigmatic nature the linguistic mode of the riddle. This homeless substance is therefore doubly disguised: already hidden, it is veiled as well by the dark speech of the riddle. Indeed, the voice enacts a darkling fate common to both the object and its riddle.

In another riddle poem, the object speaking is generally thought to be a bell (though there are other possible solutions), whose sound mimics the riddle song: "I sing round / The truth if I may in a ringing riddle."[15] Thus, the object, whatever it may be, calls itself "a ringing riddle." The thing is therefore a riddle even before it starts talking in riddles, a correspondence that suggests a certain degree of identification between poem and thing. Frequently, as I indicated in earlier examples, this identification is rooted in the phenomenon of darkness or obscurity, a quality intrinsic to the riddle or *aenigma* (and to allegory)—as the roots of these words tell us.[16] The darkness of the riddle becomes a property of the thing encrypted in the riddle, or more accurately, the dark speech of the riddle finds an image of itself in the cryptic nature of the thing it brings to life.

The puzzling identification of words and things becomes a bit more explicit when the object speaking in riddles is associated, as often happens, with reading, writing, or bookmaking. In one of the most ingenious

14. Williamson, *Feast of Creatures*, 141.

15. Williamson, *Feast of Creatures*, 62.

16. The Latin term *aenigma* (a "dark saying") derives from the Greek verb *ainissesthai,* meaning "to speak obscurely or allusively" (Liddell and Scott, *Greek-English Lexicon*). The term "riddle" (and its cognate "to read") derives, as I noted earlier, from an Anglo-Saxon verb meaning "to consider something obscure."

riddles of the Exeter Book, an inkhorn (or inkwell) speaks as an individual separated from its twin brother (the other horn), describing itself as "untwinned."[17] The melancholy inkhorn declares, "in my belly / Is a black wonder"—a trope referring to the ink that it contains. Materialized in this way, darkness appears as the material of the poem's inscription—the very substance of the riddle that is concealed in the "untwinned" thing. The "black wonder" at the core of things is thematized in another riddle on bookmaking, where the book-object describes how the quill pen "darts often to the horn's dark rim" and "with a quick scratch of power, tracks / Black on my body."[18] The darkness of writing embodied in these riddles calls to mind the dark well of the wine cup and the obscurity that binds gold to the words of its riddle.

Returning now to the problem of material substance, the first question is obvious: how are we to understand the inherent obscurity of riddles (and of lyric poetry) as a substance mirroring the darkness of things? What qualities does the substance of darkness possess (in a poem)? And what significance might the problem of literary obscurity—as distinct from obscurantism—hold for the history of metaphysical materialism? To begin to answer these questions, the term "obscurity," as it pertains to texts and especially poetry, must be dislodged from its conventionally figurative usage. "Obscurity" must be understood as a phenomenon occupying a position along a material (and ultimately metaphysical) spectrum of darkness, ranging from the unclear to the obscure to the opaque. The critical task of materializing obscurity, as a way of gauging the significance of poetry for our understanding of things, begins with the long history of the topos of darkness. In the book of Exodus, for example, the eighth plague is a swarm of locusts that "covered the face of the whole earth, so that the land was darkened" (10:15). And the darkening swarm, conceived as a body, anticipates the plague immediately following it—that of darkness itself—a "darkness which may be felt" (10:21). Evidently, there is a correspondence here between the obscure nature of the swarm and the darkness produced by the swarm, which in turn gives way to a darkness that is somehow autonomous. The autonomous dark is figured differently in the Exeter Book, where the first three poems are storm riddles, which thematize the obscurity of the riddle by configuring darkness as a pneumatic or meteorological phenomenon. Hence, the body of darkness first appears in the Exeter Book in the guise of the weather, as a body of air (corresponding to the lyric "air").

17. Williamson, *Feast of Creatures*, 147.
18. Williamson, *Feast of Creatures*, 84.

Orpheus and the Backwardness of Things

Before I delineate further the corporeal aspect of obscurity—what Milton in *Paradise Lost* calls "darkness visible"—I want to sketch a literary-historical framework for understanding the significance of obscurity as a critical concept.[19] Erich Auerbach, in his magisterial survey of Western literature, *Mimesis,* divides the European tradition into two styles, one originating with Homer and the other with the prophetic books of the Old Testament: "The two styles, in their opposition, represent two types: on the one hand, fully externalized description, uniform illumination, uninterrupted connection, free expression. . . . On the other hand, certain parts brought into high relief, others left obscure, abruptness, suggestive influence of the unexpressed."[20] Work of the latter type, Auerbach observes, is "dark and incomplete" and hence "mysterious, containing a second, concealed meaning."[21] The dark style, rooted in allegory and characterized above all by discontinuity, gives rise to the modern category of the sublime; while the descriptive mode, Auerbach states, forms the basis of realism. Although Auerbach does not directly address the literary form of the riddle—and indeed he tends to neglect lyric poetry in his analysis—his attention to the inscrutability of the parable indicates that the riddle belongs in the tradition of the dark style. The very fact that Auerbach's dichotomy of literary styles depends, in part, on the principle of obscurity indicates that the dark speech of the riddle should not be viewed as an eccentric or aberrant phenomenon in literary history.

One problem with Auerbach's model, stemming from its radical segregation of the two styles, is that obscurity never becomes palpable in his analysis of it; obscurity functions solely—and predictably—as a figurative term. Auerbach fails to corporealize the dark principally, in my view, because to do so would undermine the basic opposition in his model between obscurity and realism. Were darkness to be understood as a trope for the kind of substance produced by the apparatus of lyric poetry—that is to say, if obscurity belongs to the history of metaphysical materialism—then it

19. Here is the passage from *Paradise Lost* in which the phrase occurs:

> . . . yet from those flames
> No light, but rather darkness visible
> Serv'd only to discover sights of woe,
> Regions of sorrow, doleful shades, where peace
> And rest can never dwell.

John Milton, *Paradise Lost,* in *Complete Poetry of John Milton,* ed. John T. Shawcross (Garden City, NY: Anchor Books, 1971), lines 62–66.

20. Erich Auerbach, *Mimesis: The Representation of Reality in Western Literature,* trans. Willard R. Trask (Princeton, NJ: Princeton University Press, 1968), 23.

21. Auerbach, *Mimesis,* 15.

could not stand securely in opposition to realism (as long as the equation of realism and materialism survives). What happens to notions of style, representation, and symbolism when one restores to obscurity its corporeal properties, its substance? Are there corporeal phenomena analogous to the qualities in language that we judge to be obscure? But also: what precisely does obscurity yield in the act of reading—in the absence of clear, cognitive meaning—if not a sense, strange indeed, of poetic *materials?*

The literary-historical division at the core of Auerbach's survey reappears (in the name of darkness) in Maurice Blanchot's theory of literature, with the difference that Blanchot provides a highly suggestive material emblem for the phenomenon of literary—and specifically "Orphic"—obscurity. In his essay on the image in language, Blanchot states that "there are two possibilities for the image, two versions of the imaginary, and this duplicity comes from the initial double meaning produced by the power of the negative."[22] Literature, according to Blanchot, negates the "world" in such a way that it produces two "versions"—one ideal and the other material—of the phenomena it negates; and neither version (idea or thing) belongs to the "world." To grasp Blanchot's dichotomy correctly, one must understand the "world" in a Heideggerian sense, as the effect of a primary negation and idealization of "things," resulting in the mediated phenomenon we call the "world."[23] Literature, and more precisely the literary image, thus constitute a second moment of negation, destroying the world as we know it and exposing us to what cannot be fully grasped—that is, whatever exists in a purely ideal or purely material state. The two versions of the imaginary (i.e., the two aspects of the image) therefore correspond in Blanchot's view to whatever precedes the "world" (things) and to whatever comes after the "world" (ideas), both of which are equally remote from understanding.

Blanchot associates the aspect of the image pertaining to what precedes the world (its purely material aspect in sound or inscription) with what he calls "the word as expression of the obscurity of existence," with a moment when "literature refuses to name anything, when it turns a name into something obscure and meaningless, witness to the primordial obscurity."[24] Thus, over and against the word in its ideal, transparent,

22. Maurice Blanchot, "Two Versions of the Imaginary," in *The Gaze of Orpheus and Other Literary Essays,* by Maurice Blanchot, ed. P. Adams Sitney, trans. Lydia Davis (Barrytown, NY: Station Hill Press, 1981), 86.

23. Heidegger formulates his theory of the work of art issuing from the "rift" between the "earth" and a "world" in his essay "The Origin of the Work of Art," in *Poetry, Language, Thought.* See especially 42–44.

24. Blanchot, "Literature and the Right to Death," in *Gaze of Orpheus*, 48.

and meaningful aspect, there is, Blanchot states, "another side to literature. Literature is a concern for the reality of things, for their unknown, free, and silent existence. . . . it is the being which protests against revelation. . . . it sympathizes with darkness."[25] It is especially pertinent for our investigation of lyric that Blanchot associates the penumbral aspect of the image (which is on the side of things) with what he calls "the Orphic measure" and with "the essential night" that is "kept within the limits and the measured space of the song."[26] Hence, Blanchot refers us, like the riddles of the Exeter Book, to a darkness that is common to song and to things.

The most astonishing moment of Blanchot's theorization of poetic obscurity occurs when he compares the darkness of the image—its "elemental strangeness"—to a cadaver: "At first sight the image does not resemble a cadaver, but it could be that the strangeness of a cadaver is also the strangeness of the image." According to Blanchot, therefore, the figure of the cadaver renders what we experience as obscurity in a literary text; hence, he argues that the material aspect of a poem (not its content or meaning) is the origin of what we call obscurity in literature. The cadaverous aspect of the image is the remains of the "world" after its negation by words: "what is left behind is precisely this cadaver, which is not of the world either—even though it is here—which is rather behind the world . . . and which now affirms, on the basis of this, the possibility of a world-behind, a return backwards."[27] The analogy of the corpse thus depicts the resistance to understanding—the *backwardness*—of the orphic measure and of things prior to the "world."

At the same time, it is essential to bear in mind that, although "someone who has just died is first of all very close to the condition of a thing," Blanchot does not regard the corpse or the thing as an object. Rather, the corpse is continually transformed by "infinite erosion" and "imperceptible consumption," properties that emphasize its partial and unstable identity and that help to explain its aesthetic allure. For Blanchot calls the cadaver "this splendid being who radiates beauty" and declares, "it can very well represent an object as a luminous *formal* halo; it has sided with the *depth,* with elemental materiality."[28] The cadaver, in Blanchot's conception, effectively depicts the element of obscurity precisely because its substance is no more palpable than a halo (a phenomenon said to be woven of light and air), which is almost certainly related, in a material

25. Blanchot, "Literature and the Right to Death," 49.
26. Blanchot, "The Gaze of Orpheus," in *Gaze of Orpheus*, 101, 103.
27. Blanchot, "Two Versions of the Imaginary," 81, 82.
28. Blanchot, "Two Versions of the Imaginary," 82, 85, 83, 80 (emphasis in original).

sense, to the "beauty" radiating from the corpse. Indeed, because the cadaver is subject to "infinite erosion," thereby rendering its physical being comparable to the nebulous body of a storm (or a swarm), the material substance of a "thing" cannot easily be distinguished from the invisible substance radiating from the blurred boundaries of what exists prior to, or behind, the "world." Hence, the radiant cadaver, as Blanchot conceives it, is an emblem of the lyric substance of a poem—its obscurity—but also of the kind of body consistently produced by the apparatus of a poem.

Darkness Visible

Blanchot's emblem of the image-cadaver may appear to be eccentric or even perverse, but it displays qualities often found in a longstanding iconography of lyric substance, which concerns the representation of what Milton calls "darkness visible"—the massy light of hell. And because the luminescence of the underworld is somehow more palpable than natural light, its substance cannot be clearly distinguished from the haze of nebulous bodies. In addition, beginning with the ancient texts that feed Milton's imagery, the topos of this radiant, shadowy substance has been associated with the *pathos* of hell, with suffering. R. W. Johnson, in a study of the style of Vergil's *Aeneid* and its legacy in European lyric poetry, proves to be an indispensable guide to the classical origins of the topos of "darkness visible."[29] Though Johnson is not deliberately concerned with questions of material substance, his subtle and evocative readings of Homer and Vergil yield a rich archive of images pertaining to the material spectrum of "darkness visible." In addition, though he does not explicitly identify lyric poetry as the proper framework of his study (because the *Aeneid* is an epic poem), he readily admits that his analysis is keyed to Vergil's "famous lyricism" and that he regards the *Aeneid* as a "lyrical epic" (50, 164). Hence, his elaboration of "darkness visible" and its various permutations holds special significance for the study of lyric poetry.

In the *Aeneid,* Johnson argues, the reader encounters a "deliberately violent and disordered poetics," and further, he claims, "this deliberate

29. R. W. Johnson, *Darkness Visible: A Study of Vergil's "Aeneid"* (Berkeley and Los Angeles: University of California Press, 1976). Hereafter, page numbers are given in the text for further references to this source.

failure of images is a way of showing darkness" (59). It is not so much unmitigated darkness, however, as an amalgam of shadow and luminosity—chiaroscuro—that characterizes Vergil's *Stimmungskunst.* What Johnson calls the "negative image" of Vergil's style evokes "a trembling, fitful splendor, moving at random, overwhelmed by a space whose magnitude it can suggest but cannot illumine" (87). And there is a distinct correlation between these atmospheric conditions and the representation of unknown or unknowable phenomena (e.g., a visit to the underworld): "Vergil opts for 'unknown orders of being' and for the beautiful, filtered light that reveals realities only to hide them again" (48). Yet the "darkness visible" of the underworld becomes the light in which ordinary reality is perceived in the *Aeneid;* hence, "Vergil's hell exists both for the sake of the narrative it frames and for the sake of other kinds of realities" (89). Because it exists at the threshold of intuition—and for the sake of "other realities"—the palpable and antithetical *lux* of hell serves as the invisible material foundation of ordinary bodies.

Johnson takes great care in describing the chiaroscuro of common things (which are at the same time unknowable) as they appear in the *Aeneid,* yet he also reveals other kinds of bodies that may be latent in the trope of obscurity. For the material propensities of the dark as a figure of speech extend well beyond the failure of light that is its immediate cause. As in the storm riddles of the Exeter Book, meteorological phenomena in the *Aeneid* (storms, clouds, rainbows, mist) become forms capable of "showing" or approximating the substance of darkness.[30] These pneumatic or meteoric bodies—bodies of air—have a direct correlation to the lyric "air." In addition, Johnson cites an extraordinary passage in the *Aeneid* depicting an attempt to dislodge a beehive from a tree with a smoky torch (92). The roiling material phenomena of the swarm, the smoke, and the turbulent sound of the bees, all combine to produce a powerful approximation not only of the poem's obscurity but also of the strange substance of things as they appear in Vergilian darkness. Indeed, Johnson makes an explicit correlation between the elements of lyric and the material substance of unknowable things (which are also common things) when he refers to "the 'unknown modes of being' that Vergil, in trying to write his poem, has learned are part of its materials" (89).

30. My favorite weather in the *Aeneid* occurs when a rainbow (the goddess Iris) appears as a messenger of death; see Virgil, *The "Aeneid" of Virgil,* trans. Rolfe Humphries (New York: Scribner, 1951), book 4, lines 693–705.

Johnson's study not only corporealizes the obscurity of Vergil's text but also seeks to account for the expressivity of darkness as an emblem of material substance. That is, he attempts to discern what the idea of obscurity expresses in the existence of real bodies. Vergil's poem involves "imagining the nameless and invisible sense of what it is like to be overtaken by one's doom"—what Johnson calls "the process of becoming nothing" (98). Overtaken by darkness, a body becomes increasingly obscure, and in time, it becomes "nothing." The trope of "darkness visible" therefore depicts the substance of a body in time, or through time, and thus in flux—a process of invisible decomposition, a disappearance, recalling the "infinite erosion" of the cadaver in Blanchot's essay. Because things dwindle to nothing as darkness overtakes them in a poem, the matter of obscurity itself conversely loses its palpable character as things yield to it in time. Hence, the obscurity of the temporal object—the poem, but also the world it calls into being—reveals itself to be at once corporeal and incorporeal: the anomalous and imponderable medium of poetry itself. Yet the erosion or eclipse of things in a poem—the filtering effect of the dark—is never complete or unequivocal. As a temporal object, a body remains in obscurity, and it is precisely the invisible erosion of things that appears in poetry as a form of darkness, as a blur. Obscurity renders the appearance of things as they vanish in time: the art of disappearing.

The Metaphysics of Dust

The iconography of lyric substance constellated about the phenomenon of "darkness visible" provides a framework—remarkably stable throughout literary history—for depicting correspondences between the poem's nebulous body and certain amorphous bodies in nature. There is certainly a reflexive dimension to these correspondences—the poem sees its own body in a rainbow, a cloud of dust, a shadow, a storm—but we must also recall that pneumatic and meteorological bodies have been, since the seventeenth century, an inescapable feature of the iconography of material substance in physics. Natural philosophers have repeatedly visualized the invisible foundation of matter as a kind of weather. Hence, the corporealization of obscurity in lyric poetry frequently coincides, in its particulars, with the depiction of invisible substance in the history of metaphysical materialism.

The iconography of material substance can always be detected in poems reflecting on their own substance, on the medium of words (and things), whether it be the poetry of Vergil, of Gerard Manley Hopkins, or of the contemporary American poet Jorie Graham. The most ambitious and programmatic rendering of lyric substance in Graham's poetry occurs in her book *Materialism,* though similar concerns are evident in the titles of earlier collections, *Erosion* and *Swarm.*[31] *Materialism* juxtaposes Graham's own meditations on the mysterious texture of things with translations and "adaptations" of authors—mostly philosophers—who have had, in her view, something interesting to say about the nature of material substance: Plato, Sir Francis Bacon, Wittgenstein, Brecht, Jonathan Edwards, and Walter Benjamin (among others). In addition, the book includes a translation of canto 11 of Dante's *Inferno,* to remind us that the poet's descent into the underworld (recalling the topos of "darkness visible" that I outlined earlier) should not be isolated from the scientific discovery of a material occult (the realm of atoms) that can be represented only by imaginary forms.

Graham's anatomy of what she calls "the dream of the unified field" (the title of a poem in *Materialism,* later to become the title of her *Selected Poems*) is provoked, in part, by two questions that appear in the book: "(how can the water rise up out of its grave of matter?)— / (how can the light drop down out of its grave of thought?)—."[32] The former question, alluding to the recurrent motif of a Heraclitean river in the book, becomes "How can the scream rise up out of the grave of its matter?"[33] The book's pivot thus turns upon the impossible convergence (out of the grave) of the corporeality of the voice and the insubstantial body of light.

Versions of this impossible substance, like Milton's figure of "darkness visible," appear throughout the book as corrupt forms of *light,* which constitute the "atomic-yellow ground" of the visible world. The poet, hypnotized by a "beam" of sunlight "calling across the slatwood floor," refers to herself and "the incandescent *thing*" in the third person as "she"—the first of many palpable bodies to be gathered into the "beam."[34] In the material world of these poems, things without ostensible mass betray the presence, or passage, of time, suggesting, as we discussed earlier, that one

31. Jorie Graham, *Erosion* (Princeton, NJ: Princeton University Press, 1983); and Jorie Graham, *Swarm* (New York: Ecco Press, 1999).

32. Jorie Graham, "Event Horizon," in *Materialism,* by Jorie Graham (New York: Ecco Press, 1995), 53.

33. Graham, "Manifest Destiny," in *Materialism,* 100.

34. Graham, "Subjectivity," in *Materialism,* 25, 26.

aspect of lyric substance pertains to the substance of bodies in time. The poet calls the beam

> an unrobed thing we can see the inside of—
>   less place than time—
> less time than the shedding skin of time, the thought
>   of time.[35]

Insofar as the "beam of sun" renders (and therefore dematerializes) more palpable bodies, modeling the inscrutable passage of time that blurs, or veils, the substance of things, it recalls the insubstantial image in Yeats's "Byzantium": "an image, man or shade, / Shade more than man, more image than a shade."[36] In Graham's Byzantium, the "she" inhabiting the beam, "unrobed," appears likewise in radiant form:

> and out there, floating, on the emptiness,
>   among the folds of radio signals, hovering,
>   translucent,
> inside the dress of fizzing, clicking golden
>   frequencies—the pale, invisible flames—
> is the face of the most beautiful woman in the world.[37]

Here, the movement toward imponderable bodies revises the topos of "darkness visible" to include the ponderable light of radiation and a new division of radioactive bodies. Radiography, poised between vision and voice, thus becomes the new science of lyric substance.

Though sublimation and incorporation are magical functions of the beam's physical presence, its substance is much more likely to become evident in these poems by assuming, though never unequivocally, the properties of other, more tangible bodies. Thus, the palpable light of Graham's materialism tends to darken with air, dust, or moisture; to darken into song, storm, or flesh. In her adaptation of a passage of Plato's *Phaedo,* Graham cites Socrates on the relation of the body to "the intellectual principle, which to the bodily eye is dark and invisible." By contrast, Socrates states, "this corporeal element, my friend, is heavy and weighty and earthy and is the element of sight"; hence, the soul, when it becomes "fascinated by the body," is "cloyed with sight."[38] In Graham's reworking

35. Graham, "Subjectivity," in *Materialism,* 26–27.
36. W. B. Yeats, *The Poems,* ed. Richard Finneran (New York: Macmillan, 1983), 248.
37. Graham, "Event Horizon," in *Materialism,* 54.
38. Graham, "*From Plato's* Phaedo," in *Materialism,* 62.

of the dialectic of light and dark in her poems, the "beam" of light acquires texture—a tentative corporeal identity—by entertaining the dark:

no light—no—something
powdery, yet slick—the
continuum?—no luminosity and yet a sheen on it
which you could say is your listening
sprinkling over the green dark,
but not materially, no, a dust.[39]

The subversion of light here coincides with its granulation into darkness, or twilight, yet it also appears to be converting itself into an acoustic body, as if darkness and sound were related phenomena. Indeed, there are moments in *Materialism* when darkness appears to usurp altogether the role of the luminous beam:

the dark seems to be *composed*

. . . .

Has voice in it. A lyre? A concealed
weapon?

As if there's something in it for safekeeping, something
                                        of which I
am the paraphrase

as if lifts up above me now, a labyrinth of variegated
darks.[40]

Concealed in the dark is a paraphrase of the human body, but also a voice and a lyre.

The insubstantial beam darkens with compounds of air and dust, signifying matter, the granules of dust impending, always, in the neighborhood of sound: "morning dust, dust of the green in things, *on* things, dust of water / whirling up off the matter, mist, hoarfrost, dust over the fiddlehead."[41] If the beam is "aswarm with dust and yet / not entered by dust," then the air, impregnated by dust, functions as the matrix that permits the light (and the world) to be seen:

39. Graham, "The Break of Day," in *Materialism,* 115.
40. Graham, "The Break of Day," in *Materialism,* 123.
41. Graham, "The Break of Day," in *Materialism,* 127.

Meanwhile the transparent air
        through or into which the beam—
over the virtual and the material—
        over the world and over the world of the beholder—
glides.[42]

The body of air, the medium in which the beam makes its appearance, is also the body of music that grounds the poem:

the last note carries the air in it and is
        carried by
that air, dusty, in which the light, and the molecules of
watching, and the motes of
listening, are changes rung, rung, but upon what.[43]

In this passage, the motes (or motets) of vision and sound are suspended in a medium of air and light, which is the matrix of the turbulent substance of things as they appear in a poem.

In Graham's rhapsodic materialism, the elements of lyric substance (air, light, dust, moisture) achieve their most comprehensive form in the nebulous and dynamic bodies of the weather. And it is through the elements of this poetic meteorology that Graham's dialogue with Wallace Stevens, concerning poetry's role in the determination of material substance, becomes audible. Indeed, passages about the weather in Graham's poems often bring to mind Stevens's profound meditations on the correspondence between "the sense of poetry" and "the sense of the weather."[44] For example, Graham's poem "The Dream of the Unified Field" begins with a meditation on a snowstorm, an amorphous body that appears, and reappears, in the image of other bodies, such as "the huge flock of starlings massed over our neighborhood . . . / the black bits of their thousands of bodies swarming / then settling / overhead."[45] The poet returns repeatedly to the memory of the storm as an image of "the

42. Graham, "Subjectivity," in *Materialism,* 28–29.

43. Graham, "Invention of the Other," in *Materialism,* 132.

44. In "Adagia," Wallace Stevens writes, "Weather is a sense of nature. Poetry is a sense." Stevens, *Opus Posthumous*, ed. Samuel French Morse (New York: Alfred Knopf, 1957), 161. Stevens's materialism, inevitably overlooked or misread by critics, develops principally through his meditations on poetry's affinity with the weather. Among his many poems referring to this subject, one may consult "Extracts from Addresses to the Academy of Fine Ideas," "Like Decorations in a Nigger Cemetery," "Chocurua to Its Neighbor," "The Snow Man," "Man Carrying Thing," "A Primitive Like an Orb," and "Auroras of Autumn."

45. Graham, "The Dream of the Unified Field," in *Materialism,* 81. Hereafter, page numbers are given in the text for further references to this poem.

constant repatterning of a thing" (82) and of the mysterious inside of things, recalling the "bullioned slant" of the beam:

Filaments of falling marked by the tiny certainties
of flakes. Never blurring yet themselves a cloud. Me in it
and yet
moving easily through it. (80)

The imaginative and philosophical changes rung upon the snowstorm (which reflect the mutability of any phenomenon) coincide with the reciprocation of interior and exterior spaces. The "certainties of flakes" become bits of sleep and thought that accumulate to become the imagined objects of an interior climate:

The storm: I close my eyes and,
standing in it, try to make it *mine*. An inside
thing. Once I was . . . once, once.
It settles in my head, the wavering white
sleep, the instances—they stick, accrue,
grip up, connect, they do not melt.
I will not let them melt, they build, cloud and cloud. (85)

The nebulosity of the material storm and the solidity of intellectual objects coincide because the blind, possessive, agglutinative mode of composition is the same in both cases. Ultimately, the storm that is reassembled in the mind reveals itself to be a "possession" of history, a "splinter colony" (86). Indeed, in a startling transformation, the snowstorm becomes the "vast white sleeping geography" of the "new world" discovered by Columbus (87)—the very substance of a unified field of matter, thought, language, and history.

Counterfeit Gloom

Considered solely in terms of its conceptual horizon and its philosophical ambitions, Jorie Graham's anatomy of lyric substance might be regarded as a literary anomaly, as an eccentric and sophisticated thought experiment. Yet insofar as it dwells on—and in—the obscurity of its particular medium (the *materia poetica* of lyric), it addresses the urgent question of how poetry makes sense (and substance) of the material world. Her poetry, couched in a literary genealogy of darkness, follows the great tradition of Epicurean meditations on the nature of sense. That is to say, as rich as Graham's particular vision may be, one need not turn to poems devoted explicitly to the topic of materialism in order to discern how the medium of darkness becomes palpable in the signatures of things. Nor need obscurity be associated with virtuosity or difficulty as a prerequisite for the elaboration of lyric substance in a poem, since obscurity straddles and, in certain respects, unifies the disparate realms of literary and vernacular poetries.

The problem of obscurity, conceived as an allegory of material substance in lyric poetry, thus poses significant questions about the nature of material substance, even as it offers a fleeting glimpse of the tenuous matter of the poem itself. If we think of Blanchot's figure of the cadaver, or the "beam" of sunlight in Graham's *Materialism,* it is evident that these marvelous things (or "strange creatures," in the parlance of riddles) possess both the stable form of an object and the nebulous body of a meteoric phenomenon. The duplicity of things also appears in the object lessons staged by the Anglo-Saxon riddle: for example, possible solutions for one unsolved riddle range from swan to water to quill pen to siren. The difference between ponderable and imponderable bodies, and also the mysterious relation between them, are implicit as well in the storm riddles of the Exeter Book, which speak to us in the same fashion as the talking objects that follow them. Indeed, it is peculiar that the storm riddles, which are the first three riddles in the collection, and which pertain to nebulous bodies that are also events, should serve to introduce us to a collection of talking *objects*. Were all of the riddles to remain unsolved, however, the dark speech of the weather would not betray what distinguishes a storm from an object. The rainbow and the bucket would speak the same gibberish.

Imagining how a rainbow is like a bucket, or how a body of air precipitates more tangible bodies, might appear to be a fanciful pastime, but science suggests it is not, or not merely so. Even so, if the intuitive and nonintuitive aspects of a thing remain polarized in the discourse of scientific materialism, poetry, by contrast, excels at producing images in which the invisible foundation of matter rises to the surface of things and the mutable forms of intuition dissolve into the hidden ground of their abstraction—what Graham calls "the dream of the unified field."

Gerard Manley Hopkins, a poet notorious for the close, labored textures—and hence the obscurity—of his verse, praises what he calls "pied beauty," a rubric for contrasting phenomena that are paired or conjoined. Though, at first glance, the poem called "Pied Beauty" appears to be a simple celebration of "dappled things," it is not, on closer inspection, entirely clear why "skies of couple-colour" or a "brinded cow" might be counted among "All things counter, original, spare, strange."[46] Dappled things are "original" because they make visible the origin, the hidden foundation, of things; and they are "counter" because their appearance betrays what is antithetical to appearance—the amalgam of "pied beauty." In this sense, dappled things are "spare" because they are simple and rudimentary, but they are also excessive in their disclosure of what they do not possess, a beauty that is "past change." These ordinary things therefore betray the qualities of an invisible, mutable substance that precedes them in the image of all that is "adazzle, dim" and, more palpably, in "Fresh-firecoal chestnut-falls." And these protean substances, which hover just below the threshold of objecthood, and which nevertheless find expression in intuitive examples of "pied beauty," are emblems of "darkness visible"—of the spectacle of obscurity. In addition, by praising "all trades, their gear and tackle and trim"—perhaps the most curious example of "pied beauty" in the poem—Hopkins suggests that the insubstantial apparatus of lyric poetry somehow renders the "strange" substance of pied beauty.

The ember of pied beauty, too faint to illumine anything but itself, and therefore akin to darkness, is an effect of what Hopkins calls "light's delay." The phrase occurs in one of his so-called dark sonnets, which begins with the line, "I wake and feel the fell of dark, not day." What it means to wake into a darkness that is felt depends, in large measure, on the word "fell," a complex term with at least four disparate levels of meaning: a covering of hide; the substance known as gall (a bitter humor); a waste hillside; and a blow. The dark of wakefulness is evidently a material thing, shape-shifting and enigmatical, yet it is also a form of utterance:

This night! what sights you, heart, saw, ways you want!
And more must, in yet longer light's delay.
With witness I speak this.[47]

The poet feels "the fell of dark," and he speaks it, in the "rugged dark" of the sonnet's heavily stressed lines. Thus, the substance of darkness ranges across the material spectrum, from barren soil to liquid humor to the blows of the metrical beat.

The extraordinary texture and density of Hopkins's lines (the basis of

46. Gerard Manley Hopkins, "Pied Beauty," in *The Poetical Works of Gerard Manley Hopkins,* ed. Norman H. Mackenzie (Oxford: Clarendon Press, 1990), 144.

47. Hopkins, "St. Winefred's Well," in *Poetical Works,* 181.

their obscurity) arouse a sense of the submerged correspondence between darkness and things—the kind of enigmatical affinities that form the basis of Anglo-Saxon riddle poems. But the vocabulary and rhythm of Hopkins's lyrics, which reflect a conspicuous attempt on his part to recuperate the strong-stress metrics of Anglo-Saxon verse, are not the only aspects of his poetry to evoke the sensibility of the riddle. The bold, but sometimes inscrutable, physiognomy of Hopkins's verse recalls the materialism of the riddle as well in its use of uncommon conceits to render common things, not to mention the *substance* of things. The most ambitious and sustained example of this method occurs in "The Wreck of the Deutschland," the first great expression of Hopkins's mature style. The poem recounts the sinking of a passenger ship (and the drowning of five nuns on board) by a powerful storm "between midnight and morning of December 7" in 1875.[48] It is not the ship, however, but the storm and the darkness mingled with it that compel the poet's attention. The long night at sea and the storm consume nearly a quarter of the poem's thirty-five stanzas, so that the storm becomes the material and figurative matrix of the poem's theology.

Instead of starting with an ordinary object and allowing the object, through the technical and figurative operations of the poem, to decompose, to dissolve into the invisible substance of its material foundation, the method of Hopkins's materialism, by contrast, starts with an image of the penumbral substance of things—a storm—in order to bear witness to the objectification of matter through language. A number of the poem's features invite the reader to view it as a storm riddle, after the Anglo-Saxon riddle poems. Indeed, "The Wreck of the Deutschland" actually contains several short riddles that are very close in form to those found in the Exeter Book. Here is one of them:

"Some find me a sword; some
The flange and rail; flame,
Fang, or flood." (121)

Were we to supply the exhortation "Say who I am" at the end of these lines, the poem could easily be mistaken for an Old English riddle (which indeed it may be, given the quotation marks). The riddle creature, in this

48. This reference to the timing of the storm—at night—occurs in the poem's dedication (to the five drowned nuns). Hopkins, "The Wreck of the Deutschland," in *Poetical Works*, 119. Hereafter, page numbers are given in the text for further references to this poem.

case, is Death (the solution supplied by the poet, who adds, "storms bugle his fame").

If we are to read "The Wreck of the Deutschland" as a storm riddle, as a parable of theological materialism, then we must listen more carefully to Hopkins's echo of a storm riddle in the Exeter Book. Here is the voice of the storm in the Anglo-Saxon text:

Sometimes I swoop down, whipping up waves,
Rousing white water, driving to shore
The flint-gray flood, its foam-flanks flaring
Against the cliff wall. Dark swells loom
In the deep—hills on hills of dark water,
Driven by the sea, surge to a meeting of cliffs.[49]

And here is Hopkins's description of the imagined (and perhaps borrowed) storm of his allegory:

For the infinite air is unkind,
And the sea flint-flake, black-backed in the regular blow,
Sitting Eastnortheast, in cursed quarter, the wind;
Wiry and white-fiery and whirlwind-swivelled snow
Spins to the widow-making unchilding unfathering deeps. (122)

Though the two texts diverge in significant ways (Hopkins, for example, imagines a snowstorm), the evocation of "dark swells" is central to both passages. And Hopkins's phrase "sea flint-flake" is almost certainly an adaptation of the Anglo-Saxon epithet "flint-gray flood." A few lines later, he refers to "the cobbled foam-fleece" of the sea (123), again perhaps echoing the Exeter riddle. Generally, the alliterative patterns and strong-stress meter shared by the two poems heighten one's sense of resounding forms and intertextual play.

Though the Anglo-Saxon tradition appears to furnish Hopkins with the imagery and prosodic effects necessary to evoke the storm's fatal character, the speaker of Hopkins's poem recoils from the task of imagining what lies beyond the scope of his experience or knowledge. The storm therefore remains a mystery, a conundrum, whose resolution is uncertain. Allied with an unknown—and perhaps unknowable—event, words abandon the speaker; the poem begins to unravel:

49. Williamson, *Feast of Creatures*, 60.

But how shall I . . . Make me room there;
Reach me a . . . Fancy, come faster—
Strike you the sight of it? look at it loom there. (126)

The problem here is similar to that faced by Vergil or Milton in trying to depict the underworld, for the storm that Hopkins seeks to represent is indeed a kind of hell on earth. That is to say, the storm becomes, for Hopkins, the place in which one discovers the protean substance of "darkness visible."

Hopkins's solution to the problem is at once surprising and familiar; he declares,

There was a single eye!
Read the unshapeable shock night
And knew the who and the why;
Wording it how but by him that present and past,
Heaven and earth are word of, worded by?— (126)

The poet therefore finds his footing again, so to speak, and acquires the power to envision what has taken place in the dark by assuming the "single eye" of God, the one true witness to the event. (This is the surprising part of the poet's answer to the conundrum posed by the storm.) Even more important, for our purposes, the act of imagination or representation is conceived in terms of reading and textuality. Hence, the unknown materials of the storm—the "unshapeable shock night"—are assimilated to the turbulent substance of the poem. And that is the familiar part of the poet's solution to representing the storm. For we have already seen, on several occasions, how a poem is inclined to discover the nature of its own materials in the substance of darkness and the weather. In Hopkins's great poem, not only is there continual attention to problems of language and speech, but the storm's furious body (air, snowflake, thunder, stress, darkness) begins somehow to resemble the dainty materials of the poem: "Storm flakes were scroll-leaved flowers, lily showers—sweet / heaven was astrew in them" (124). The storm becomes a kind of toy, its "black-about air" at once the poem's breath and the "searomp over the wreck" (123). The "storm's brawling" becomes a "madrigal start" (123), and the fearful "dark" rhymes with "the uttermost mark" (127)—with writing.

In Hopkins's storm riddle, the wind, called out of its name, becomes "the burl of the fountains of air" (123), and night is converted to the poem's obscurity, to "counterfeit gloom" (in Milton's memorable image). The insubstantial engine of lyric therefore turns darkness into a thing, an artifact. And this is the aim of a riddle: the dark speech veiling the object coalesces—once the riddle is solved—into an image of the object itself. Yet obscurity, in a literary sense, is itself already an artifact: the glowing remains of darkness apprehended by language. Heidegger's equation of naming with *lighting* comes to mind, so that we may understand obscurity—what passes for material substance in poetry—to be the erosion of the particular darkness of things by their names, producing a metaphysical compound of language and matter, *logos* and phenomenon. Naming the dark makes darkness visible, and this conversion from substance to object is always a matter of artifice.

In conclusion, I want to return to the question of what significance the principle of lyric substance may hold for metaphysical materialism and for materialist criticism in literary studies. Most immediately, the correlation between the way science makes sense of material substance (by depicting the invisible) and what matters about the world in a poem should encourage criticism in the humanities to abandon uncritical assumptions about the nature of material substance. Unless the critical methodology is strictly empirical—an orientation fundamentally alien to literary criticism—the reality of matter must always remain uncertain, always a problem that needs to be taken into consideration. Hence, the study of material cultures, for example, should never take for granted the material integrity of its objects.

Finally, although one is not likely to ascribe to poetry the authority and explanatory power usually reserved for science, this antinomy also obtains within science itself, between theoretical physics and more empirical models or disciplines. Hence, the question of what sort of reality should be ascribed to the underworld of quantum mechanics (in contrast to the way bodies behave in Newtonian space) resembles debate about the significance of poetry for our conception of physical reality. Which is more real, physics repeatedly asks, the unreal substance of subatomic matter or the mutable appearance of things in perceptual space? It is not inconceivable that it may one day appear reasonable to assimilate our understanding of ordinary bodies to the invisible—and sometimes incommensurable—features of material substance (as science envisions it). So, too, we may one day grant to lyric substance (what poetry makes of the world) an authority it possesses today only in the realm of speculation—the only certainty, perhaps, it will ever possess.

THREE

Lost Laboratories of the Sphinx

The more closely one looks at a word, the greater the distance from which it looks back. KARL KRAUS

Enigmatography

The term "modernism" calls to mind, justifiably, a complex program of experimentation in the arts, yet the decades of the 1930s and 1940s (the period of so-called late modernism) saw the emergence of critical and aesthetic categories that have resisted historical and theoretical analysis, in part because of their uncertain relation to the formalist legacy of modernism. I am referring to the aesthetic ideology of *kitsch* and to the poetic or philosophical principle of the enigma (the latter having entirely escaped the purview of critical assessments aimed at producing a *new* modernism). Although the submerged correspondences between kitsch and enigmatic expression remain beyond the scope of this chapter, it is essential to note that both concepts emerged in response to the gradual dissolution of the historical avant-garde and to the development of fascism in Europe. The idea of kitsch, on the one hand, first appeared in the writings of Hermann Broch and Clement Greenberg as a countersign of fascism and, more polemically, in opposition to avant-garde practice—an opposition that is deeply unstable.[1] The figure of the riddle, on the other hand, functions in the writings of Heidegger, Benjamin, and Adorno (among others) as a means of addressing the broader implications of obscurity, whether in modern art and literature or in traditions (Presocratic philosophy, Baroque allegory) associated obliquely by these authors with modernity.

Adorno, in particular, makes bold claims about the significance of the riddle for comprehending the nature of art, declaring, for example, that "all art works are riddles."[2] Moreover, he observes, "Hermetic art works tend to be rebuked for being unintelligible. Actually, their unintelligibility is a confession that all art is enigmatic" (179). Adorno's approach to the figure of the riddle, intimated by his rejection of common judgments about the significance of obscurity, is antihermeneutical. He is not interested in the possibility of solving riddles or in reconciling *Verstehen* (understanding) and obscurity. Rather, he states, "The enigmatic quality renders the very notion of *Verstehen* problematic" and, more pointedly, "Aesthetics cannot hope to grasp works of art if it treats them as hermeneutical objects. What at present needs to be grasped is their unintelligibility" (77, 173). As the phrase "at present" in the latter statement suggests, Adorno views the "enigmatic quality" of art as integral, more precisely, to *modern* art: "As the work (under the auspices of modernism) posits unintelligibility as expression, increasingly destroying the intelligible moment, the traditional hierarchy of understanding is shattered. Its place is taken up by the reflection on the enigmatic quality of art" (476). Under the "auspices" of modernism, the possibility of solving, or understanding, the riddle gives way to reflection on the work's essential obscurity, on the apotropaic conditions of the riddle. Under the regime of the modernist enigma, one finds "art acquiring meaning by giving expression to its glaring lack of meaning" (185). The "glaring" riddle of modern art therefore distinguishes itself by making a spectacle of obscurity. Adorno deploys the figure of the riddle in his efforts to characterize modern art, yet by neglecting to emphasize or examine the inherently *verbal*

1. Broch's earliest writing on kitsch appears in a section entitled "Der Kitsch" of a larger essay "Das Böse in Wertsystem der Kunst" (Evil in the Value System of Art), published in the journal *Neue Rundschau* in August 1933. Broch revised these ideas for a lecture at Yale in 1950, which was published as "Einige Bemerkungen zum Problem des Kitsches" (Notes on the Problem of Kitsch) in Hermann Broch, *Gesammelte Werke* (Zurich: Rhein-Verlag, 1955), 6:295–309. In 1939, Clement Greenberg published his polemical essay "Avant-Garde and Kitsch," reprinted in his *Art and Culture: Critical Essays* (Boston: Beacon Press, 1961). On the unstable opposition between kitsch and avant-garde, see Daniel Tiffany, "Kitsching the *Cantos*," *Modernism/Modernity* 12, no. 2 (2005): 329–337.

2. T. W. Adorno, *Aesthetic Theory*, trans. C. Lenhardt, ed. Gretel Adorno and Rolf Tiedemann (London: Routledge and Kegan Paul, 1984), 176. Hereafter, page numbers are given in the text for further references to this source.

nature of the enigma, he misses an opportunity to situate the broader significance of the riddle in a correspondence between the enigma and modern *poetry*.

Walter Benjamin, by contrast, in a brief essay on the "riddle" of profane objects, never diverts his attention from the specifically verbal operation of the riddle, even when it functions as "a symbol of noncommunication."[3] In his view, the "mystery" of profane objects—that is, "the insoluble aspect of the artifact or event"—can be "redeemed" only by understanding the object as a word, a *Rätselwort,* by disclosing the analogy between word, riddle, and being: "For precisely as word all being exists in a state of mystery by virtue of the symbolic force of the word, and in an ambiguous sense—which is constitutive for the nature of the riddle, the key to the riddle [*Rätselwort*]—is not only its solution, as the thing that thwarts it, but also its intention, its precondition, its foundation and the 'resolution' of the intent to puzzle that is concealed in it."[4] Benjamin argues here that the "being" of every profane object reveals its mystery (or its "share" of the mystery of things) only insofar as it exists as a word—a "riddle word"—which is at once the precondition, the intention, and the foundation of the object. Significantly, the riddle word is more than the object's "solution" or its explanation: it "redeems" the object by disclosing the grounds of its enigmatic nature in a purely formal sense. Benjamin, like Adorno, is concerned, not with solving riddles, but with the objective conditions, the operation, of the enigma. For Benjamin, however, the enigmatic nature of the *word,* in particular, determines the "mystery" of the object. By assuming the condition of a word, the profane object becomes a riddle.

Benjamin's modeling of the "mystery" of being after the word—a *Rätselwort*—calls to mind Heidegger's revisionary account of Presocratic efforts "to secure Being in the essence of language."[5] Searching the fragmentary verse of Parmenides and the aphorisms of Heraclitus, Heidegger recovers the forgotten metaphysics of the λόγος, he explains, from the "depths of a riddle": "thinking changes the world. It changes it in the ever darker depths of a riddle. . . . The riddle has long been propounded to us in the word, Being."[6] Heidegger undertakes a "series of unprece-

3. Walter Benjamin, "Riddle and Mystery," in *Selected Writings,* by Walter Benjamin, ed. Marcus Bullock and Michael W. Jennings (Cambridge, MA: Belknap Press of Harvard University Press, 1996), 1:268.

4. Benjamin, "Riddle and Mystery," 267.

5. Martin Heidegger, "Logos (Heraclitus, Fragment B50)", in *Early Greek Thinking,* by Martin Heidegger, trans. David Farrell Krell and Frank A. Capuzzi (New York: Harper, 1975), 77.

6. Heidegger, "Logos," 78.

dented readings of these texts in order to disclose what he calls—quite deliberately—"the riddle of Being."[7] Emphasizing repeatedly the "enigmatic fullness" and "riddling" character of the thought of Parmenides and Heraclitus, Heidegger scours these texts for "enigmatic key words" (*Rätselworter*)—the same term used by Benjamin in reference to modern allegory—to serve as the pivots of his exegesis. Furthermore, like Benjamin, he focuses on the verbal properties of the riddle (manifest in the style of the texts under consideration) to demonstrate the fundamental correspondences between λόγος and Being. Thus, concerning the nature of Being, "the fundamental trait of presencing itself is determined by remaining concealed and unconcealed."[8] Correspondingly, "λόγος is *in itself and at the same time* a revealing and concealing."[9] The revealing self-concealing of the riddle—analogous to what I have called the spectacle of obscurity—therefore expresses, and conjoins, the homologous structures of λόγος and Being. In the end, what Heidegger, like Benjamin, calls the riddle's "mystery"—its "invisible shining"—pertains, not to any possible solution or to its content, but to its paradoxical operation: "the shining of the lighting is in itself at the same time a self-veiling—and is in that sense what is most obscure."[10]

One discovers, as I have indicated, a general consonance and multiple reverberations among what one might call the "enigma variations" of Adorno, Benjamin, and Heidegger. Adorno, for example, like Heidegger, emphasizes the open secrecy of the riddle: "art as a whole is a riddle. Another way of putting this is to say that art expresses something while at the same time hiding it" (176). More specifically, he explains: "I am using the term 'enigma' not in a loose sense, denoting some general ambiguity, but in the precise sense of a riddle or puzzle. While puzzles may not represent explicit and objective solutions, they do have potential solutions. Now, art works are puzzles in this sense. Every one is like a *Vexierbild* [picture puzzle], vexing the viewer whose defeat is a foregone conclusion. . . . Like art it hides something while at the same time showing it" (178). Significantly, by using the analogy of a picture puzzle to illustrate his conception of the enigma, Adorno discloses the *vernacular* origins of the riddle, thereby linking the principle of obscurity to an aesthetic ideology that departs from the criteria of "literary" or "literate" poetry. In philosophical terms, Adorno's general understanding of art and (by implication) of the riddle as an "aesthetic monad" coincides with his determina-

7. Martin Heidegger, "The Anaximander Fragment," in *Early Greek Thinking*, 58.
8. Martin Heidegger, "Aletheia (Heraclitus, Fragment B16)," in *Early Greek Thinking*, 106–107.
9. Heidegger, "Anaximander Fragment," 58 (emphasis in original).
10. Heidegger, "Aletheia," 123.

tion of enigmatic "expression"—the term used by Adorno throughout his discussion of the riddle.[11] That is to say, the hermeticism of the vernacular artifact (the picture puzzle) is indistinguishable from its expressiveness—a condition demonstrating the open secrecy of the riddle.

Adorno's reference to Leibniz's monadology and its theory of metaphysical expression helps to explain a curious analogy for what may be described as the *perceptiveness* of the enigma: "To solve a riddle in art is to identify the reason why it is insoluble—which is the gaze art works direct at the viewer. They demand to be understood in terms of their substance" (178–179). The reference here to the *substance* of the riddle confirms my thesis regarding the modernist preoccupation with the *metaphysics* of the riddle, yet the notion of the artwork, or riddle, gazing back at the viewer evokes, more precisely, Leibniz's theory of "monadic perception": a nonrelational transaction that is characteristic of all entities, animate or inanimate, and that constitutes the very substance of being.

These difficult concepts, especially the notion of the gaze of the artifact, are more familiar to us from Benjamin's theory of modern allegory and one of its spin-offs, the bewitching "aura" of the object—conceptions which are dependent, as Benjamin acknowledges, on Leibniz's theory of monadic perception and on the poetological research of early German Romanticism: "'Perceptibility,' as Novalis puts it, 'is a kind of attentiveness.' The perceptibility he has in mind is none other than that of the aura. Experience of the aura thus rests on the transposition of a response common in human relationships to the relationship between the inanimate or natural object and man. . . . To perceive the aura of an object we look at means to invest it with the ability to look at us in return."[12] In a footnote to this passage, Benjamin contends that words, like objects, possess a kind of "attentiveness" and, further, that "this endowment is a wellspring [*Quellpunkt*] of poetry. . . . Words, too, can have an aura of their own."[13] Attributing to words a monadic "aura"—the capacity to gaze back at the reader—therefore identifies the verbal metaphysics of the riddle as one of the hidden sources (a "wellspring") of poetry.[14]

11. Adorno's reference to the "aesthetic monad" appears in the context of his discussion of art as a riddle. See Adorno, *Aesthetic Theory*, 180.

12. Walter Benjamin, "Some Motifs in Baudelaire," in *Charles Baudelaire: A Lyric Poet in the Era of High Capitalism*, by Walter Benjamin, trans. Harry Zohn (London: Verso, 1983), 148.

13. Benjamin, "Some Motifs in Baudelaire," 148 n. 90.

14. Benjamin's choice of the term *Quellpunkt* (wellspring) is significant, as it echoes Hölderlin's famous poem "The Rhine," which refers to the source (*den Quell*) of the Rhine as a riddle (*Rätsel*), claiming "Ein Rätsël ist Reinentsprungenes" ("Pure of source is the riddle").

Rhapsodic Measures

Beyond these philosophical reflections on the nature of the riddle, one does indeed find literary and critical evidence of the significance of riddles, or enigmatic expression, for modernist poetry. Guy Davenport, for example, introducing his translation of the fragments of Heraclitus (known in antiquity for his "riddling" style), asserts: "His presence as a spirit in both modern poetry (Eliot, Pound, William Carlos Williams, Hopkins) and in modern physics makes him peculiarly a twentieth-century guide, one of our *daimons*."[15] On the cover of his book, Davenport reproduces a sketch of a Cubist "head in bronze"—a minacious, ambiguously human figure—reminding the reader that the epithets associated with Heraclitus's work signal an identification with the riddling Sphinx of antiquity. The "*daimon*" of modernist poetry evoked by the forbidding bronze head thus alludes at once to Heraclitus and to the figure of the Sphinx.

Marshall McLuhan, as well, makes a case for the influence of the fragmentary texts of the Presocratics (especially Empedocles) on a group of leading modernists—on T. S. Eliot, in particular: "His devotion to the Pre-Socratic philosophers is evident in his citation of them, but it is Empedocles whose vision pervades *The Waste Land* and *Four Quartets*. Eliot was not alone in his recourse to Empedocles. It would be quite easy to show how deeply W. B. Yeats and Ezra Pound and James Joyce had also studied Empedocles."[16] Dismissing—perhaps unjustly—the verse drama *Empedocles on Etna,* published by Matthew Arnold in 1852, McLuhan traces the literary dissemination of Empedocles' philosophy-in-verse to Lewis Carroll's Humpty Dumpty, who impersonates the *Sphairos* (the cosmic egg) of Empedocles' metrical thinking:

> Must a name mean something? Alice asked doubtfully.
>
> Of course it must, Humpty Dumpty said with a short laugh: *my* name means the shape I am.[17]

15. *Herakleitos and Diogenes,* trans. Guy Davenport (Bolinas, CA: Grey Fox Press, 1979), 9. Fragments of Heraclitus recur in Pound's *Cantos,* while T. S. Eliot places one of Heraclitus's aphorisms concerning the λόγος at the beginning of "Burnt Norton" in *Four Quartets.*

16. Marshall McLuhan, "Empedocles and T. S. Eliot," introduction to Helen Lambridis, *Empedocles* (University: University of Alabama Press, 1976), viii.

17. Lewis Carroll, *Through the Looking Glass,* cited in McLuhan, "Empedocles and T. S. Eliot," vii. With regard to Arnold's *Empedocles on Etna,* one should note that Arnold would certainly have been aware of Hölderlin's *The Death of Empedocles,* a verse drama written in three distinct (and unfinished) versions between 1797 and 1800.

To McLuhan's mind, the Presocratic Humpty Dumpty is an invention of the *logician* Charles Dodgson, but also a poetic vision of Lewis Carroll's: "The Nursery world of myth and mutations was where Empedocles first established a beachhead in the Victorian age."[18]

Modernist intuitions, or variations, of the riddle remain embedded in the long history of debate about the difficulty of modern poetry—a context yielding little insight, however, into the specific features of the riddle as a poetic model. Received ideas about lyric poetry (even when it is associated with the avant-garde) continue to veil the curious affinities of the modernist enigma, not to mention the eccentric genealogy of the riddle. Any serious consideration of the riddle as an enduring but occluded source of poetry must begin with the mythical figure of the Sphinx, whose riddles bear little resemblance to conventional forms of poetry in antiquity, yet who is described by Euripides as chanting a "song" (μέλος) and by ancient commentators as composing "deadly melodies" (μοῦσα θανόντων).[19] Sophocles refers to the monster as "the Sphinx of intricate song" (ποικιλωδός), calling her, more precisely, a *rhapsode* (ῥαψωδός), the Homeric term for the "singer of tales," the epic poet.[20] Following the implications of these judgments, one would want to include the riddle of the Sphinx among those ancient writings (Pindar's odes, the aphorisms of Heraclitus) whose obscurity is judged to be a "constitutive element" of their significance.[21] Ancient commentary therefore reveals that the Sphinx was identified in antiquity (by fifth-century Athenians) as a singer or poet and, further, by implication, that the αἴνιγμα (riddle) may be understood as a kind of poetry.[22] Yet it is far from clear what sort of poetry her riddle exemplifies, or what type of poet the Sphinx may be—questions, I want to argue, that play a larger role than we imagine in the history of poetry and poetic genres.

By calling the Sphinx a *rhapsode,* the classical Greek term for the Homeric singer, Sophocles apparently seeks to place the Sphinx in the epic, or post-epic, tradition, even as he appears to suggest that Oedipus solves the riddle because he recognizes it as a departure from epic, the prereq-

18. McLuhan, "Empedocles and T. S. Eliot," vi.

19. Euripides' comment can be found in line 1506 of *The Phoenician Woman* (also known as *The Phoenissae*), and the reference to "deadly melodies" appears in the Scholiast to line 50 of *Phoenissae.*

20. Sophocles, *Oedipus the King,* lines 130 and 391.

21. John Hamilton names Pindar and Heraclitus, though not the Sphinx, as figures whose work is characterized by George Steiner's category of "ontological obscurity." Hamilton, *Soliciting Darkness* (Cambridge, MA: Harvard University Press, 2003), 4.

22. Ancient Greek provides two different terms for the verbal device of the riddle: αἴνιγμα and γριφος. As the term αἴνιγμα appears to include other types of utterances (such as oracles), the precise nature of the riddle of the Sphinx (characterized as an αἴνιγμα) raises basic questions about the relation between riddles, songs, and other types of "dark sayings."

uisite for his hermeneutic success. On the face of it, the correspondence between ἔπος and αἴνιγμα is peculiar, if not bizarre, because of the wildly divergent scales of epic poetry and the riddle—though one would not want to rule out the possibility that certain features of epic poetry could, under certain conditions, occur on the scale of the question, the aphorism, the miniature. In addition, the correlation of Sphinx and *rhapsode* does not appear to rely on the formal implications of the verb ῥάπτω (to sew or stitch together) or on the compositional methods implied in this term. Liddell and Scott conjecture that Sophocles may have called the Sphinx a *rhapsode* because she declaims her song—the deadly riddle—in public, like the Homeric singer of tales.[23] The implications of this possible affinity for the poetic tradition are at once profound and subversive: the riddle, one of the archetypes of poetic obscurity, would appear in this light to be an instrument—at once provocative and inscrutable—of public, and even civic, discourse (if one takes seriously the function of epic poetry). Furthermore, the model of the *rhapsode* implies that the singer of riddles belongs to a *vernacular* tradition of poetry that is both performative and itinerant.[24] The qualities associated with this riddling, post-epic genre of poetry—a genre subsequently overshadowed by traditional lyric—persist with surprising stability in later manifestations of the rhapsodic genre. Indeed, the hybrid character of the Sphinx herself—part human, part lion, part bird—may be construed as a figure for the anomalous genre of poetry she practiced in the streets of Thebes.

To characterize the poetry of the Sphinx—and the riddle itself—as "rhapsodic" diverges sharply from contemporary usage of the term (and its cognate "rhapsody"), associated with exaggerated enthusiasm and feeling. For the rhapsodic nature of the Sphinx and her riddling songs shared certain technical and performative features with epic poetry: the notorious riddle itself, for example, was apparently composed in hexameters, the meter of the Homeric epics.[25] At the same time, the original

23. Liddell and Scott, *Greek-English Lexicon,* s.v. ῥαψωδός, 716.

24. On the vernacular methods of the epic singer, see Albert Lord's classic work *The Singer of Tales* (Cambridge, MA: Harvard University Press, 1960). In the Classical period of Greek antiquity, the rhapsode had become essentially a professional (and sometimes ridiculed) reciter or performer. My use of the term, by contrast, emphasizes the archaic sense of the rhapsode as a composer and itinerant poet. For an account of Plato's ambivalent accommodation of the rhapsodic hymn, see Gregory Nagy, *Plato's Rhapsody and Homer's Music* (Cambridge, MA: Harvard University Press, 2002).

25. The earliest record of the riddle's text appears in a fragment of a lost play by Euripides. See John Vaio, "The New Fragments of Euripides' *Oedipus,*" *Greek, Roman, and Byzantine Studies* 5 (1964): 44. Line 6 of *Oxyrhynchus Papyri,* document 2459, frag. 2, indicates specifically that the Sphinx chanted the riddle in "hexameters." The Euripidean citation, which supplies only portions of five lines, is later confirmed by Athenaeus (AD 200), whose version of the riddle appears in five full hexameter lines (Athenaeus 10.456b).

term, "rhapsody," in its epic context (a poem stitched together from various elements) does not comprehend fully the monstrosity of the riddling, post-epic verse practiced by the Sphinx.

To grasp the nature of the rhapsodic measures of the Sphinx, one must turn to analogous, and correspondingly anomalous, figures such as the Sirens (another hybrid of human and animal), whose dangerous song orbits the epic tradition—almost as a kind of gossip—in idiosyncratic ways. For, although the song of the Sirens is known principally for its spellbinding quality, part of its allure for Odysseus derives from its premonitory aspect: the Sirens promised to inform Odysseus of the fates of all his Greek comrades in Troy (*Odyssey* 12.189–190). In addition, the Sirens, like the rhapsode and the Sphinx, practice their art in a fluid, haphazard place—the open sea—reminding us of the perplexing but obviously significant relation between rhapsody, obscurity, and the construction of public space. Further, the Sirens' rumored response to Odysseus's successful resistance to their song—suicide—recalls the fate of the Sphinx when Oedipus solves the infamous riddle.[26] The explanation for these parallels between Siren and Sphinx lies in a more fundamental correspondence between the types of songs they compose, a shared practice from which we may hope to define more clearly the post-epic conjugation of riddle and rhapsody (in the original, Homeric sense of the term).

What kind of strange song is it, exactly, issuing from the mouths of the Sirens and the Sphinx? What new model, or genre, of poetry is articulated for posterity by the poetic practice of these mythological figures? In addition to the unexpected associations with the epic tradition, the enigmatic songs of the Sphinx and the Sirens share a common origin in the ancient tradition of metrical charms (ἐπῳδαί) or "binding spells" (αγωγή).[27] Recent scholarship has gathered evidence of a "venerable tradition of hexametrical charms" in antiquity—a genre of poetry composed, like the riddle of the Sphinx and the epic verses of the *rhapsode,* in hexameters.[28] A central feature of ancient Greek magic and medical lore, these hexametrical charms were designed to elicit erotic desire or affection in the beloved (hence the "binding" nature of the spell), often by seeking to induce physical suffering, by torment; that is, by applying—sympathetically, of course—"the whip of persuasion."[29] In addition, these bind-

26. On the suicide of the Sphinx, see Robert Graves, *The Greek Myths* (Harmondsworth: Penguin, 1960), 2:10; on the suicidal nature of the Sirens, see 245, 361.

27. The scholarship of Christopher A. Faraone treats these little-known materials in various guises. See especially his *Ancient Greek Love Magic* (Cambridge, MA: Harvard University Press, 1999), 1–30.

28. Faraone, *Ancient Greek Love Magic,* 74 n. 145.

29. Faraone, *Ancient Greek Love Magic,* 60.

ing spells were often performed with the aid of various accessories: the magical "perforated strap" (κεστός) lent by Aphrodite (along with a few charmed words) to her favorites and also the ἰύγξ (root of the English word "jinx"), an emblem of torment consisting of a live bird pinned to a small wheel. By extrapolation, then, one might argue that the dangerous songs of the Sirens and the Sphinx—along with the genre of poetry following from their monstrous example—were fashioned in the spirit of the *jinx,* at the same time that these songs were revising the rhapsodic measures of epic.

The pragmatic dimension of the hexametrical charms (and hence their importance to a kind of literary speech-act theory) may be discerned in the etymologies of the very names of the Siren and the riddler. The word "Siren" derives from the Greek verb (σειρά) meaning "cord" or "rope"—hence the binding power of the Sirens' song. Indeed, in Xenophon's *Memorabilia,* Socrates calls the Sirens' song an ἐπῳδή (erotic incantation) used to attract and bind men, precisely like a love charm.[30] One must bear in mind that the "flowery meadow" of the Sirens is littered with the corpses of their victims, lured to their island by "honey-sweet" song. Similar powers may be ascribed, it appears, to certain kinds of riddles, for the Greek term γριφος (riddle) also means a "snare" or "trap." Indeed, the power to bind and captivate gives the Sphinx her name, which derives from the verb σφίγγω (root of the English word "sphincter"): to bind fast, to strangle, to throttle.[31] One might presume that the name reflects her preferred means of killing the hapless citizens of Thebes (one by one, as each encounters the riddle's obscurity), yet the term γριφος (along with the example of the Sirens) suggests that we are meant to understand the riddle itself as a verbal snare, an incidence of erotic magic that comes in the form of a question, a means of captivation.

The affinities between these different types of verbal "snares" suggest that we should understand the riddle as a kind of binding spell that may be broken by a single word, the *Rätselwort*—that is, by solving the riddle. This view is in keeping with the myth of Oedipus and the Sphinx, in which Apollo (the tutelary god of the Delphic oracle) sends the Sphinx to plague the city of Thebes by posing her riddle to its citizens and murdering them one by one, as each fails to supply the magical keyword, the solution. Surprisingly, the idea of the riddle as a spell or charm that may be broken by a single word persists in the modernist variations of the enigma. Adorno,

30. Xenophon, cited in Faraone, *Ancient Greek Love Magic,* 131.

31. Samuel Coleridge extends the implication of this root to its limit, calling the riddle of the Sphinx a "fart." Coleridge, *The Notebooks of Samuel Taylor Coleridge,* ed. Kathleen Coburn, vol. 1, *1794–1804, Text* (Princeton, NJ: Princeton University Press, 1957), journal entry 1184.

for example, refers to "the word that breaks the spell [*das lösende Wort*] of the riddle" (178). The significance of this view for studies of poetry is articulated in hermeneutical terms by Paul de Man, whose definition of a riddle may be understood as a belated variation of the modernist enigma: "A riddle is not, in itself, out of the reach of knowledge, but is temporarily hidden from knowledge by a device of language that can, in turn, be deciphered only by another operation of language. . . . The poem is not ritual, mystery, or prayer, but a text to be interpreted and inviting the reader's answer, as all riddles do."[32] De Man's insistence on distinguishing the riddle from "mystery" (probably a response to Benjamin's coupling of "riddle and mystery") is useful because it emphasizes the *verbal* continuity between the production and reception of the enigma, the movement from question to "answer," from obscurity to solution.

De Man fails, however, to address more closely the problem of the riddle's obscurity, especially the potentially fatal effects of its spellbinding appeal to the listener. For behind the allure of the riddle, behind its rhapsodic measures, lies the threat of death: an effect of *poesis* that is all but inexplicable—a mystery—in modern terms. The riddle of the Sphinx is not merely apotropaic in its terrifying effects but *apocalyptic,* as it combines the promise of revelation and the threat of annihilation. In this respect, the operation of the riddle of the Sphinx captures a moment of *public* discourse when a certain kind of *terror* must be counted among the effects of poetry. Sophocles, for example, describes the Sphinx as a "virgin with curved talons" (γαμψώνυχα παρθένον), a bird of prey.[33] Indeed, there can be little doubt that the citizens of Thebes, plagued by the "glaring," random minstrelsy of the Sphinx, existed in a state of terror prior to the achievement of Oedipus—not unlike the citizens of a modern city terrorized by a serial killer before his (or her) capture. As a poet, the ancient Sphinx may thus be compared to the riddling serial killers and cryptographers of modernity (the Zodiac Killer or the Unabomber), each producing a vernacular strain of "poetry" (in their cryptic letters to the public) recalling the apotropaic allure of the Sphinx and her single, compulsively reiterated poem (akin perhaps to birdsong).

The modern reader's difficulty in comprehending, much less recovering, the dread once inspired by the riddle of the Sphinx reveals a modern aporia in the magical and aesthetic powers attributed to poetry. Yet it is precisely our distance from the archaic riddle (all riddles are distant, one

32. Paul de Man, "The Riddle of Hölderlin," in *Critical Writings, 1953–1978*, by Paul de Man, ed. Lindsay Waters (Minneapolis: University of Minnesota Press, 1989), 206.

33. Sophocles, *Oedipus the King,* line 1199.

could argue) that renders modern art enigmatic, according to Adorno: "The configuration of mimesis and rationality is the enigmatic image of art. It is a product of history. Art is what is left over after the magical and cult functions of archaic art have fallen by the wayside" (185). Art *becomes* a riddle—something incomprehensible—with the sublimation of its magical properties.

Efforts to find modern analogies for the public ordeal of the ancient riddle bring to mind nightmarish scenes of the classroom transformed into a court and site of execution: the hapless reader or student is put to death—on the spot—for not understanding a poem, for not solving the riddle. Ludicrous as these analogies may appear to be, they remind us that the general air of perplexity and anxiety surrounding poetry for the modern reader is neither trivial nor contingent. Though it may, as Adorno argues, be a product of history, the vexation induced by the obscurity of a poem cannot—or should not—be overcome or eliminated from the modern reader's experience. On the contrary, as Adorno contends, the incomprehension of the philistine is the truest demonstration of art's "enigmatic quality": "One among several reasons for wanting to study people who have no artistic sensibilities at all is that they exemplify the enigmatic quality of art in an especially striking way. . . . Unbeknownst to themselves, they represent an extreme form of criticism of art while at the same time showing up art's truth" (177).

Giorgio Agamben sees in the riddle of the Sphinx an allegory of "the barrier between signifier and signified that constitutes the original problem of signification" (an "origin" reconfigured by Heidegger in his alignment of riddle and λόγος). Only with difficulty, however, does the relation between language and dread enacted by the riddle become evident in Agamben's account: "the enigma belongs to the sphere of the apotropaic, that is, to a protective power that repels the uncanny by attracting it and assuming it within itself."[34] Agamben suggests in a note to this statement that *death* occupies the place of the uncanny in the parable of the Sphinx. In other words, the risk of death posed by the riddle defers death itself. Confronted by the unyielding obscurity of a poem, one faces—thereby keeping at bay—the presence of death.

The uncanniness at the heart of the riddle finds expression in a num-

34. Giorgio Agamben, *Stanzas: Word and Phantasm in Western Culture,* trans. Ronald L. Martinez (Minneapolis: University of Minnesota Press, 1993), 138. Agamben fails to note the source of his basic thesis concerning the uncanniness of the riddle: Heidegger's correlation of the fate of Oedipus and the uncanniness (*Unheimlichkeit*) of Being—which is exemplified by the revealing self-concealing of the riddle. Heidegger, *Introduction to Metaphysics,* trans. Ralph Mannheim (New Haven, CT: Yale University Press, 1959), 150–151.

ber of particular ways. There is the trope of genealogy: Oedipus, an unwitting perpetrator of incest, solves the enigma of a monster engendered by incestuous relations, for the Sphinx herself is said to be the offspring of her mother, Echidne, and her own brother, Orthrus (the two-headed hound of Geryon).[35] Indeed, the obscurity of the riddle itself is sustained by the uncanniness of the riddle creature: the human interlocutors of the Sphinx in Thebes find death for failing to recognize their own human image in the "monster" portrayed by the riddle (a creature with two, three, or four legs, at various times of the day). In fact, the trope of the monster—its true identity undeciphered—extends to the genre of the riddle itself: a rhapsodic amalgam of epic and incantational verse, a form incognito. The question of form pertains as well to the uncanniness of death: the riddle carries the art of the rhapsode to near extinction. The collected works of the Sphinx amount to a single poem—a mere quatrain—in the form of a question. In the alluring and menacing refrain of the Sphinx, we discover the ends of poetry—its possible extinction—which is yet another manifestation, with particular significance for modernity, of the terror sown by the riddle, yet another way of posing apocalypse in words.

Hex

The figure of the rhapsode, the itinerant composer of epic verse, became by most accounts little more than a performer following the emergence of new forms of poetry and discourse during the Archaic period in Greece (the period between the Epic and Classical ages). At the same time, according to some of the commentary I cited earlier, the figure of the Archaic rhapsode—the itinerant poet—underwent complex and often-surprising developments, becoming in the figure of the Sphinx, for example, a singer of *riddles*. The idea that the poetics of the riddle is somehow implicated in the historical demise, or transformation, of epic poetry finds corroboration in ancient biographies of Homer, whose death was said to have been precipitated by his failure to solve a riddle.[36] One anonymous biographer of Homer, echoing other ancient sources, writes: "They say he died on the island of Ios after finding himself helpless because he was unable to solve a riddle of the fisherboys. This is it: What we caught we left behind, and

35. Hesiod, *Theogony,* lines 306–332.

36. I am grateful to Greg Thalmann for referring me to this anecdote and for his helpful suggestions (and corrections) in response to an early draft of this chapter.

what we missed we carry."[37] Homer, it is said, had been warned by another kind of riddle, by the Delphic oracle—years before the incident took place—to "beware the young boys' riddle."[38] Further, the fatal effects of the riddle in Homer's life recall the dreadful consequences of the riddle of the Sphinx—at least for those unable to solve the enigma.

One should also bear in mind that the equation of rhapsode and riddler—indeed, the very idea that the Sphinx is a singer, a poet—may be an invention of the Classical period, since it was Sophocles and Euripides who envisioned her as a bird of prey, who drew attention to her deadly *melodies,* her suicidal nature. In this respect, the mythical figure of the Sphinx, as we know her, is a historical back-formation, a projection that is enormously helpful in tracing "the path of song" and, more specifically, the path of the rhapsode from its epic pedigree to a figure of persistent but oscillating—and sometimes inscrutable—modernity.

The eccentricity of the rhapsodic measures of the Sphinx reflects the ferment of a historical period in which the Homeric rhapsode (as a composer) gradually assumed the disparate features of its afterlife—its life after epic. The Archaic period saw the emergence of philosophical—that is, antimythological—thinking, alongside what would become the predominant mode of Western poetry: lyric monody. Insofar as ancient lyric poetry was a reaction against the impersonal, backward-looking features of epic, one must emphasize that rhapsodic verse (including its elaboration beyond the scope of traditional epic) was distinctly different from ancient lyric poetry. At the most basic performative level, poetry composed in hexameters was delivered *without* musical accompaniment, following the example of the epic tradition, in contrast to lyric poetry, which was always recited with musical accompaniment.[39] Thus, the principal mode of modern poetry recitation—the unadorned voice—has affinities with the performance of ancient epic and its curious generic offspring (such as the riddle), though the unadorned voice now sometimes falsely evokes—in the absence of musical accompaniment—a lost tradition of lyric poetry. For the rhapsodic measures of the unadorned voice—the songs of the rhapsode, the riddler, and the Siren—were

37. Martin L. West, ed., *Homeric Hymns, Homeric Apocrypha, Lives of Homer,* Loeb Classical Library (Cambridge, MA: Harvard University Press, 2003), 437. The solution to the fisherboys' riddle is "lice."

38. West, *Homeric Hymns,* 325.

39. One should note that epic poetry continued to be composed, somewhat erratically, down through the Hellenistic period. In addition, "lyric" is not a term of archaic origin. On the performative features of hexametrical verse, see James W. Halporn, Martin Ostwald, and Thomas G. Rosenmeyer, *The Meters of Greek and Latin Poetry* (Indianapolis: Bobbs-Merrill, 1963), 16.

always a *rival* of lyric poetry, never the remains of its supposed partition from music.

The hexametrical terrain of a rhapsodic countertradition (only loosely associated with the legacy of the rhapsode as a performer or actor) encompassed then not only pseudo-epic (the remains of epic) but the *pharmakos* of the binding spell (exemplified by the Sirens' song) and the deadly guessing game of the riddle.[40] In the latter two genres, one listens to the song of the unadorned voice at one's peril—the kind of song one might be advised *not* to listen to. Oddly, in the case of the Sirens' song, the "substance" of the song has a material relation to the deliberate act of *not* listening to the song. For Odysseus prepares "beeswax" to stop the ears of his crew against the "honey-sweet" song of the Sirens—one product of the bees functioning as antidote to another—as if the "substance" of song and the substance causing deafness were elements of a sensorial, or poetic, continuum (*Odyssey* 12.187, 199).

The curious torsion of the rhapsodic measure yields as well the elegiac couplet, a metrical innovation consisting of one conventional hexameter line and a second line of five dactyls, one short of a full hexameter (a line of two truncated half-hexameters). The riddle of the Sphinx, composed in brief hexameter lines, may thus be construed as the mythical origin of the elegiac couplet, with piercing effects that recommend elegiac meter as the preferred vehicle for the poetic epigram.[41] The elegiac couplet may stand alone—a poetic monad—when it is exemplified by the riddle, the epigram, or the pithy speech of oracles (often composed in verse); yet the elegiac couplet also forms the basis of strophic (or stanzaic) composition, in contrast to the continuous hexameters (stichic composition) of epic poetry. In this mode, the elegiac meter becomes the vehicle for two ostensibly divergent genres, drinking songs and poems of a reflective nature, sometimes combined in a single composition.[42] The elegiac measures of the drinking song attest to the vernacular origins of the rhapsode—the itinerant singer of tales—for the drinking song is a familiar epic device, a convivial prelude to games of wit and reflection, including the posing of riddles.

40. The term *pharmakos* in Greek can mean "poison," "drug," or "incantation." See Faraone, *Ancient Greek Love Magic,* 7.

41. Halporn, Ostwald, and Rosenmeyer, *Meters of Greek and Latin Poetry,* 12–13. The modern poetic elegy combines features of the funerary epigram and the poem of reflection.

42. As an example of this type of elegiac combination, Hermann Fränkel cites two elegies by Archilochus, which begin with "an exhortation to drink. This is no accident; the gathering of men to drink was the normal occasion for poetic instruction and reflection." Fränkel, *Early Greek Poetry and Philosophy: A History of Greek Epic, Lyric, and Prose to the Middle of the Fifth Century,* trans. Moses Hadas and James Willis (New York: Harcourt Brace Jovanovich, 1975), 152 n. 1.

Ransom in a Voice

In her capacity as a poet—with one short and ineradicable "song" to her name—the Sphinx of Greek antiquity is often treated by Classical and Hellenistic writers as if she, a monster, had actually lived: no clear distinction exists, for her followers, between the mythical figure and the poet whose obscure "style" influenced various poetic "experiments" during the Archaic period. One of the trademarks of her poetic practice is of course its capacity to produce a kind of dread in the listener, associated with the enunciation of the riddle song. Though the expressive transactions between poetry and dread may be lost on the modern reader, the correlation between captivation, terror, and the female voice in Greek myth—and indeed in the Sphinx herself—does in fact remain accessible to readers of modern poetry. Like the wailing voices of the Sirens and their cousins, the Harpies, the enigma of the Sphinx is a song requiring circumvention or appeasement. Yet during the historical development of the enigma as a literary genre in antiquity, a notable suppression of the riddling effect of dread may be observed to coincide with the suppression of the female voice in the riddle song. For one of the earliest collections of riddles assembled in antiquity (the one hundred Latin "enigmas" of Symphosius, dating to the fifth century AD) displays neither the fatality nor the female voice of the Archaic riddle (except for the female personification of some of the riddle creatures).[43] Though its origins and motivation cannot be precisely determined, the suppression of the element of dread and of the female voice in the enigma helps to explain the unmistakable (and strangely productive) conversion of the riddle into a literary trifle or toy—a transformation which nevertheless preserves the vernacular conditions of its dissemination by the Sphinx.

If the repression of the female voice of the enigma becomes, then, a general feature of enigmatology, it also allows for some truly extravagant lapses in the injunction against poetry's synthesis of whimsy and dread. Emily Dickinson, for example—one of literary history's greatest riddlers—coaxes the enigma into modernity in part by thematizing and refashioning the economy of dread associated with the ancient riddle song. Some of her best-known poems are riddles—though not always recognized as such—and she loves to remind her reader what type of riddle she prefers:

43. Symphosius's selection of a "century" of riddles (one hundred in number) became the template for many later collections of riddles, including the foundational medley of Anglo-Saxon riddles in the Exeter Book manuscript. The length of this format suggests that it may be the underlying paradigm for the customary length (sixty to one hundred pages) of a collection of lyric poems by a single author.

The Riddle we can guess
We speedily despise—
Not anything is stale so long
As Yesterday's surprise.[44]

Again and again she voices her preference for the secret that resists disclosure:

The Suburbs of a Secret
A Strategist should keep,
Better than on a Dream intrude
To Scrutinize the sleep. (1245)

In addition, Dickinson's preference for the extremities of the visible spectrum—"Best things dwell out of sight" (998)—sometimes produces a parable of obscurity yielding a poetic doctrine of the riddle:

I see thee better—in the Dark—
I do not need a light—
The Love of Thee—a Prism be—
Excelling Violet—

I see thee better for the Years
That hunch themselves between—
The Miner's Lamp—sufficient be—
To Nullify the Mine— (611)

Here, the poet's faculty (or perhaps the poem itself—a prism, a miner's lamp) allows her to "see in the dark"—a kind of darkness dispelling the dark—finding the distance of years to be an aid to vision "Excelling Violet."

Dickinson calls the enigma she seeks—and inscribes—by many names:

I would not paint—a picture—
I'd rather be the One
Its bright impossibility
To dwell—delicious—on— (505)

44. Emily Dickinson, *The Complete Poems of Emily Dickinson*, ed. Thomas H. Jackson (Boston: Little, Brown, 1952), poem 1222. Hereafter, all numbers referring to this publication refer to poems, not pages, and are given in the text.

In its contrariness, the "bright impossibility" dwelling in the unpainted picture is another trope for the visible darkness relished by the poet. Indeed, contrariness lies at the heart of Dickinson's attraction to riddles:

Some things that fly there be—
Buds—Hours—the Bumblebee—
Of these no Elegy.

Some things that stay there be—
Grief—Hills—Eternity—
Nor this behooveth me.

There be that resting, rise.
Can I expound the skies?
How still the riddle lies! (89)

Only that which stays *and* remains, that which is visible and invisible—like the phantom object of "elegy"—can become, for Dickinson, the object of a riddle.

In another poem, Dickinson declares, "I probed Retrieveless things," and further, "I tried to think a lonelier Thing / Than any I had seen . . . An Omen in the Bone" (532). The correlation of riddle and elegy focuses here on the trope of the "Omen in the Bone," which is also one of the portals through which the economy of *dread* enters Dickinson's construction of the riddle. One of Dickinson's best-known riddles—about "a narrow Fellow in the Grass"—ends with the following stanzas:

Several of Nature's People
I know, and they know me—
I feel for them a transport
Of cordiality—

But never met this Fellow
Attended, or alone
Without a tighter breathing
And Zero at the Bone. (986)

The "Omen in the Bone" of the earlier poem—and more narrowly the letter *O*—become here figures of dread ("Zero at the Bone") aroused by the unnamed riddle creature.

Inhabiting distances "Further than Guess can gallop / Further than Riddle ride," the voice of Dickinson's enigmatology confesses:

I lived on Dread—
To Those who know
The Stimulus there is
In Danger—Other impetus
Is numb—and Vitalless—

The modern poet rediscovers the dread and sublimity associated with the riddle of the Sphinx, yet she dramatically restructures its economy by internalizing the dread once reserved for the hapless stranger who heard the riddle enunciated by the Sphinx—the dread that paralyzed the entire population of Thebes (as long as the riddle remained unsolved). Furthermore, the archaic dread hovering about the enigma (akin to the modern sublime) becomes a narcotic—a dangerous *pleasure*—keeping the modern poet alive.

Dickinson is not above rationalizing dread ("Apprehensions—are God's introductions," 797), yet she is more inclined to call "Anticipation / A Dice—a Doubt—" (886). In one of her many bird riddles, the song pouring from its "anticipation" becomes unbearable and divides in two:

You'll know Her—by Her Voice—
At first—a doubtful Tone—
A sweet endeavor—but as March
To April—hurries on—
She squanders on your Ear
Such Arguments of Pearl—
You beg the Robin in your Brain
To keep the other—still— (684)[45]

In a frank anatomy of guessing and seeing in the dark—of riddling—Dickinson reveals the degree to which the poet's internalization of dread becomes a key element in the formulation of modern lyric subjectivity:

You see I cannot see—your lifetime—
I must guess—

45. In another of her bird riddles (poem 760), the poet calls the unnamed creature a "Winged Beggar," once again alluding to a kind of song—a beggar's chant—requiring appeasement.

How many times it ache for me—today—Confess

. . . .

But I guess guessing hurts—

Here the atmosphere of dread that once held the city of Thebes in thrall, like a spell waiting to be broken, becomes the riddle's modern affect: "I guess guessing hurts . . . her translated faces / Teasing the want / It—only—can suffice!" (253).

Dickinson elaborates and indeed literalizes the *economy* of dread by identifying a certain element in her song as a kind of lyric "ransom":

Silence is all we dread.
There's Ransom in a Voice—
But Silence is Infinity.
Himself have not a face. (1251)

Here, we have all of the elements of the modern enigma: the "silence" of the unsolved riddle, the "dread" it inspires, and the "translated faces" of the riddle object. The enigma becomes an abduction, and the poet's song—its painful "guessing"—serves to "ransom" the absent "face." In another of Dickinson's riddles, the last line declares, "I've ransomed it—alive—," yet the riddle creature is never named or revealed (762). Hence, the lyric "ransom" is not the same as a solution to the riddle. For the modern poet is at once abductor and ransomer of the riddling "face"; the poem is both riddle and "ransom." Just as the modern enigma incorporates the dread of the ancient listener, so it usurps the stranger's painful guess, ransoming a face that never comes into view. The riddle goes unsolved by the riddler precisely because the dreaded silence of the enigma holds the lure of "infinity"—a prospect synthesizing captivation and ransom, riddle and solution, obscurity and substance.

Elegiac Questions

The evening of song delivered by the epic rhapsode always began, Hermann Fränkel notes, with a question: "In the established manner of the rhapsode, the narrative was to be set going by questions."[46] The binding song of the Sphinx, composed in elegiac hexameters in the form of a question, suggests that these queries were not merely a prelude to song but ele-

46. Fränkel, *Early Greek Poetry and Philosophy,* 326.

ments in the rhapsode's poetic production. Indeed, the form of the riddle indicates that a significant poetic innovation occurred with the rhapsodic incorporation of the question, a speech act akin to the inquisitive mode of solicitation. It might also be argued, however, that the enigmatic questioning of Man by the Sphinx merely condenses the demythologizing tendency already well under way in the *Odyssey,* where Odysseus is more demonstrably "human"—more real, so to speak—than any figure in the *Iliad.*

This vital tendency of the rhapsodic tradition, where song and critique converge in enigmatic questioning, contributed to the formation of a new mode of questioning, at once provocative and charismatic: the unprecedented inquiries of itinerant "philosophers." The hexametrical signature of these reflective writings bears some relation, it appears, to a lost epic, or pseudo-epic, called the *Margites,* which was composed, anomalously, in elegiac couplets.[47] A number of the most important practitioners of the new, reflective discourse (Xenophanes, Parmenides, Empedocles) composed their "philosophy" in hexameters—in elegiac couplets, more precisely—a polemical adaptation of the epic tradition, standing in contrast to the contemporaneous innovation of "lyric" poetry (which was not composed in hexameters). The new "philosophizing rhapsodes" must have sounded strangely modern and archaic all at once. Indeed, the boundaries in the Archaic period between various emergent poetries (lyric, incantational, post-epic rhapsody) and the new "philosophy" (a term that did not yet exist) were far from distinct. Prior to the invention of the term φιλό-σοφος (philosopher) by Pythagoras, the word σοφός could mean either "sage" or "poet."[48]

Aside from the hexametrical platform (the metrical signature of the unaccompanied voice), which unifies the diverse components of the rhapsodic tradition, one can detect the features of an oracular, or enigmatic, *style* straddling the realms of poetry and philosophy, verse and prose. Sophocles, for example, describes the Sphinx as "chanting oracles in verse" (χρησμῳδόν), recalling perhaps Apollo's sponsorship of her domination of Thebes.[49] Evidence that the Sphinx became an early

47. Some ancient sources claim that the *Margites* was composed by Homer immediately prior to hearing the oracle's warning about the riddle that would one day bring about his demise. West, *Homeric Hymns,* 325. The correlation of the riddle with a pseudo-epic composed in elegiac couplets—in association with Homer's death—appears to prefigure the eccentric afterlife of epic verse.

48. On the Pythagorean distinction of the term φιλόσοφος, see John Burnet, *Early Greek Philosophy* (London: A. and C. Black, 1958), 277–278. The usage of σοφός to mean "poet" continues well into the fifth century: "when Pindar in the fifth century speaks of σοφοί, he usually means poets." Fränkel, *Early Greek Poetry and Philosophy,* 239. The origin of the term appears to refer to "practical mastery" of a given subject, lending support to its association with poesis.

49. Sophocles, *Oedipus the King,* line 1200.

paradigm in the history of philosophical "style" appears in the epithets assigned to Heraclitus by the critical tradition: he is called ὁ Σκοτεινός (the Obscure) and his writing is described as αἰνικτής (riddling).[50] Indeed, one of his most famous aphorisms, pertaining to the Delphic oracle's mode of signification, appears to function not only as a critical assessment of the riddling properties of oracular utterance but as a veiled description of his own philosophical style: "The lord whose oracle is in Delphi neither speaks nor conceals, but gives signs [tokens]" (οὔτε λέγει οὔτε κρύπτει ἀλλὰ σημαίνει).[51] In its riddling mode of signification, the oracle therefore provides "tokens" of the hidden λόγος underlying all of nature, which constitutes the ground of being itself.

Although Heraclitus cast his "tokens" in prose (a fairly new invention in the sixth century BC, retaining many of the features of verse), the oracular, or enigmatic, "style" of early philosophy descends inevitably from poetry and, more specifically, from the rhapsodic tradition. Indeed, since Nietzsche's genealogical revision of the Presocratics in *Philosophy in the Tragic Age of the Greeks,* it has been fashionable to view the philosophies of Heraclitus and Parmenides as possessing "a peculiar logic derived from rhapsodic forms of expression."[52] In other words, Presocratic "philosophy"—the term itself may be misleading—possesses, it is said, a distinctive worldview more in keeping with poetry (with Homer and post-epic experimentation) than with science or the later, pragmatic discourse of Aristotle. Heidegger, the most influential advocate of this view, calls the thought of Heraclitus and Parmenides *dichterisch* (poetical), yet he also claims, in keeping with generally held views, that the thinking of Parmenides determines "the essence of Western thought down to the present day."[53] Thus, it is not unusual for a contemporary critic or philosopher to identify Parmenides as the first true philosopher of the Western tradition and, at the same time, to call his text a "poem."[54]

50. These terms are cited in G. S. Kirk and J. E. Raven, *The Presocratic Philosophers* (Cambridge, MA: Cambridge University Press, 1957), 184.

51. Kirk and Raven, *Presocratic Philosophers*, 211 (frag. 93).

52. Nietzsche's unfinished and posthumously published essay was written about the time of *The Birth of Tragedy* (published in 1872). Alexander P. D. Mourelatos, *The Route of Parmenides* (New Haven, CT: Yale University Press, 1970), 36 n. 76.

53. Heidegger, *Introduction to Metaphysics,* 144. The comment by Heidegger about Parmenides (from the essay "Was heisst Denken?") is cited by Jean Beaufret, *Le poème de Parménide* (Paris: Presses Universitaires de France, 1955), 8. Beaufret's book elegantly reviews and elaborates the Heideggerian position on the Presocratics. Heidegger's view of Parmenides as the "first philosopher" stems from Hegel's judgment: "genuine philosophizing began with Parmenides." Cited in Martin Heidegger, "Moira (Parmenides, VIII, 34–41)," in *Early Greek Thinking,* 83.

54. A passage by Mourelatos illustrates perfectly these inadvertent, critical contradictions: "The poem represents both the culmination and the demise of the earliest, dogmatic-speculative phase of Greek philosophy; he is, without doubt, the first critical and reflective philosopher, the first philoso-

Fetters, Jinx, Logic

The conventional—and evidently fractured—critical perspective on the writings of Parmenides raises important questions about distinctions between poetry and philosophy in the Archaic period of Greek literature, yet it also raises questions, more importantly for my purposes, regarding *contemporary* assumptions about the difference (or lack thereof) between poetry and philosophy. In other words, how is it possible that contemporary scholars and critics can identify a text as being both a poem and a paradigm of philosophical discourse without violating certain basic critical criteria? In fact, the *form* of Parmenides' text makes it impossible *not* to regard it as a poem, since it is composed entirely in epic hexameters, adhering closely to the four-cola structure of the Homeric line.[55] Nor are there any appreciable metrical or formal differences between the narrative "Proem," or introduction, and the more didactic segments of the poem.[56] In addition, Parmenides develops several poetic motifs, or themes, familiar from the epic tradition, deploying them not so much as images, narratives, or symbols but, according to Mourelatos, as a "logical calculus" of the unprecedented ideas and procedures encountered by the reader of the poem.[57] Indeed, it is indubitably clear that Parmenides intended to write an epic poem of sorts, as Fränkel confirms: "Many of the elementary points will be misunderstood, and much of what is best, most salient, and most vital in the philosophical doctrine will be missed, so long as we do not make the resolve to read the work as an epic poem of the period in which it was composed."[58] Yet Parmenides' appropriation of the rhapsodic tradition is every bit as strange in its experimental thrust as the deadly question posed—in hexameters—by the Sphinx: another jinxing rhapsody, "a composition which sounds at once too modern and too archaic."[59]

pher in the proper sense of the word; he is the father of Western rationalism, even the kind of rationalism (in spite of Parmenides' intention perhaps) that has found its fulfillment in modern, theoretical physics." Mourelatos, *Route of Parmenides,* xi. Note the use of the word "poem" at the outset of Mourelatos's declaration. Poets as well are sometimes inclined to view Parmenides' text as poetry. The contemporary American poet Heather McHugh, for example, initiates her reflection on the Presocratics by declaring, "Parmenides of all the ancient poets is the most alert to the problems posed by acts of language-making." McHugh, "What We Make of Fragments," in *Broken English,* by Heather McHugh (Hanover, NH: Wesleyan University Press, 1993), 82.

55. See Mourelatos, "Appendix I: Parmenides' Hexameter," in *Route of Parmenides,* 264–268, on the colometric features of Parmenides' verse. See also his more general discussion of the composition and vocabulary of Parmenides' poem, 2–11.

56. Mourelatos, *Route of Parmenides,* 265.

57. Mourelatos, *Route of Parmenides,* 44.

58. Hermann Ferdinand Fränkel, *Wege und Formen frühgreichischen Denkens* (157), cited in Mourelatos, *Route of Parmenides,* 1.

59. Mourelatos, *Route of Parmenides,* 265.

The most prominent motif drawn from the Homeric texts is that of the journey: Parmenides' poem presents the words and thoughts of a *traveler,* a figure identified only as the κοῦρος (the youth), whose "speaking-and-thinking horses" set him on "the famous road of the goddess who leads the man who knows through all cities."[60] The mysterious goddess offers the youth σήματα (8.2)—the same term used by Heraclitus to refer to the "tokens" of the oracle—to guide him on his way. More than one scholar has discerned a parallel between Odysseus and the κοῦρος—(the most substantial link to the epic tradition) with particular attention given to the Circe-Tiresias episode (the journey to the underworld), especially the correlation between Circe, in her role as πομπη (guide), and the route-giving "goddess" of Parmenides' poem.[61] Havelock finds as well an allusion to the song of the Sirens in Parmenides' demonstration of the delusional "Way of Seeming" (δόξα), contrary to the "Way of Truth": a "deceitful ordering of my epic words."[62] In addition, however, to these epic correspondences—and deformations—one should bear in mind that the figure on the road in Parmenides' poem evokes Parmenides' own vocation as an itinerant philosopher, not to mention the streetwise practice of the Sphinx (the public nature of her queries and her occupation of the streets of Thebes).[63]

The conditions of itinerancy and the road (ὁδός) motif (a word used numerous times by Parmenides in his poem) point beyond the thematic links between Homer and Parmenides to more basic philological correspondences between rhapsody and reflection, poetry and philosophy, in the Greek mind. For the route followed and recounted by the κοῦρος is not simply a physical road; it is πολύφημος (1.2), a road of "much speaking" (or "much singing") and, in a phrase emphasizing its ambiguous place and substance, "a road of enquiry that exists for thinking" (2.2). An epic formula, ὁδὸν καὶ μέτρα κελεύθου, referring to the "road and the measures of the route," captures not only the dual aspect of the road, at once material and immaterial, but its explicit correlation to the "measures" (μέτρα) of song.[64] Indeed, not surprisingly, the "Proem" supplies

60. Parmenides, in Kirk and Raven, *Presocratic Philosophers,* 266, frag. 1, lines 2–4. Citations from Parmenides' poem in the text will henceforth be identified by fragment number and line number (e.g., 1.2–4).

61. See Eric A. Havelock, "Parmenides and Odysseus," *Harvard Studies in Classical Philology* 63 (1958): 137–138.

62. Parmenides, 8.52; Havelock, "Parmenides and Odysseus," 143 n. 59.

63. Parmenides, born in the southern Italian city of Elea, was said to be an "itinerant philosopher" (a view reinforced by the reference in the "Proem" to the "man who knows" passing through many towns; 1.2). Plato claims that Parmenides visited Athens (sometime between 450 and 445 BC) and conversed with Socrates. See Burnet, *Early Greek Philosophy*, 169, 172 n. 1.

64. The formula is cited by Mourelatos, *Route of Parmenides,* 20.

a verbal map, a *topography* of the road leading to a place from which "no news ever returns" (πανaπευθέα) or, as the youth declares, "as far as my heart desires" (2.6, 1.1). Scholars acknowledge that a coherent mapping of the youth's route to "the gates of the paths of Night and Day" (1.11) depends, at the very least, on "a curious feat of celestial mechanics," with the implication that "the topography of the journey is blurred beyond recognition" (though "the blur is intentional").[65] Blurry topography would seem to be the inevitable condition of a road that is also a way of singing or thinking—indeed, the complex trope of the ὁδός in Parmenides' poem appears to depend on a discursive *topology* uniting geography and teleology, rhapsody and reflection, poetry and philosophy.

The topology of the ὁδός in Parmenides' poem bears directly on a lively philological debate about the correlation between the Greek word for the rational faculty of the mind, νοῦς, and the word νόστος, referring at once to the geographical "return" of the Greek heroes from Troy and to the poetic telling of that "return" (by a rhapsode or singer). Mourelatos, for example, finds etymological evidence for "a bridge from the theme of Odysseus' νόστος in Homer to the Kouros' journey in Parmenides."[66] Indeed, without overlooking the distinction between νόστος as a "return" and ὁδός as a route moving in one direction only—a one-way street—Douglas Frame (the first scholar to make a convincing philological case for the νοῦς-νόστος connection) assembles evidence from Parmenides' "Proem" as corroboration of his thesis about the myth of the "return" in Greek epic. He notes that the term ὁδός is "collocated" in several passages of Parmenides' poem with the verb νοεῖν (to think) and the noun νόημα (thought, reflection), evidence that Parmenides' poem "plainly reveals the primitive source of the word for the rational faculty."[67] At the same time, Frame asserts that the correlation between ὁδός and νοεῖν, between wandering and thinking, in Parmenides is more than a literary motif and indeed that it is independent of the Homeric text: "Parmenides has done more than recognize and remember 'a slight overtone of allegory' in the *Odyssey*. For what appears in Homer actually reflects a deep and important etymological connection, and when Parmenides recaptures this connection so fully, we cannot believe that he has been entirely dependent on Homer."[68] In other words, by composing his groundbreaking reflec-

65. Mourelatos, *Route of Parmenides,* 15–16. The "curious feat," according to Havelock, would be "a sort of reverse Phaeton." Havelock, "Parmenides and Odysseus," 134–135.

66. Mourelatos, *Route of Parmenides,* 43.

67. Douglas Frame, *The Myth of the Return in Early Greek Epic* (New Haven, CT: Yale University Press, 1978), 159–160.

68. Frame, *Myth of the Return,* 172.

tions as an epic poem set on the road, Parmenides demonstrates the inescapable verbal correspondence between wandering and singing, homelessness and reflection; between, as his poem asserts to such devastating effect, being and thinking (εἶναι and νοεῖν).

In their analyses of Parmenides' appropriation and revision of epic poetry, Havelock, Frame, and Mourelatos all leave unexamined a significant—and fairly obvious—aspect of the νοῦς-νόστος etymology: the term νόστος, as I indicated earlier, can refer both to the actual return, or homecoming, of a Greek hero and to a song, or rhapsodic account, of that return.[69] Failure to attend to the philosophical context of this double meaning in Parmenides' text—especially to the role of poetry in the νοῦς-νόστος formation—overlooks the central figurative demonstration of Parmenides' most famous and polemical thesis: τὸ γὰρ αὐτὸ νοεῖν ἐστίν τε καὶ εἶναι (3, "Thinking and being are the same thing.")[70] For the equivalence of νόστος as "return" and νόστος as "song of the return" (as event *and* its poetic representation) provides a remarkably faithful analogue of the equivalence of being and thinking in Parmenides' system—an equivalence that becomes more binding as Parmenides drafts the rhapsodic measures bearing the "icy tremor of abstraction" (as Nietzsche characterizes it) determining the *path* of his thinking.[71]

Just as the epithet πολύτροπος can mean "much-wandering" or "very wily," so the ambiguity of the word νόστος discloses a range of affinities that lead more deeply into the nexus of the rhapsodic tradition, to the curious affinity between the song of return and the song of the Sirens. In *Odyssey* 11.100, for example, Tiresias begins his conversation with Odysseus in the underworld by observing, "You are striving for a honey-sweet return" (νόστον δίζηαι μελιήδεα), a statement referring to either Odysseus's homecoming or a song about his return. Evidence for the latter can be found in the word μελιήδεα (honey-sweet), a term closely related to the epithet μελιγηρυν for the "honey-voiced" song of the Sirens, which is itself "an epic recitation."[72] This affinity between the song of the Sirens and the epic song of return (νόστος), which "charms" its listeners, pro-

69. Gregory Nagy refers to "*nostos* as not only 'homecoming' but also 'song about a homecoming.'" Yet he also makes a somewhat broader claim (in reference to *Odyssey* 1.326–327): "*nostos* here designates not only the homecoming of the Achaeans but also the epic tradition that told about their homecoming." Nagy, *The Best of the Achaeans: Concepts of the Hero in Archaic Greek Poetry* (Baltimore, MD: Johns Hopkins University Press, 1979), 35 n. 2 and 97 n. 2.

70. Because this statement occurs as a single-line fragment and because of its syntactic ambiguity, Mourelatos declines to offer an "interpretation" of this line. Mourelatos, *Route of Parmenides,* xv.

71. Friedrich Nietzsche, *Philosophy in the Tragic Age of the Greeks,* trans. Marianne Cowan (Washington, DC: Regnery Gateway, 1962), 70.

72. Fränkel, *Early Greek Poetry and Philosophy,* 9.

vides critical insight into the type of song—boundless and yet binding—that Parmenides sings and that necessarily underlies his conception of νοεῖν (thinking).

In addition to the unnamed goddess who sets the youth on the road in Parmenides' poem, the youth encounters a powerful female deity described variously as "Justice," "Necessity," and "Fate," who holds the keys to the "gates of Night and Day" and who mysteriously binds what-is (ἐόν) "in fetters" (8.26). Mourelatos explains: "The polymorph deity is not canonical. This particular combination of hypostases is unknown to Homer or Hesiod. But there is an unmistakable motif of locks, chains, and bonds."[73] Appropriately, Mourelatos examines references to Fate and Necessity in the epic tradition to illustrate the binding λόγος of the unfamiliar goddess, yet he neglects to consider that the irresistible constraint of her *logic* (which drives the reasoning of Parmenides' poem) may be related to the binding song of the Sirens and, hence, to the rhapsodic genre of the binding spell (including the riddle). From this perspective, the irresistible logic of Parmenides' reasoning must be understood as a noetic variation of the metrical charm, or *jinx,* which places the world of appearances (the "Way of Seeming" in the system of Parmenides) under the magical regime of νοεῖν (logic), thereby revealing the invisible reality of what-is. The prospect of such a transformation is, of course, terrifying to all (including the youth, who must use "soft words" to persuade the formidable goddess of many faces to open the gates) and creates an atmosphere of dread reflecting the "much-punishing" (πολύποινος) nature of the hybrid deity. In this placeless place, from which no news ever returns, the freakish divinity of the new logic brings to mind the cold monstrosity of the Sphinx, as well as the apocalyptic space in which she operates, governed by revelation and fatality, by illumination and constraint.

The affinities between the song of wandering (νόστος) and the song of the Sirens provide critical insight as well into the promiscuous yet confining space conjured by the rhapsode, not to mention the varieties of experience associated with wandering, which inform the Greek concept of mind (νοῦς). For the notion of wandering reflection most certainly evokes the condition of homelessness, or exile, characterizing not only the experience of Odysseus but the vicissitudes of the itinerant rhapsode and philosopher. The example of the Sirens further specifies that the rhapsodic (and public) space of reflection be random, or promiscuous, in its address, yet calculated (and destructive) in its effects. Like the riddle of the Sphinx, the ordeal of public rhapsody is irresistible, at first: honey-sweet and com-

73. Mourelatos, *Route of Parmenides,* 26.

pulsively reiterated, like birdsong, a serial song. Many of the properties of rhapsodic reflection are in fact captured by the term πολύτροπος, "much-turning," "much-wandering," qualities associated at once with the road, with the song of the road, and with reflection. This endless turning or coiling defines a path, or a song, that obscures its own destination: a labyrinth, a snare, a logic.

Blow-Up

The winding road traveled by the rhapsodic thinker ends in a catastrophic event, an orphic apocalypse, which destroys the certitude of sensuous appearance (by "an icy tremor of abstraction") and reveals, according to Parmenides, the equivalence of being and thinking. Logic becomes a tool, a rhapsodic form, of derealization. More specifically, since Parmenides' conception of thinking (νοεῖν) derives etymologically from notions of poetic reflection (that is, from actual songs of wandering and homelessness), his equation of being and thinking—the inaugural moment of Western rationalism—reveals itself as the touchstone of a metaphysics that is essentially *verbal* in nature, a conception of being grounded not simply, as Heraclitus declares, in the λόγος but in the *poetic* word.[74]

Heidegger, as I indicated earlier, understands the "word" looming behind Parmenidean νοεῖν to be a *riddle word:* λόγος assuming the *form* of a riddle. More precisely, "what the enigmatic key word [*Rätselwort*] of the saying silently conceals" is "the relation between thinking and Being."[75] Moreover, given the compound of poetic and enigmatic reflection, the "riddle of Being" (that is, the formulation of Being as a riddle, as a verbal enigma) carries within it an apocalypse pertaining as well to poetry itself: for if the riddle or the wayfarer's song or the rhapsodic question expands infinitely (in substance or in principle) to ground the totality of being itself, then poetry as such risks becoming nothing by encompassing everything—a tautology. Dissolving in its own reflection, poetry offers a metaphysical *solution,* yet it also becomes an instrument of *dissolution* in complex ways, thereby fulfilling a public experiment involving disparate genres and forms.

The metaphysical crisis precipitated by and reflected in Parmenides' poem coincided, I have argued, with a crisis of literary and discursive

74. In fragment 50, for example, Heraclitus states, "Listening not to me but to the Logos it is wise to agree that all things are one." Kirk and Raven, *Presocratic Philosophers,* 188.

75. Heidegger, "Moira (Parmenides, VIII, 34–41)," 92.

forms: the emergence of new poetries following the revision of ancient epic; the invention of prose; the vigorous experimentation occurring at the limits of rhapsody; the development of hybrid forms mixing poetry, philosophy, and other discursive genres. All of this activity presumes, it must be emphasized, a more general crisis in the nature of *form* itself; the revealing self-concealing form of the riddle, when understood as a premonitory relic of the epic tradition that combines magic (in a technical sense) and philosophical inquiry, embodies, in its relation to the activity of reflection, this general crisis of form.

An apocalypse of poetic form and metaphysical substance (a development skirting and subverting the *lyric* tradition) is of course not a theological event but a set of circumstances that recurs periodically in literary history but is often obscured by the dominant lyric tradition—even when lyric poetry is profoundly affected by such developments. I am suggesting that one may discover throughout literary history a kind of episodic countertradition which replicates the formal and philosophical conditions of the rhapsodic constellation of antiquity. Founded upon the ruins of epic and encompassing the various genres of the unadorned voice (the riddle, the oracle, the binding charm), the rhapsodic poem takes possession of public space as a materialization of reflection, acting as an instrument of poetic or philosophical *terror*—a terror that is "honey-sweet." Frequently contesting and enriching the conditions of lyric, rhapsodic poetry is experimental—to the point of self-sacrifice—promiscuous, wildly synthetic, agitational, reflective, and founded upon the conditions of itinerancy. Suspended between jinx and logic, rhapsodic poetry survives historically either by rarefaction—diagramming an "icy tremor of abstraction"—or by disappearing into the vernacular, that is, into the vernacular conjugation of song, reflection, and agitation.

The task of understanding the concept of a *modernist* enigma, with which I began this chapter, becomes less intractable if we bear in mind the genealogical relation of the rhapsodic mode to the poetics of the riddle. For the enigma variations of Benjamin, Adorno, and Heidegger (who directly invokes the rhapsodic philosophy of Parmenides) can be placed in the context of a larger historical development—modernism—which betrays many of the basic features of rhapsodic invention. Reflexive, experimental, agitative, and heterogeneous in its materials, the poetry of the modern avant-garde coincides with, and frequently alludes to, a crisis in conceptions of metaphysical substance, precipitated in part by the development of quantum mechanics but also by the emergence of the modern technical media. Many of the leading figures in Anglo-American modernism (Ezra Pound, T. S. Eliot, Gertrude Stein) were speculative critics in the mold of the rhapsodic poet-philosopher, a figure relayed to them perhaps by Matthew Arnold's *Empedocles on Etna* but also embodied more fully in the philosophical personae of Walter Pater, Oscar Wilde, and Friedrich Nietzsche. In addition, the task of reinventing epic for modernity (undertaken by Pound, Stein, William Carlos Williams, Charles Olson, and others) frequently involved mixing genres and disciplines, thereby following the contours of the rhapsodic paradigm. Indeed, some of the most important legacies of experimental and vernacular modernism—including some of the poets associated with Objectivism (Louis Zukofsky and Lorine Niedecker especially) and the poet-theorists of contemporary Language Poetry—are perhaps best understood as expressions of modern rhapsody.[76]

The premises of rhapsodic invention reassert themselves in the discourse of modernism in other ways as well. It is no accident that Walter Benjamin wrote his fragment-essay "Riddle and Mystery" shortly after completing his dissertation on the theory of art formulated by Novalis and Friedrich Schlegel. For the concept of Romantic irony, one of the principal icons of the discourse of poetic self-reflection, reactivates the λόγος of the ancient riddle. In one of the many "fragments"—a problematic innovation in poetic form—composed by the Athenaeum group, Friedrich Schlegel writes, "irony is the only involuntary and yet completely deliberate dissimulation. It is equally impossible to feign it or divulge it."[77] More succinctly, "Irony," Schlegel asserts, "is the form of paradox."[78] The paradox of the open secret—so important to formulations of the modernist enigma—reappears after antiquity in the Romantic discourse of poetic reflection: "In this sort of irony, everything should be playful and serious, guilelessly open and deeply hidden."[79] Wit—the "genial" form of irony—displays the properties of a riddle, one could argue, because "wit is a prophetic faculty," a statement recalling, but also revising, the oracular function of the riddle in antiquity.[80]

At the core of the Jena Circle's poetic program is Schlegel's thesis that

76. For a Chomskian reading of the "deep structure" of Language Poetry, which addresses unwittingly the metaphysical fallout of the rhapsodic experiment, see Oren Izenberg, "Language Poetry and Collective Life," *Critical Inquiry* 30 (Autumn 2003): 132–159.

77. *Friedrich Schlegel's "Lucinde" and the Fragments,* trans. Peter Firchow (Minneapolis: University of Minnesota Press, 1971), Lyceum frag. 108. All references to fragments use the numbering and titles of collections of fragments (Lyceum, Athenaeum, Ideas) of this edition. The numbering of the Firchow translation uses, in turn, that of the German edition of Schlegel's complete works: *Kritische Friedrich Schlegel Ausgabe* (Paderborn-Darmstadt, 1958–).

78. Schlegel, Lyceum frag. 48.

79. Schlegel, Lyceum frag. 108.

80. Schlegel, Lyceum frag. 126. In Lyceum fragment 96, Schlegel declares, "A good riddle should be witty; otherwise nothing remains once the answer has been found."

art is a "medium of reflection" in which new centers (works of art) are continually forming. Revising Fichte's equation of reflection and being (a thesis in accord with Parmenides' famous equation of thinking and being), Schlegel emphasizes a second order of reflection ("the thinking of thinking"), which is distinct from intellectual positing or intuition (and from unconscious intuition): "Intellectual intuition," as Benjamin explains, "is thinking that produces its object; reflection in the Romantics' sense, however, is thinking that produces its form"—that is, the form of thinking.[81] Schlegel, like Fichte, understood that "reflection is always reflection of a form," yet he takes a decisive step by equating the primal schema of reflection (the thinking of thinking) with *aesthetic* form. Further, he characterizes reflection as a *medium,* stressing (with Novalis) the *mediality* of the absolute (conceived as reflection) and hence its affinity with art. The origin of the doctrine of modern formalism in the arts thus turns on a radical change in the meaning of the term "form": "The Romantics, unlike the Enlightenment, did not conceive of form as a rule for judging the beauty of art, or the observance of this rule as a necessary precondition for the pleasing or edifying effect of the work. Form did not count for the Romantics either as a rule in itself or even as dependent on rules."[82] This crisis in the general concept of form, which abandons rules altogether, produces, as might be expected, a crisis in the integrity of aesthetic forms and genres—a development replicating the conditions of the rhapsodic experiment in antiquity.

The very concept of "experiment," which becomes so important to the doctrine of modern formalism, acquires a novel, aesthetic application in the Romantic debate on the nature of reflection. Fichte characterizes reflection as an "experiment," a definition exposing the correlation of the empirical and figurative aspects of the term "observation" (a term with close affinities to Leibniz's concept of monadic "perception"). In the writings of Novalis, empirical observation, fused with reflection, becomes (in Benjamin's phrase) "magical observation": "observation fixed in its view only the self-knowledge nascent in the object; or rather it, the observation, *is* the nascent consciousness of the object itself."[83] Hence, by implication, "Experiment consists in the evocation of self-consciousness and self-knowledge in the things observed."[84] In these astonishing hypoth-

81. Walter Benjamin, *The Concept of Criticism in German Romanticism,* in *Selected Writings,* 1:128.

82. Benjamin, *Concept of Criticism,* 148.

83. Benjamin, *Concept of Criticism,* 148. Benjamin discusses Fichte's concept of reflection and experiment on 147 and cites Novalis on experiment: "The process of observation is at the same time a subjective and objective process, an ideal and a real experiment" (148).

84. Benjamin, *Concept of Criticism,* 148.

eses, a method of experiment fusing perception and reflection exposes a metaphysics of *thinking things*. Experiment therefore becomes the instrument of a theory of reciprocal expression, derived principally in this case from Leibniz's "Monadology." Like monads, works of art are forms—centers of reflection—which mirror all other forms. Hence, the modern doctrine of formalism in the arts promises to deliver through reflection—through continuous experiment—a "peculiar infinity" of expressive (i.e., "magical") correspondences between forms (which are denied relations as objects).

In the aesthetic ideology of the Athenaeum group, poetry becomes the form of the dissolution of all forms, the paradigm of reflection (since reflection is a medium), and the principal means of "experiment." In a famous and lengthy "fragment," Schlegel writes:

> Romantic poetry is a progressive universal poetry. Its aim isn't merely to reunite all the separate species of poetry and put poetry in touch with philosophy and rhetoric. It tries to and should mix and fuse poetry and prose, inspiration and criticism, the poetry of art and the poetry of nature; and make poetry lively and sociable, and poeticize society. . . . It alone can become, like the epic, a mirror of the whole circumambient world, an image of the age. And it can also—more than any other form—hover at the midpoint between the portrayed and the portrayer, free of all real and ideal self-interest, on the wings of poetic reflection, and can raise that reflection again and again to a higher power, can multiply it in an endless succession of mirrors.[85]

As this passage demonstrates, the rhapsodic dissolution of forms and genres (encompassed, nevertheless, by "epic") depends on what Blanchot calls "the almost abstract demand made by poetry to reflect itself and to fulfill itself through *its* reflection."[86] By reflecting only itself—that is, by reflecting only the medium of reflection—the possibility for the reflection of forms becomes infinite in poetry: "an endless succession of mirrors." All forms, by virtue of their reflexivity, become "poetry."

The alignment of poetry, reflection, and experiment transforms poetry into an abyss, a "mirror" promoting the collapse of generic distinctions, a destructive whim extending, in Schlegel's view, to disciplinary boundaries as well: "If you want to penetrate into the heart of physics, then let yourself be initiated into the mysteries of poetry."[87] Even more broadly, he declares, "The whole history of modern poetry is a running commentary

85. Schlegel, Athenaeum frag. 116.
86. Maurice Blanchot, "The Athenaeum," trans. Deborah Esch and Ian Balfour, *Studies in Romanticism,* Summer 1983, 165.
87. Schlegel, Ideas frag. 99.

on the following brief philosophical text: all art should become science and all science art."[88] The impulsive, totalizing gestures of these statements (virtually meaningless in themselves) implicate poetry in a progressive abstraction of all phenomena, a synthesis rivaling the metaphysical crisis induced by Parmenides' rhapsodic experiment. Although Schlegel and Novalis characterize the infinite blow-up of poetry as "progressive" and even revolutionary, one could also assert that the revolutionary "word"—the infinitizing of poetry—is fantastically destructive and indeed apocalyptic in its aim to "mix and fuse" all forms and, more ominously, to "poeticize society." It would not be an exaggeration, I think, to describe the scope of poetry's hypothetical "penetration" into the mundane as *totalitarian*. Indeed, Schlegel refers at times to "transcendental poetry," that is, to "the unconscious and unformed poetry which stirs in the plant and shines in the light, smiles in the child, gleams in the flower of youth."[89] At this level of abstraction, the infinitizing of poetry in early Romanticism recalls the verbal metaphysics of the Heraclitean λόγος and the Parmenidean νοεῖν: "the poetry of poetry" unifies all things to such an extent that the substance of being can be no different from the "substance" of poetry. The revolutionary character of this verbal substance ensures, however, that "poetry" is never far removed from terror. (Louis XVI was beheaded in Paris only five years prior to the publication of the first issue of the *Athenaeum*.) In the case of the Jena Circle, whose members produced so little actual poetry, the apocalyptic value of infinitizing poetry, which restores poetry's integrity by revealing its ancient and recurring link to Western metaphysics, becomes evident only with the sacrifice of poetry as a material form.

Retracing the basic contours of the rhapsodic experiment in antiquity, the metaphysical crisis evident in the Romantic doctrine of "transcendental poetry" is accompanied by a transformation of the general concept of form, but also, as I have indicated, by a crisis of aesthetic, or poetic, *forms*. Recalling "the state of disintegration and fermentation" characterizing Alexandrian poetry in antiquity, Romantic poetry pursues a "nameless art," experimenting with "peculiar new combinations and compounds," seeking "a form, however, whose distinctiveness resides almost exclusively in its formlessness."[90] "A philosophy of poetry," according to Schlegel, "would waver between the union and the division of poetry, between

88. Schlegel, Lyceum frag. 115.

89. Friedrich Schlegel, "Dialogue on Poetry," in *"Dialogue on Poetry" and Literary Aphorisms*, by Friedrich Schlegel, trans. Ernst Behler and Roman Struc (University Park: Pennsylvania State University Press, 1968), 54. Athenaeum fragment 238 treats the concept of "transcendental poetry."

90. Schlegel, "Dialogue on Poetry," 64.

poetry and practice, poetry as such and the genres and kinds of poetry; and it would conclude with their complete union. . . . The keystone would be a philosophy of the novel."[91]

If the Romantic debate about poetic form reaches its catastrophic conclusion in the alignment of poetry with a "philosophy of the novel," one should bear in mind that the synthetic principle of the Romantic "novel" appears in a variety of different guises, from Novalis's (and Tieck's) renovation of the *Märchen* (fairy tale) to Schlegel's flirtation with the anomalous and unrecoverable genre of ancient pantomime: "The pantomimes of the ancients no longer exist. But in compensation, all modern poetry resembles pantomimes."[92] Significantly, the idea of the novel is invoked more often, as we have seen, under the name "epic" and, more specifically, in reference to something Schelling calls "speculative epic."[93] Schlegel calls the parodic legacy of epic—which would include Parmenides' "speculative epic"—"a rhapsody, with deep understanding in seeming incoherence."[94] Friedrich Gundolf, a scholar whose lectures Walter Benjamin attended in Berlin (and whose book *Goethe* Benjamin reviewed in 1917), describes Schlegel's "Dialogue on Poetry" as being composed of "rhapsodies" which present the author's thoughts "in apparently incoherent succession"—a model of composition used as well by aphoristic writers such as Diderot and Nietzsche.[95]

The rhapsodic mode of composition informs Schlegel's interest in the genre of the "project" (a term that has survived in our own contemporary critical parlance): "A project is the subjective embryo of a developing object. . . . The feeling for projects—which one might call fragments of the future—is distinguishable from the feeling for fragments of the past only by its direction: progressive in the former, regressive in the latter."[96] This description of the "project" betrays the synecdochal relation between totality and fragment that motivates Romanticism's most important (and perhaps only) innovation in poetic form: the fragment. Just as the rhapsodic experiment of antiquity sees epic composition crystallized in the hexametrical riddle of the Sphinx, so the epic ambitions of the Athenaeum group bear fruit in the form of the poetic fragment.

91. Schlegel, Athenaeum frag. 252.

92. Schlegel, Athenaeum frag. 69.

93. Phillipe Lacoue-Labarthe and Jean-Luc Nancy, *The Literary Absolute*, trans. Philip Barnard and Cheryl Lester (Albany: State University of New York Press, 1988), 79.

94. Schlegel, "Dialogue on Poetry," 63.

95. Friedrich Gundolf, *Romantik* (Berlin, 1931), 45ff. Cited in Ernst Behler and Roman Struc, "The Position of Friedrich Schlegel's *Dialogue on Poetry* within the Romantic Movement," in Schlegel, *"Dialogue on Poetry" and Literary Aphorisms,* 10.

96. Schlegel, Athenaeum frag. 22.

At the same time, although it would be accurate to say that the Romantic fragment first appears as a new element in the spectacle of ancient, literary "ruins," and that it reveals the "progressive" inclination of the ancient model, one must emphasize, as Schlegel does, the essential difference between ancient and modern fragments: "Many of the works of the ancients have become fragments. Many modern works are fragments as soon as they are written."[97] The key to this Romantic fragment, which addresses the ontological status of the fragment, can be found in a phrase of Chamfort's, converted by Schlegel into a maxim: "the wise man must confront fate always *en état d'épigramme*."[98] From this observation, one may infer that the fragmentariness of the modern fragment is not a property of the verbal artifact but rather the product of a state of mind, a *form* conferred upon language (which is itself a medium) by reflection.

This distinction helps to explain why the modern fragment, even if it possesses no determinate formal properties, may be characterized as a poetic *form*. As a discrete form, the reflective condition of the fragment illustrates perfectly the Romantic conception of form in general. From one perspective, as a verbal *object,* the fragment forms a totality, an aesthetic monad: "A fragment, like a miniature work of art, has to be entirely isolated from the surrounding world and be complete in itself."[99] Yet as a *form*—and this is where the scholarly method of philology comes into play—the paleographic fragment always relates to the absent parts of the whole of which it forms a fragment. (Indeed, the line of fracture defining the fragment may be said to represent, indexically, the adjoining fragments.) For, as Philippe Lacoue-Labarthe and Jean-Luc Nancy observe, "to write the fragment is to write fragments."[100] That is to say, though a fragment always forms a totality, it always also exists, like the monad, in an aggregation of fragments. (In the case of the Athenaeum fragments in particular, this formal aggregation reflected the social production of the work, which was a collective and anonymous enterprise—part of the revolutionary praxis of the Romantic experiment.) As a verbal object, the fragment is without relations to other fragments: the fragment, it may be said, is windowless. Yet as a *form,* as a refrain in the medium of reflection, the poetic fragment reflects all other fragments in a "peculiar infinity" of expressive correspondences.

As a form of prophecy, defined not by its content but by its techni-

97. Schlegel, Athenaeum frag. 24.

98. Schlegel, Lyceum frag. 59.

99. Schlegel, Athenaeum frag. 206.

100. Lacoue-Labarthe and Nancy, *Literary Absolute,* 43–44.

cal and pragmatic qualities, the Romantic fragment fulfills the rhapsodic legacy of experimentation by *avoiding* fragmentariness for its own sake.[101] Instead, the rhapsodic fragment appears, according to Lacoue-Labarthe and Nancy, as "a piece struck by incompleteness," so that "every fragment is a project: the fragment-project does not operate as a program or prospectus but as the *immediate* projection of what it nonetheless incompletes."[102] To convert incompletion into a verb—to incomplete—captures the riddling essence, according to Blanchot, of an actuality that is never *there:* "unfinished books, unfulfilled works. Perhaps. Unless one of the tasks of Romanticism was precisely to introduce a totally new mode of fulfillment and even a veritable conversion of writing. The power for the work to be and no longer to represent, to be everything, but without content or with virtually indifferent content."[103] Schlegel himself associates the equation of being and "infinite poetry," exemplified by the fragment in the catastrophic fulfillment of the rhapsodic experiment, with uselessness and, at the same time, with a turbulent "substance": "When with equal attention one observes the purposelessness and the lawlessness of modern poetry as a whole and the great excellence of its individual parts, the mass of this poetry appears to be a sea of struggling forces in which the particles of dissolved beauty, the pieces of shattered art, clash in a confused and gloomy mixture."[104] Bearing in mind the historical proximity of the apocalyptic events in France to Schlegel's observations, one cannot fail to discern the political implications of a poetic substance rivaling the general "gloom," at once "lawless" and meteoric in its imagined materiality. The coupling of gothic horror and political agitation in "particles of dissolved beauty"—in the nebulous form of the fragment—revives for modernity the rhapsodic amalgam of poetry, reflection, and agitation.

101. Schlegel's conception of poetic irony as a form of prophecy calls for a model of "divinatory criticism": "The romantic kind of poetry is still in its state of becoming; that, in fact, is its real essence: that it should forever be becoming and never perfected. It can be exhausted by no theory and only a divinatory criticism would dare to try to characterize its ideal." Athenaeum frag. 116.

102. Lacoue-Labarthe and Nancy, *Literary Absolute,* 41, 43.

103. Blanchot, "The Athenaeum," 165.

104. F. Schlegel, "On the Study of Greek Poetry," cited in Lacoue-Labarthe and Nancy, *Literary Absolute,* 51.

FOUR

Lyric Monadologies

Insensible perceptions are as important to pneumatology as insensible corpuscles are to natural science.

G. W. LEIBNIZ, *NEW ESSAYS ON HUMAN UNDERSTANDING*

In all predicates in which we see the fossil, it sees us.

NOVALIS, *GRAINS OF POLLEN*

Words often understand themselves better than do those who use them.

FRIEDRICH SCHLEGEL, "ON INCOMPREHENSIBILITY"

Genetic Obscurity

Starting from the premise that lyric obscurity shares certain expressive and ontological properties with other modes of obscurity, my examination of the rhapsodic paradigm in antiquity (ranging from the "deadly melodies" of the Sphinx to the binding measures of Parmenides) indicates that the *jinx* of obscurity in verse adheres not only to certain sociological conditions (homelessness, itinerancy, anonymity) but to various permutations of metaphysical substance associated with the concept of *logos*. A more complete analysis of the innate obscurity of metaphysical substance remains necessary, however, in order to identify the applications of obscurity as a philosophical concept, to disclose the ontological foundation of lyric obscurity, and to formulate a kind of grammar for the idioms and precincts of sociological obscurity.

Leibniz's theory of monadic substance, because of its reliance on linguistic concepts and because of its impact on Romantic poetics and modern philosophy, offers an ideal platform for demonstrating the general significance of Heidegger's thesis concerning the interrelation of poetry and metaphysics. Further, just as the concept of obscurity tethers the disparate realms of poetic language, metaphysics, and social being, Leibniz's theory of symbolic expression, which presumes the condition of obscurity, serves as what he calls the "Ariadne thread" marking a path through the labyrinth of his philosophical interests: logic, metaphysics, physics, social theory. The thread of "equivocal expression" unites the unreality of the phenomenal world (bodies, language, social existence) to its inscrutable but logical substance. In addition, because of the essential discontinuity of monadic substance, and because of the absolute hermeticism—the windowlessness—of every monad, Leibniz's conception of being offers a model of obscurity which discounts the possibility of actual effects produced by obscurity—the spectacle of obscurity—in order to give a rigorous account of expressive relations (without causal interaction) between solipsistic entities. A new Leibniz thus emerges as the tutelary figure of a universal poetics of obscurity, according to which the world becomes a demimonde within the camera obscura of the monad.

Leibniz's metaphysical doctrine holds that nothing is real but "monads," simple entities without parts, possessing "neither extension, nor shape, nor divisibility"—that is, without sensory or material properties.[1] Monads, according to Leibniz, are "incorporeal automata," consisting solely of perception and appetite; indeed, perception (a term used by Leibniz in a manner requiring careful explanation) *is* substance in a world defined by mindlike, immaterial entities.[2] Though monads (the "true atoms of nature") are beings of reason, they supply, in aggregate, the a priori conditions of all material bodies—a conception granting only partial reality to matter (insofar as it may be understood as a "mode" of monadic perception) and subjecting the status of material entities to endless debate.[3]

"Each monad," according to Leibniz, "is a living mirror, or a mirror endowed with internal action, which represents the universe."[4] Substance therefore, according to Leibniz, is essentially a *medium,* a mirror in constant flux. Yet monads have no direct, or causal, interaction with

1. G. W. Leibniz, "The Principles of Philosophy, or, the Monadology" (1714), in *Philosophical Essays*, by G. W. Leibniz, ed. and trans. Roger Ariew and David Garber (Indianapolis: Hackett, 1989), 213.

2. Leibniz, "Monadology," 215.

3. Leibniz, "Monadology," 213.

4. G. W. Leibniz, "Principles of Nature and Grace, Based on Reason," in *Philosophical Essays,* 207.

other monads or with the phenomenal reality designed—and perceived indirectly—in concert with other monads. Hence, perception, the very substance of monads, occurs without external influence: a paradox defining the essential lyricism—that is, the obscurity—of monadic being. Monads do, however, have relations, in a manner of speaking, with other monads, though such relations consist solely of expressive correspondences, or harmonized perceptual states. All monadic relations are therefore *immanent* relations. For theorists of the sublime and for the writers associated with the Jena Circle of German Romanticism, Leibniz's theory of the solipsistic perception of monads and his explanation of relations between these hermetic substances—each with its own imperfect perspective on the universe—provided the basic terms for a model of lyric expression founded upon obscurity.

Certain basic features of the aesthetic ideology of modern poetry, including its polemical acknowledgment of lyric obscurity, first began to appear in essays, dialogues, and collections of aphorisms by German writers in the latter part of the eighteenth century. These writings on the nature of poetry reveal a significant debt to the speculative metaphysics and theories of logic developed by Leibniz. In fact, the development of aesthetics as a concept and, later, as a philosophical discipline bears the particular imprint of Leibniz's ideas during this crucial period of its formulation. Alexander Baumgarten, for example, the first writer to use the term "aesthetics" (in 1735, in his essay "Philosophical Meditations on Some Matters Pertaining to Poetry"), was known principally as an explicator of Leibniz's philosophy.[5] Later, members of the Jena Circle, especially Novalis and Friedrich Schlegel, found in Leibniz's concept of the monad a compelling, though sometimes cryptic, model of aesthetic form. Thus, the Romantic revival of Leibniz's philosophy cannot be isolated from the momentous changes in thinking about poetry (and in poetry itself) that occurred during this period and that authorized the proliferation and naturalization of obscurity in the most innovative forms of modern poetry.[6]

5. Baumgarten's essay can be found in a selection of his writings: *Reflections on Poetry,* trans. Karl Aschenbremer and William Holther (Berkeley and Los Angeles: University of California Press, 1954).

6. Were one to seek a contemporary analogy for Leibniz's influence over the Jena Circle and its followers, one would want to consider the fascination exercised by Wittgenstein's thought over certain contemporary writers (and scholars) associated with the school of Language Poetry. Marjorie Perloff's book *Wittgenstein's Ladder* (Chicago: University of Chicago Press, 1996) offers both an illustration and an exposition of Wittgenstein's appeal to post-Objectivist sensibilities. The "Wittgenstein effect" in contemporary poetry emanates, like the Romantic vortex around Leibniz, from an eccentric conjugation of poetry and logic—though certainly this recent episode is less momentous in its effects than the earlier doctrine of "poetic logic" (Hölderlin's phrase). Wittgenstein was, after all, essentially a logician, whose early thinking was influenced (via his teacher, Bertrand Russell) by Leibniz.

Leibniz is known today principally as one of the founders of modern logic, as perhaps the greatest mathematician among the major European philosophers (he was the inventor of infinitesimal calculus), and for his metaphysical system, summarized near the end of his life in a text known as the "Monadology." Leibniz's readership since the early twentieth century has therefore consisted primarily of philosophers debating his theories of language, logic, and metaphysics. At the same time, we must recall that the reception and transmission of Leibniz's work—not to mention its original audience—have always been an eccentric affair. Leibniz relied for much of his career on aristocratic patronage, a circumstance that sometimes influenced the composition and presentation of his work, as Peter Fenves notes: "the *Theodicy,* like many of Leibniz's more extensive writings (in French), is directed toward the edification of princesses."[7] Much of his work, moreover, originally saw the light of day (often posthumously) with the support of figures such as R. E. Raspe, the author of the Baron Munchausen tales, who published Leibniz's *New Essays on Human Understanding* in 1765, a milestone in the establishment of Leibniz's reputation (almost fifty years after his death). Catherine Wilson writes: "Sometimes appreciation for Leibniz seemed based in a kind of aestheticism—the *Theodicy* was already for Swiss Charles Bonnet in 1748 a kind of toy or ornament, rather than a truth-bearing philosophical apparatus. He describes it as 'a kind of telescope, which showed me another universe, which presented to me an enchanted perspective . . . almost magical.'"[8] Condillac complained that Leibniz's "Monadology," consisting of nothing but "metaphors, finally, got lost in the infinite."[9] Hegel called Leibniz's philosophy a "metaphysical novel," and Bertrand Russell, who introduced Leibniz to modern readers, called the "Monadology" a "kind of fantastic fairy tale."[10]

It was indeed Leibniz's "Monadology" (a treatise of about twelve pages written in French in 1714) which attracted the interests of Novalis, Friedrich Schlegel, and other Romantic writers associated with the *Athenaeum* magazine toward the end of the eighteenth century. For the young

7. Indeed, Peter Fenves adds, the *Theodicy* (1706) was dedicated to the recently deceased queen of Prussia, daughter of Leibniz's most important patron, the Electress Sophia. The queen of Prussia was also the recipient of letters outlining Leibniz's conception of "clear but confused perception," the nucleus of his theory of monadic obscurity. Fenves, *Arresting Language: From Leibniz to Benjamin* (Stanford, CA: Stanford University Press, 2001), 289–290 n. 91.

8. Catherine Wilson, "The Reception of Leibniz in the Eighteenth Century," in *The Cambridge Companion to Leibniz,* ed. Nicholas Jolley (Cambridge: Cambridge University Press, 1995), 467.

9. Etienne Bonnot de Condillac cited in Wilson, "Reception of Leibniz," 455.

10. Hegel cited in Fenves, *Arresting Language,* 284 n. 68; Bertrand Russell, *A Critical Exposition of the Philosophy of Leibniz* (1900; London: George Allen, 1937), xiii.

experimentalists of the *Frühromantik* in Germany, the appeal of Leibniz's ideas could not be separated from his philosophical *style*.[11] Schlegel, placing Leibniz "among the greatest masters" of a "thoroughly material wit," describes his manner of writing and thinking as falling between science, philosophy, and poetry: "The most important scientific discoveries are bon mots of this sort—are so because of the surprising contingency of their origin, the unifying source of their thought, and the baroqueness of their casual expression. . . . The best ones are *echappés de vue* into the infinite. Leibniz's whole philosophy consists of a few fragments and projects that are witty in this sense."[12]

From Leibniz's attempt to free mathematics from geometric intuition, Schlegel, who was instrumental in what might be called "a cult of infinity" among the members of the Jena Circle, deduced a "language of infinity" (corresponding to the "necessary fiction" of infinitesimal calculus) in the guise of the poetic fragment. Indeed, Schlegel's most important stylistic innovation (practiced in concert with his friend Novalis)—the literary-philosophical fragment—clearly takes inspiration not only from the *philosophy* of the monad but from the monadological *style* of Leibniz's treatise: "A fragment, like a miniature work of art, has to be entirely isolated from the surrounding world and be complete in itself."[13] Moreover, the fragment and the *riddle* are united in Schlegel's mind by the substance of wit—a monadic substance—which somehow exceeds its comprehension: "A good riddle should be witty; otherwise nothing remains once the answer has been found."[14]

Though Leibniz's "witty" philosophical style—a "chemical wit," in Schlegel's phrase—furnished a cool example of the new aesthetic ideology of the enigma, his appeal to the Jena Circle was not primarily stylistic. At a moment in literary and cultural history when the I-know-not-what of aesthetic experience was being redefined in revolutionary ways, the "new Leibniz" emerged as *the* philosopher of the German counter-Enlightenment, a rallying point—in part for his ostensibly unsystematic approach—of anti-Kantian views. Probably most important to the new models of lyric sensibility (and lyric form) developed by Schlegel and his counterparts was Leibniz's theorization of "perceptions we do not

11. The role of the *idea* of philosophical style in Leibniz's thought is carefully delineated by Fenves in the first chapter of his book *Arresting Language*, 13–32.

12. *Friedrich Schlegel's "Lucinde" and the Fragments*, trans. Peter Firchow (Minneapolis: University of Minnesota Press, 1971), Athenaeum frag. 220. All references to fragments use the numbering of this collection.

13. Schlegel, Athenaeum frag. 206.

14. Schlegel, Lyceum frag. 96.

apperceive," an idea anchoring the first systematic model of subliminal, or unconscious, experience.[15] In addition, Leibniz's theory of monadic perception, a psychology of ontological substance, provided the philosophical rationale for placing sensation, intellection, and feeling on a continuum, so that perception and feeling might be regarded as "confused" forms of thinking—and thinking as a species of "perception." In this respect, the "Monadology" provides the basis for eighteenth-century conceptions of *sentimentality*, a discourse of "intellectual feelings" and, hence, of objects, places, or events infused with emotional reflection.

One could therefore begin to conceive of perceptions that are "clear, but confused"—a formulation of ontological substance (since perception *is* substance in the "Monadology") reliant on a complex rhetoric of clarity and obscurity: a model commensurable, Leibniz discerned from the outset, with the emerging aesthetic of the sublime. What's more, the obscurity of monadic perception (its subliminality and perspectival nature) is not simply unavoidable but constitutive of individual substances. In the context of this dynamic transvaluation of obscurity, the evocative monad became for Fichte a model of the self, for Novalis a template of the natural object (think of Keats's negative capability), and for Schlegel a principle of aesthetic form.[16] The psychological inflection of monadic substance thus activated a series of transitive relations between Romantic conceptions of subjectivity, objecthood, and aesthetic form—all oriented around the axis of poetological research.

The essential features of the Romantic Leibniz survived into the twentieth century in surprising ways. The Marxist critic Georg Lukacs, for example, called the work of art "eine fensterlose Monade" (a windowless monad) in an early essay on aesthetics, published in 1917.[17] The most illustrious (and discreet) modern student of the "Monadology" in its Romantic aspect was, curiously, another Marxist, Walter Benjamin—an indication, perhaps, of the latent sociological prospect of the monad. Benjamin's dissertation director, Richard Herbertz, published a book on Leibniz, *Die Lehre vom Unbewussten im System des Leibniz* (The Doctrine of the Unconscious in the System of Leibniz) in 1905, a work that almost certainly influenced Benjamin's dissertation, "The Concept of Criticism

15. On the origin and historical vicissitudes of Leibniz's theory of unconscious perception (which has no mechanism of repression), see Jonathan Miller, "Going Unconscious," *New York Review of Books*, 10 April 1995.

16. Walter Benjamin discusses these adaptations of monadological principles in his dissertation, "The Concept of Criticism in German Romanticism," reprinted in *Selected Writings*, vol. 1, *1913–1926*, by Walter Benjamin, ed. Marcus Bullock and Michael W. Jennings (Cambridge, MA: Harvard University Press, 1996), 134–135, 147.

17. Georg Lukacs, "Die Subjekt-Objekt Beziehung in der Ästhetik," *Logos*, 1917–1918, 14–28.

in German Romanticism" (which views the "medium of reflection" posited by Schlegel and Novalis as essentially monadological).[18] Though Benjamin's career as a Leibnizian idealist reached its peak—and breaking point—in his formulation of the guiding principles of *The Origin of the German Mourning Play* in the mid-1920s, his thinking never lost its Leibnizian cast.[19]

Though one may rightfully place these works of Herbertz and Benjamin (and Lukacs) in a genealogy of the Romantic Leibniz, one must also regard them as elements in a distinctive, *modern* revival of Leibniz in the early twentieth century, which proceeded along an axis that is significantly different from the orientation of the Romantic Leibniz. Though not entirely bereft of literary qualities, the modern Leibniz was, at least initially, a Leibniz among the philosophers, acknowledged for his seminal contributions to the philosophy of language, to modern logic, and for his critique of mathematics (through his invention of infinitesimal calculus). Two books, published nearly simultaneously, ignited a ferocious debate about the significance of Leibniz's work: *La logique de Leibniz d'après des documents inédits* (1901) by Louis Couturat and *A Critical Exposition of the Philosophy of Leibniz* (1900) by Bertrand Russell.[20]

Within a matter of several years, substantial contributions to the modern Leibniz renaissance had appeared from major European philosophers: Edmund Husserl's *Logische Untersuchungen* (Logical Investigations) in 1900; Ernst Cassirer's *Leibniz' System in seinen wissenschaftlichen Grundlagen* (The Scientific Foundation of Leibniz's System) in 1902; as well as Herbertz's book on *petites perceptions* in 1905.[21] A second reappraisal of Leibniz's

18. Richard Herbertz, *Die Lehre vom Unbewussten im System des Leibniz* (1905; repr., New York: Olms, 1980).

19. The monadological schema of the *Trauerspiel* book appears in the book's notoriously difficult "Epistemo-critical Preface." See Walter Benjamin, *The Origin of German Tragic Drama,* trans. John Osborne (New York: Verso, 1977). In 1923, when he was writing the book, Benjamin wrote to his friend Christian Rang describing his regard for "Leibniz's entire way of thinking, his idea of the monad, which I adopt for my definition of ideas." Letter to Florens Christian Rang, 9 December 1923, in *Selected Writings,* 1:389. The most explicit contemporary account of Benjamin's monadological method appears in Siegfried Kracauer's 1928 essay "On the Writings of Walter Benjamin," in *The Mass Ornament: Weimar Essays,* by Siegfried Kracauer, ed. and trans. Thomas Y. Levin (Cambridge, MA: Harvard University Press, 1995), 259–264. In addition, Benjamin's correlation of riddles and names (the verbal counterpart of the monad) in a fragment written in 1921, "Riddle and Mystery," reveals a distinctive feature of Benjamin's monadology. *Selected Writings,* 1:267–268.

20. Russell once declared, "I often have imaginary conversations with Leibniz, in which I tell him how fruitful his ideas have proved." *The Autobiography of Bertrand Russell* (Boston: Little, Brown, 1967), 280.

21. Cassirer's book presents a detailed comparison of the philosophies of Kant and Leibniz, while Husserl's work laid the foundations of phenomenology, in part, by attacking the psychologism of contemporary theories of logic. Both Cassirer's and Husserl's books have been reprinted in numerous editions. See Ernst Cassirer, *Leibniz' System in seinen wissenschaftlichen Grundlagen,* ed. Marcel Simon

thought, stimulated in part by debate over the philosophical implications of quantum mechanics, emerged in the 1920s: Hans Reichenbach, writing in Berlin at the same time that his friend Walter Benjamin was drafting his monadological critique of the *Trauerspiel,* invoked Leibnizian metaphysics in his polemical—and politically charged—attacks on the principle of causality.[22] In addition, Alfred North Whitehead drafted the most comprehensive modern monadology (addressing the "metaphysics of experience") in the lectures constituting *Process and Reality* in 1929.[23]

Although the Leibniz renaissance of the early twentieth century (the Leibniz of logical positivism and Wittgenstein's Vienna Circle) rarely reached beyond the precincts of analytic philosophy or philosophically minded criticism, it is principally the constellation of topics and specialized vocabulary of the Analytic Leibniz—rather than the Romantic Leibniz—that supplied the arts with the terms for a model of lyric expression. While the Romantic Leibniz emerges from debate about the hermeticism and the inviolability of the monad—about the *absence* of relations among monads—the modern, Analytic Leibniz is consumed by the puzzle of monadic relations, by the enigma of solipsistic perception, and by plausible explanations of mass phenomena (whether bodies or other forms of collectivity) in a universe made up of monads. And it is precisely the question of hermetic or solipsistic relations which bears most directly on the transitivity of lyric obscurity.[24]

Ariadne's Thread

In certain fundamental respects, Leibniz's metaphysic sustains the equation of *logos* and being integral to Parmenides' theory of metaphysical substance, thereby anticipating Heidegger's claim—in his modern revival

(Hamburg: Meiner, 1998); and Edmund Husserl, *Logical Investigations,* ed. Dermot Moran, trans. J. N. Findlay (New York: Routledge, 2001).

22. Among Reichenbach's writings on Leibniz, see his essay "The Theory of Motion according to Newton, Leibniz, and Huyghens" (1924), in *Selected Writings,* by Hans Reichenbach, vol. 2, *1909–1953,* ed. Maria Reichenbach and Robert S. Cohen, trans. Elizabeth Hughes Schneewind (Dordrecht: Reidel, 1978), 48–65. On the charged political implications of Reichenbach's arguments in the 1920s (in the context of National Socialism)—which may be compared to the political implications of Benjamin's monadology—see Paul Forman, "Weimar Culture, Causality, and Quantum Theory, 1918–1927," in *Historical Studies in the Physical Sciences,* ed. Russell McCormmach (Philadelphia: University of Pennsylvania Press, 1971), 87–91. Forman notes that Max Planck devoted the annual public session of the Prussian Academy of Sciences in 1922 to "their spiritual founder, Leibniz" (92).

23. Alfred North Whitehead, *Process and Reality* (Cambridge: Cambridge University Press, 1929).

24. Bertrand Russell reports that he "first realized the importance of relations when . . . working on Leibniz." Russell, *My Philosophical Development* (London: Allen and Unwin, 1959), 48.

of metaphysics—that "language is the house of Being."[25] Furthermore, the "Monadology," Leibniz's most concise exposition of his metaphysical theories, may, from the standpoint of its preoccupation with symbolic logic, be described as a treatise on *enigmatology,* insofar as its theory of substance rests on a model of "equivocal expression." Recalling the function of poetic language in the Anglo-Saxon riddles, verbal obscurity, as Leibniz conceives it, expresses the nonintuitive properties of being, which lie beyond reach of the senses. Just as the materialism of the riddle continually reverts to an iconography of immaterial substance, so the discontinuity of monadic substance—borrowed from atomism—becomes a vehicle for the derealization of corporeal phenomena.

Because the basic strands of Leibniz's thought (symbolic logic and metaphysics) betray the influence of his early thinking about artificial languages and his lifelong interest in natural languages (etymology in particular), one must bear in mind that his formulation of ontological substance and his understanding of logical procedures reflect, essentially, a conception of *linguistic* being. Further, the various aspects of Leibniz's thinking are unified by efforts to identify elementary forms (e.g., monads) and to describe the syntax of relations (the "art of combinations") between these forms. In each of these philosophical domains, Leibniz's analytic project yields a methodological "device" capable of navigating by "calculation" and with "the aid of signs" what he calls "the labyrinth of the continuum" (the maze of phenomenal appearance) or other structures characterized by obscurity—such as the branching of historical languages, or the "labyrinth of freedom."[26] The labyrinth, we should recall, however, is a form "inviting dalliance, but never complete understanding."[27]

In keeping with the rhetoric of labyrinthine forms, Leibniz often refers to the analytic key, or calculus, as the "thread of Ariadne," echoing his conception of the "Ariadne thread" of etymology.[28] Most impor-

25. Martin Heidegger, "Letter on Humanism," in *Basic Writings*, trans. David Farrell Krell (San Francisco: HarperCollins, 1993), 217.

26. The phrase "labyrinth of the continuum" appears in Leibniz, *Theodicy: Essays on the Goodness of God, the Freedom of Man, and the Origin of Evil* (1710), trans. E. M. Huggard (La Salle, IL: Open Court, 1985), 53.

27. L. E. Loemker, introduction to *Philosophical Papers and Letters*, by G. W. Leibniz, ed. L. E. Loemker, 2nd ed. (Dordrecht: Reidel, 1969), 14.

28. Donald Rutherford remarks on Leibniz's use of phrases such as "the thread of Ariadne" or "thread of meditation" to describe his conception of symbolic logic. Rutherford, "Philosophy and Language in Leibniz," in *Cambridge Companion to Leibniz*, 258 n. 17. Leibniz's reference to the "Ariadne thread" of etymology appears in a letter to Ludolf (1687). Leibniz, *Sämtliche Schriften und Briefe,* ed. German Academy of Sciences (Berlin: Akademie Verlag, 1923–), series 1, 5:31. Cited in Hans Aarsleff, "The Study and Use of Etymology in Leibniz," in *From Locke to Saussure: Essays on the Study of Language and Intellectual History,* by Hans Aarsleff (Minneapolis: University of Minnesota Press, 1982), 94–95, 100 n. 42.

tantly, and consistently, Leibniz conceives of the calculus—the Ariadne thread—as a system of "rational writing," a "philosophical language," or, more commonly, a "universal characteristic":

No one should fear that the contemplation of signs will lead us away from the things in themselves; on the contrary, it leads us into the interior of things. We often have confused notions today because the signs are badly arranged, but then with the aid of signs we will easily have the most distinct notions, for we will have at hand *a mechanical thread of meditation,* as it were, with whose aid we can easily resolve any idea whatever into those of which it is composed.[29]

So great are the analytic powers of this "mechanical thread of meditation" (elsewhere compared to the inventions of the microscope and the telescope) that Leibniz describes it as a "guiltless kind of magic."[30] Though Ariadne's thread reveals itself to be a "mechanical"—that is, logical—instrument, allowing one to *calculate* one's way out of the maze, the magical thread, and the riddling topography of the labyrinth, remain, in essence, linguistic phenomena.

In the early part of his career, Leibniz devoted attention to a wide array of grammatological phenomena: cryptography, cartography, heraldry, numismatics, ancient writing systems, and the alphabet of the deaf. Shaped by these inquiries, the basic features of his theory of monadic substance (and its relation to the phenomenal world) first appeared in his critique of language and logic. For Leibniz believed that "language is to be regarded as the bright mirror of the understanding," a trope recalling his assertion that the monad is a "living mirror" of the universe (and a trope that would become a cornerstone of modern language philosophy).[31]

29. Leibniz, letter to Tschirnhaus, May 1678, in *Philosophical Papers and Letters*, 193 (emphasis added). The phrase "mechanical philosophy" refers, in the seventeenth century, to the new critical philosophy associated with the revival of atomism (and with Descartes in particular), which is to be contrasted with Scholasticism, or the "common philosophy." Discussion of Leibniz's phraseology of the *charactéristique* can be found in Rutherford, "Philosophy and Language in Leibniz," 228–230, 256–257 n. 12.

30. Referring to his "invention" of the "universal characteristic" Leibniz offers a number of analogies for its analytic potency: "My invention includes the whole use of reason, a judge for controversies, an interpretation of notions, a balance of probabilities, a compass which will pilot us through the ocean of experience, an inventory of things, a table of thoughts, a microscope to scrutinize the closest objects, a telescope to individuate those most distant, a general calculus, a guiltless kind of magic, a kind of writing that everybody will read in his own language." Leibniz, *Sämtliche Schriften und Briefe,* series 1, 2:167–169. Cited in Paolo Rossi, "The Twisted Roots of Leibniz' Characteristic," in *The Leibniz Renaissance,* by Paolo Rossi (Florence: Olschke Editore, 1985), 289.

31. Leibniz cited in Aarsleff, "Study and Use of Etymology in Leibniz," 85. The metaphor of language as a mirror appears as well in Leibniz, *New Essays on Human Understanding*, ed. and trans. Peter Remnant and Jonathan Bennett (Cambridge: Cambridge University Press, 1996), 3.7.6. Wittgen-

Indeed, the modern revival of Leibniz was launched with Russell's contention that "Leibniz's philosophy was almost entirely derived from his logic."[32] We must bear in mind, however, that Leibniz's earliest thinking about logic appears in a prospectus for a universal language, *On the Art of Combinations* (1666). Rossi confirms the verbal orientation of *De arte combinatoria:* "The characteristic, as Couturat pointed out, was not initially conceived under the form of an algebra or of a calculus, but under the form of a universal tongue or writing."[33] Hence, the foundational role of logic in Russell's thesis must be referred, ultimately, to Leibniz's thinking about language and systems of writing. Even when the logical calculus displaced the universal characteristic in Leibniz's thinking (though the two projects are never entirely distinct), its organizing principle, the "subject-predicate logic," betrays its linguistic origin.

The essential point to bear in mind is that one can trace the foundational premises of the "Monadology" (immanence and expression) back through the subject-predicate logic (the predicate inheres in the subject) to the "art of combinations" informing Leibniz's model for a universal characteristic. Leibniz himself acknowledges that any conception of simple form, including the monad, cannot be explained without reference to his theory of symbolic characters: "I maintain that all simple forms are mutually compatible. This is a proposition of which I cannot give proof without explaining the basis of my symbolic logic [*caractéristique*] thoroughly."[34] In Leibniz's view, therefore, the symbolic character of ordinary words—conceived etymologically—exemplifies the subliminality of monadic substance. The logic of expression unites speech (Latin *fare*) and fate (*fatum*).[35]

Leibniz's later writings testify to the importance he gives to natural language in his metaphysical conceptions, seeking not only to find, through etymology, the Ariadne thread out of the labyrinth of natural

stein's picture theory of language (conceived under the influence of Leibniz) is one of the inaugural moments of modern language philosophy.

32. Russell, *Critical Exposition of the Philosophy of Leibniz,* v.

33. Rossi, "Twisted Roots of Leibniz' Characteristic," 277. Michel Serres, in his two-volume exposition of Leibniz's thought, makes an even broader claim for "l'importance dans le leibnizianisme de la philosophie du langage," with reference, predictably, to the universal characteristic and the *combinatoire,* yet he also states: "Expliquer le leibnizianisme par modèles mathématiques ou modèles linguistiques est une seule et meme chose." Serres, *Le système de Leibniz et ses modèles mathématiques* (Paris: Presses Universitaires de France, 1968), 2:508 n. 1.

34. Leibniz cited in Hide Ishiguro, *Leibniz's Philosophy of Logic and Language* (Cambridge: Cambridge University Press, 1990), 56.

35. The principles of a "rational" etymology imply, according to Peter Fenves, "an infinite language in which there is no distinction between saying so and being so." Fenves, *Arresting Language,* 29–31.

languages but to view the distillation of natural languages as the Ariadne thread leading out of the "labyrinth of the continuum"—that is, the maze of phenomenal reality. On this latter point, Leibniz declares, "No one should fear that the contemplation of signs will lead us away from the things in themselves; on the contrary, it leads us into the interior of things."[36]

The Infinity of Small, Hidden Springs

Deeply imbued with his thinking about language and symbolic logic, Leibniz's thesis concerning the inherent obscurity of metaphysical substance finds expression in his theory of monads. Monadic perception is the incorporeal substance that permeates all sensory phenomena in the universe, as well as being the substance of relations between entities (monads) that have no interaction with one another. The concept is central to Liebniz's metaphysics, yet a notion of perception without consciousness or sensory properties (in the case of bare monads) remains puzzling and even paradoxical. Indeed, the I-know-not-what of monadic substance is, like Heidegger's conception of Being, inherently enigmatic, a riddle without a solution: the nonsensuous and unconscious perception intrinsic to a material object is no less puzzling, for example, than the existence of matter and material phenomena in a universe composed solely of monads—which have no material properties.

Leibniz's thinking about language, in addition to providing the general armature for his metaphysics, influences in precise and dramatic ways his theory of monadic perception. For example, in his view, the obscurity associated with monadic perception can be compared to the necessary residue of incomprehension generated by the symbolic functions of readership and textuality. Indeed, monadic perception, according to Leibniz, is best understood as a form of reading (which supplies its own inscription): "It is therefore these present perceptions, along with the regulated tendency to change in conformity with what is outside, which form the musical score which the soul reads."[37] Here the monad (or soul) comprises at once the musical notation (or logical inscription) of the phenomenal world and the "reader" of the score: an illustration of the fact that expression and perception coincide in substance—even in the mindless realm of bare monads. A similar equation of perception and expression in the

36. Leibniz, letter to Tschirnhaus, in *Philosophical Papers and Letters,* 193.
37. Leibniz, *Philosophical Papers and Letters,* 580.

act of monadic "reading" can be found in Leibniz's observation that "a soul can read in itself only what is distinctly represented there; it cannot unfold all its folds at once, because they go to infinity."[38] (The dark "folds" to which he refers here are the unconscious elements, or *petites perceptions,* of monadic substance.)

Routinely using the phrase "Il est ecrit dans le monad" (in the letters to Arnauld, for example), Leibniz suggests that the monad may be compared to a *crypt* whose interior is engraved with inscriptions evoking an external world. Further, in the "Monadology," he contrasts the more limited (and hence obscure) perception of the individual monad ("a soul can read in itself only what is distinctly represented there") with a fully omniscient "reader," God: "he who sees all can read in each thing what happens everywhere, and even what has happened or what will happen."[39] Conceived as a form of reading, monadic perception is at once partially omniscient and "blind or symbolic": a way of knowing things—a "blind knowledge"—linking reading, in an ordinary sense, to all symbolic procedures.[40]

Monadic perception is obscure for reasons which Leibniz takes great care to explain. In the first place, monadic substance (the substance of all things) is obscure because its perception of the universe (a mirror, or replica, of all that exists) is limited by its particular *perspective* on the universe: each monad, according to Leibniz, is "a mirror endowed with internal action, which represents the universe from its own point of view and is ordered as the universe itself."[41] The individual "point of view" of each monad does not limit its perception to only "a part of things"—in other words, it expresses the universe in its entirety—yet "this representation is confused as to the *detail* of the whole universe, and can only be distinct for a small portion of things." What, then, does the monad perceive? The answer is, astonishingly, the entire universe, with varying degrees of clarity and obscurity—sometimes in ways that are both "clear" and "confused" at the same time. Accordingly, Leibniz argues, "Monads are limited, not as to their objects, but with respect to the modifications of their

38. Leibniz, "Monadology," 221.

39. Leibniz, "Monadology," 221.

40. Leibniz maintains that most of our thinking is "blind or symbolic; we use it in algebra and arithmetic and indeed almost everywhere." Leibniz, *Philosophical Papers and Letters*, 292.

41. Leibniz, "Principles of Nature and Grace," 207. Elsewhere, Leibniz explains the perspectival substance of the monad in terms of a pictorial space anticipating the principles of cubism: "Just as the same city viewed from different directions appears entirely different and, as it were, multiplied perspectively [*sic*], in just the same way it happens that, because of the infinite multitude of simple substances, there are, as it were, just as many different universes, which are nevertheless only perspectives on a single one, corresponding to the different points of view of each monad." Leibniz, "Monadology," 220.

knowledge of them. Monads all go confusedly to infinity, to the whole; but they are limited and differentiated by the degrees of their distinct perceptions."[42] Monadic perception therefore combines infinity and confusion, omniscience and obscurity.

Taking these conditions into account, Gilles Deleuze argues that the "Monadology" forms "a 'symbolic' philosophy of expression, in which expression is inseparable from the signs of its transformations, and from the obscure areas in which it is plunged."[43] Emphasizing the inherent obscurity of symbolic expression—and hence of monadic substance—in Leibniz's metaphysic, Deleuze concludes: "*Such a symbolic philosophy is necessarily a philosophy of equivocal expression.*"[44] From this statement, one may infer that monadic substance is itself equivocal, insofar as it reflects the nature of symbolic expression.

The combination of omniscience and obscurity in monadic substance pertains not only to the general economy of metaphysical perception but, as Leibniz contends, to individual states of perception: "Each distinct perception of the soul includes an infinity of confused perceptions."[45] Offering a memorable analogy for the combination of clarity and confusion—the chiaroscuro—characterizing all monadic perception, Leibniz states, "Each soul knows the infinite—knows all—but confusedly. It is like walking on the seashore and hearing the great noise of the sea: I hear the particular noises of each wave, of which the whole noise is compared, but without distinguishing them."[46] Based on these views, Leibniz developed a precise terminology to designate the various qualities of perception (and combinations of qualities) occupying the spectrum of monadic perception, thereby sowing the seeds of a doctrine of "clear but confused" perception that would later be appropriated by theorists of the sublime and of Romantic poetry.[47]

The clear but confused admixture of the substance of monadic perception becomes less perplexing if we substitute material atoms for monads. Viewed through the prism of the metaphysical materialism of atomist doctrine (the standard reference for the nature of substance), our per-

42. Leibniz, "Monadology," 220–221.

43. Gilles Deleuze, *Expressionism in Philosophy: Spinoza,* trans. Martin Joughlin (New York: Zone Books, 1992), 329.

44. Deleuze, *Expressionism in Philosophy,* 329 (emphasis in original).

45. Leibniz, "Principles of Nature and Grace," 211.

46. Leibniz, "Principles of Nature and Grace," 211.

47. Leibniz offers his most succinct account of types of perception in his correspondence with the queen of Prussia. Leibniz, *Philosophical Papers and Letters,* 547–549. Bertrand Russell gives a useful summary of the terminology: "Knowledge is either *obscure* or *clear.* Clear knowledge is *confused* or *distinct.* Distinct knowledge is *adequate* or *inadequate.*" Russell, *Critical Exposition of the Philosophy of Leibniz,* 167–168 (emphasis in original).

ception of a material body is at once "clear and confused," in the sense that we apprehend clearly (more or less) its sensible properties while its inscrutable substance (atoms) remains obscure, unknowable, to us. Each distinct perception is fed by what Leibniz calls "an infinity of small, hidden springs."[48] His famous illustration of our clear but confused perception of the roar of the sea is likewise a physical analogy for the subliminality of monadic perception.

Bearing in mind the correspondence between monadic and sensible perceptions, Leibniz goes so far as to claim that "*sensible* qualities are in fact *occult* qualities. . . . And although they are familiar to us we do not understand them the better for that; as a pilot understands no better than another person the nature of the magnetic needle which turns toward the north, although he has it always before his eyes in the compass."[49] The idea that manifest qualities are somehow obscure betrays the essential inversion of materialism which lies at the heart of the "Monadology" (and its lyric affinities): "Every accident is a kind of abstraction; only substance is concrete."[50] From this perspective, insensible substances are "concrete," while material bodies are mere abstractions, accidents, or "modes of things." One must bear in mind, however, that the "occult" properties of material bodies derive from, or correspond to, a metaphysics of equivocal expression, which functions inevitably like a language machine fueled by obscurity—a machine Leibniz builds around the term *fatum,* in which *speech* determines *fate.*[51]

Lucifer's Element, or the Secrets of the Sublime

In order to appreciate fully Leibniz's observations about the aesthetic connotations of the subliminality of monadic substance (that is, his references to music, architecture, etymological harmonies, and the principle of the sublime), one must first possess a thorough understanding of the doctrine of monadic perception. As the sole substance of monads, perception constitutes the monad's only possible relation with anything outside itself. Accordingly, changes within a monad from one perception

48. Leibniz cited in Roger Ariew, "G. W. Leibniz, Life and Works," in *Cambridge Companion to Leibniz,* 42 n. 27. In "Monadology," Leibniz refers to the "infinity of small inclinations and dispositions of my soul"—that is, to the infinity of the monad's *petites perceptions* (217).

49. Leibniz, "On the Supersensible Element in Knowledge, and On the Immaterial in Nature," in *Leibniz: Selections,* ed. Philip P. Weiner (New York: Scribners, 1951), 356 (emphasis in original).

50. Leibniz, *Philosophical Papers and Letters,* 605.

51. Leibniz addresses the correlation between *fatum* and *fare* in *Philosophical Papers and Letters,* 122.

to another constitute the only possible form of monadic action.[52] More importantly, for the history of poetics, Leibniz's theory of monadic "perception" is obscure, in part, because it does not involve, in its most rudimentary form, the experience of sense perception, or sensation; which is to say, it erodes the absolute distinction (dear to Kant) between thinking and perceiving—an idea of explosive importance for Romantic poetics and epistemology. The riddle of solipsistic perception helped to fuel as well the modern revival of interest in Leibniz, whose characterization of monadic perception as "miraculous, or marvelous," prompted Bertrand Russell to explain: "Perception is marvelous, because it cannot be conceived as an action of the object on the percipient, since substances never interact. Thus, although it is related to the object and simultaneous with it (or approximately so), it is in no way due to the object, but only to the nature of the percipient."[53] In a sense, as Fabrizio Mondadori observes, "it is *as if* what is perceived (whatever it may be) were not there at all: given the denial of causal interaction, what is (said to be) perceived might as well melt into thin air."[54] More radically, the metaphysical doctrine of monads implies that "the being or reality of material things consists solely in the fact that they are perceived."[55]

Leibniz's theory of perception, which determines the nature of monadic relations (and, by implication, the scope of lyric expression), diverges most sharply from standard definitions of "perception" by its rejection of any causal relation between a monad and the "objects" of its perception: "Monads perceive what passes without them by what passes within them."[56] Thus, each monad is an image (a "mirror endowed with internal action") of the universe only in the sense that it *multiplies* the world by its mirroring—not in the sense that its perceptions (or reflections) resemble the sensory world. In its mirroring function, monadic perception therefore "involves" the world in such a way that it produces "a multitude in the unity or simple substance."[57]

52. Leibniz explains that "a monad, in itself and at a moment, can be distinguished from another only by its internal qualities and actions, which can be nothing but *perceptions* (that is, the representation of the composite, or the external, in the simple) and its *appetitions* (that is, its tendency to go from one perception to another), which are the principles of change." Leibniz, "Principles of Nature and Grace," 207 (emphasis in original). Elsewhere, he states that "this is all one can find in the simple substance—that is, perceptions and their changes." Leibniz, "Monadology," 215.

53. Russell, *Critical Exposition of the Philosophy of Leibniz*, 132.

54. Fabrizio Mondadori, "Solipsistic Perception," in *Leibniz: Critical and Interpretive Essays*, ed. Michael Hacker (Minneapolis: University of Minnesota Press, 1982), 32 (emphasis in original).

55. Donald P. Rutherford, "Phenomenalism and the Reality of the Body in Leibniz's Later Philosophy," *Studia Leibnitiana* 22, no. 1 (1990): 15.

56. Leibniz, *Philosophical Papers and Letters*, 711.

57. Leibniz, "Monadology," 214.

In accordance with the mirror analogy, Leibniz calls monadic substance "represented being," an observation suggesting that monads exhibit what may be described as a "presupposition of mediality."[58] Each monad may thus be described as a medium. Indeed, the "Monadology" may be read as a prehistory of modern media and, more specifically—given its preoccupation with immaterial substance—as a doctrine of *lyrical* media. At the same time, monads are logical substances, if nothing else—or logical media.

The eccentricity of monadic perception is not, however, defined solely by its solipsistic nature; it is perplexing as well because of its universality, its metaphysical status as the only true substance of all phenomena. By this definition, monadic perception must be characteristic of *all* entities, including objects and creatures without minds—not to mention the materials of language and other sign systems (with the implication that words are *perceptive,* in addition to being perceptible). Conscious perception can therefore never be more than a tiny fraction of all monadic perception: the perceptions intrinsic to a doorknob—and to most entities—are not merely perceptions without awareness but perceptions requiring no presence of mind whatsoever! The mirror analogy of monadic perception must therefore pertain to a field of *unconscious* expression (the basis, as I indicated earlier, of the subliminality of monadic substance). Leibniz warns the reader in this regard: "it is good to distinguish between *perception,* which is the internal state of the monad representing external things, and *apperception,* which is *consciousness,* or the reflective knowledge of this internal state, something not given to all souls, nor at all times to a given soul."[59] Hence, the kind of perception common to all monads—minds and objects alike—is not merely senseless (without sensory origin) but mindless.

Distinguished from apperception and from *sensation* (defined as "a perception accompanied by memory"), unconscious perception (the domain of *petites perceptions,* as Leibniz refers to them) constitutes the sole substance of what he calls "bare monads"—substances without awareness or memory. Bare monads, like the souls of animals "when their perceptions are not sufficiently distinct to be remembered," exist in a stupor resembling death, "as happens in a deep, dreamless sleep or in a fainting

58. Leibniz, "Monadology," 221; Friedrich Kittler, *Discourse Networks, 1800/1900,* trans. Michael Meteer, with Chris Cullens (Stanford, CA: Stanford University Press, 1990), xiii. In Kittler's more recent work, influenced by Paul Virilio, his thesis concerning the militarization of perception in modern society conforms in certain basic respects to the doctrine of monadic perception (though he is describing a material phenomenon).

59. Leibniz, "Principles of Nature and Grace," 208.

spell"—a condition of complete obscurity.[60] In this obscure condition, the psychology of ontological substance evokes the mind in a state of *shock,* at once windowless and untouchable: the unconscious domain of naked, slumbering monads. Hence, the "bare" substance of the universe exists in a dormant, or suspended, state, according to Leibnizian metaphysics, though the slumbering existence of simple monads does not imply the absence of perception or an interruption in the continuous correspondence between all monads. On the contrary, "separated by their internal actions," monads correspond with one another—mechanically and interminably—at an infinite remove.

The profound obscurity of perceptions intrinsic to objects (to bare monads) descends as well, at times, on the conscious substance of rational souls (monads capable of reflection). Leibniz writes: "we experience within ourselves a state in which we remember nothing and have no distinct perception; this is similar to when we faint or when we are overwhelmed by a deep, dreamless sleep. In this state the soul does not differ sensibly from a simple monad."[61] Hence, the rational soul may consist, at moments, of nothing more than the dormant substance of objects—an indication of the consistency and explanatory power of Leibniz's metaphysic. Even the conscious perceptions of the rational soul are sometimes half asleep, plagued by the obscurity of bare substance.

How then can perception be explained in a universe without causal interaction between substances (a question essential as well to the "blind knowledge" of poetry)? While the solipsistic nature of monadic perception—the very substance of things—seems, at first glance, to be far removed from concerns about poetry and poetics, one might begin to narrow this gap by noting that a basic correspondence exists between Leibniz's theory of monadic relations and the relational properties attributed by Kant to poetry and to poetic knowledge of the world: "Poetry fortifies the mind: for it lets the mind feel its ability—free, spontaneous, and independent of natural determination—to contemplate and judge phenomenal nature as having *aspects that nature does not on its own offer in experience either to sense or to understanding*."[62] Poetry thus "contemplates" properties of "phenomenal nature" (the sensory world) which are not derived from sensory experience—a model of lyric "contemplation" with obvious similarities to the solipsistic perception of monads.

Lyrical knowledge of the sensory world, like monadic perception, is

60. Leibniz, "Principles of Nature and Grace," 208.

61. Leibniz, "Monadology," 215.

62. Immanuel Kant, *Critique of Judgment,* trans. Werner S. Pluhar (Indianapolis: Hackett, 1987), part 1, book 2, section 53, 196–197 (emphasis added).

"miraculous" because it is senseless, because it does not rely on a causal relation to the object. Poetic knowledge, like monadic perception, is *immanent.* Indeed, given the influence of Leibniz's thinking on early Romantic formulations of aesthetic experience, it is not unlikely that Kant's conception of poetic knowledge owes something to the riddle of monadic substance—a metaphysics of autistic experience yielding a revolutionary discourse of aesthetic form. Whether or not Kant's model of aesthetic judgment is essentially solipsistic, the problematic of lyric obscurity acquires new significance, and systematic implication, by passing through the logical calculus (not to mention the "chemical wit") of Leibniz's monadology.

The solipsism and subliminality of monadic perception pertain in significant ways to modern conceptions of lyric obscurity. Subliminality in particular, which anchors Leibniz's principle of "clear but confused perception," figures as a central feature of Leibniz's observations about the aesthetic connotations of monadic substance. More precisely, he views the arts as intuitive models of the subliminality of monadic substance. Referring to "intellectual pleasures known confusedly"—the basic condition of monadic perception—he states: "Music charms us, even though its beauty consists only in the harmonies of numbers and in a calculation that we are not aware of, but which the soul nevertheless carries out."[63] Architecture as well offers a paradigm of unconscious but expressive harmonies: "The pleasures that sight finds in proportions are of the same nature, and those caused by the other senses amount to something similar."[64] Thus, the subliminal pleasures of music and architecture arise from the obscurity of harmonic structures whose "numbers" escape us (though they remain susceptible to analysis). Thus, the aesthetic form of music veers toward the condition of noise—the "great noise of the sea"—but also toward the implicit calculations, or metrics, of lyric poetry. And the obscurity of these submerged designs "charms" us: a power of attraction or movement, akin perhaps to the "appetition" of insensible monads.

The particular resonance of the term "harmony" for Leibniz may stem, in part, from his usage of it in reference to linguistics and the correspondences revealed by etymology.[65] For Leibniz, the innate "harmony of lan-

63. Leibniz, "Principles of Nature and Grace," 212.

64. Leibniz, "Principles of Nature and Grace," 212.

65. Concerning the most active phase in Leibniz's thinking about natural languages, Hans Aarsleff writes: "between 1695 and 1700 he wrote ten long letters to Sparfvenfelt that are almost exclusively concerned with linguistic matters . . . and some of the very last letters Leibniz wrote, in October of 1716, were devoted to his linguistic studies." Further, "during his last years, Leibniz planned publi-

guages" becomes evident by comparing etymological samples between, for instance, "the languages of the interior of Scythia."[66] Hence, the task of etymology is to reveal the "harmony" of disparate tongues: an innate structure, or calibration, which becomes a prime analogy for the preestablished harmony of monadic perceptions.

In a metaphysics of equivocal expression, all signs may be obscure, but they are never arbitrary. The harmonic structure of etymology therefore unifies the subliminal elements—the hidden "folds"—of *individual words*. By tracing what he calls "the canals of tropes" leading to the origin of a word—tropes resembling the *petites perceptions* of monadic substance—Leibniz seeks to reconstruct a philosophically and, as the historical evidence indicates, poetically significant language expressing all that can be known about the world: a paradise of inviolate names.[67]

Individual words, like monads capable of reflection, are at once clear and confused, manifest and subliminal. To cite one of Leibniz's favorite tropes for the chiaroscuro of monadic substance, language impresses us as being at once intelligible and turbulent, distinct and obscure: "almost as it looks in a pond at a distance, where we might see the confused and, so to speak, teeming motion of the fish in the pond, without discerning the fish themselves."[68] The obscurity of language (and of poetry) therefore corresponds to the "teeming motion" of subliminal and expressive harmonies lying beneath the intelligible aspect of words.

Leibniz advances the idea of a language that functions *expressively*, an idea with obvious implications for the problem of lyric obscurity: "To anyone who wanted to speak or write about any topic, the genius of this language will supply not only the words but also the things. The very name of any thing will be the key to all that could be reasonably said or thought about it or done with it."[69] Even more strikingly, the monadic name contains, or expresses, even what one does *not* know about a thing (includ-

---

cation of parts of the vast collection of etymological material he had gathered over the years. Edited by Eckhart, it appeared in 1717, as *Leibnitii Collectanea Etymologica*." The "Monadology," we should recall, was written in 1714, two years before Leibniz's death. Aarsleff, "Study and Use of Etymology in Leibniz," 86.

66. The phrase "harmony of languages" appears frequently, according to Aarsleff, in Leibniz's etymological studies, especially in his correspondence from the 1690s till his death. Aarsleff, "Study and Use of Etymology in Leibniz," 85.

67. Fenves discusses the significance of the phrase "canals of tropes" in Leibniz's linguistic investigations. Fenves, *Arresting Language*, 25. Leibniz's etymological project (to recover an ideal, philosophical vocabulary from the materials of natural language) will be recognizable to contemporary readers in the philosophical etymologies of Heidegger, especially his violent translations of Greek terms.

68. Leibniz, "Monadology," 222.

69. Leibniz, *Sämtliche Schriften und Briefe*, series 2, 1:420. Cited in Rutherford, "Philosophy and Language in Leibniz," 231.

ing its etymological affinities): "The name 'gold' . . . signifies not merely what the speaker knows of gold, e.g., something yellow and very heavy, but also what he does not know, which *may* be known by someone."[70] In other words, the monadic name may express qualities of a thing that are *unknown to all* speakers of a language—a language of facts but also of secrets.

Leibniz took a strong interest in poetry (demonstrated by his composition of verses in Latin, French, and German), and it is in one of his own Latin compositions that one discovers an intricate and amusing emblem of his theory of expressive etymology. In a lengthy poem on the death of his former protector, Duke Johann Friedrich of Brunswick, Leibniz devotes a section to the discovery of phosphorus by Hennig Brand in 1669. Illustrating his thesis about the unreliability of natural languages, he contemplates the disjunction between the proper name of the Prince of Darkness, Lucifer, and its Latin roots, *lux* and *ferens,* which mean "light bearing"—the same as the Greek term for the newly discovered element, phosphorus.[71] Quite obviously, the biblical figure bearing the name Lucifer bears little or no relation to the meaning of the name's Latin roots. Thus, the arbitrary or, let us say, ironic proper name of the prince of the underworld manifests in the most perverse way the dubiety—that is, the obscurity—of natural languages and, I would argue, of expression itself.

Leibniz's reference to phosphorus as an "immortal emblem of the blessed soul" (Immortale animae referens emblema beate) suggests that Lucifer's element, phosphorus, expresses the chiaroscuro of monadic substance, its equivocal expression of light and dark (and its immortality). The monadic signature becomes legible as well in the designation of phosphorus as the "fire unknown to Nature itself" (Ignotum, Natura, Tibi, ni doctior illum)—a quality evoking the monad's self-containment and its cryptic relation to the phenomenal world.

The subliminal, equivocal, and even antithetical properties of the name Lucifer find expression more significantly in Leibniz's thinking about the aesthetic principle of the sublime. Indeed, the etymology of the word "sublime" (Latin *sub* + *limen,* "below the threshold"), by inverting the word's conventional associations with loftiness and elevation, illustrates the equivocation at the core of Leibniz's doctrine of expressive substances: the *sublime* cannot be distinguished from the *subliminal.* Hence,

70. Leibniz, *New Essays on Human Understanding,* 3.9.24.

71. Leibniz, *Gesammelte Werke: Aus den Handschriften der Königlichen Bibliothek zu Hannover,* ed. Georg Heinrich Pertz, 4 vols. (1843–1847; repr., Hildesheim: Olms, 1966), 4:38. Fenves cites an untitled dialogue of 1677 in which Leibniz discusses the arbitrariness of Lucifer's name. Fenves, *Arresting Language,* 37–39.

the equivocation—that is, the obscurity—of the word "sublime" invites us to view the world that is reflected in the dark glass of the monad as an *underworld,* as the expression of an abject dimension of the sublime.

Leibniz was living in Paris when Nicolas Boileau published the earliest complete translation—with a brief but influential preface—of Longinus's *On the Sublime* in 1674. Two years later, shortly before leaving Paris in 1676, Leibniz wrote an important essay in Latin entitled "On the Secrets of the Sublime." The Latin word for "secrets," *arcana,* appears as well in an alternative title he considered for the essay: "The Elements of an Arcane Philosophy."[72] Profiting from the supplemental interrelation of these two titles, one can discern an emblem of the essay's implicit thesis, alluding to a correspondence between diverse modes of secrecy: the arcane "elements" of sublime experience; the *petites perceptions* of monadic substance; and the "sublime style" (a principle introduced by Boileau) of Leibniz's own "arcane philosophy."

Written during a seminal, early period of Leibniz's career, when he was drafting the basic ideas for the metaphysical system that would be summarized much later in the "Monadology" in 1714, Leibniz's essay on the sublime indicates that he quickly recognized in the aesthetic principle of the sublime an intuitive model of the subliminality of monadic substance. Although Leibniz says nothing directly about poetry's relation to the "secrets" of the sublime, later theorists of the sublime clearly grasped the implications of his argument, developing more explicitly the correlation between lyric obscurity and the expressive harmonies of the sublime. Edmund Burke, author of the widely influential *A Philosophical Enquiry into the Origin of our Ideas of the Sublime and the Beautiful* (first published in 1757), goes so far as to adopt Leibniz's iconic terms (such as "distinct" or "confused" perceptions) in analyzing the monadic structure of certain categories of words.[73] The innate obscurity of these types of words becomes in turn the basis for Burke's brief discussion of the sublime effects of poetry (achieved through *expression* rather than description): "so little does poetry depend for its effect on the power of raising sensible images,

72. Leibniz, "On the Secrets of the Sublime, or on the Supreme Being," in *De Summa Rerum, Metaphysical Papers, 1675–1676,* by G. W. Leibniz, trans. with notes by G. H. R. Parkinson (New Haven, CT: Yale University Press, 1992), 21–33. Parkinson notes the existence of the alternative title (23). Parkinson also includes in this volume an outline (produced by Leibniz in 1676) for a projected essay entitled "On the Secrets of Things" (89–90).

73. Discussing the *lack* of understanding generated by what he calls "compounded abstract words" (such as virtue, liberty, or honor), Edmund Burke contends that nobody gains even a "general idea" of their meaning, "for if he had, then some of the particular ones [i.e., "particular modes of action"], thought indistinct perhaps, and confused, might come soon to be perceived. But this, I take it, is hardly ever the case." Burke, *A Philosophical Enquiry into the Origin of Our Ideas of the Sublime and the Beautiful,* ed. James T. Boulton (Notre Dame, IN: University of Notre Dame Press, 1968), 164.

that I am convinced it would lose a considerable part of its energy, if this were the necessary result of all description."[74]

Lessing's *Laocoön*, published in 1766 and directly influenced by Burke's treatise, develops a far more comprehensive account of the correlation between lyric obscurity and the principle of expression (the key to the aesthetic category of the sublime): "I do not deny to language altogether the power of depicting the corporeal whole according to its parts. . . . But I do deny it to language as the medium of poetry."[75] In this brief genealogy of the concept of the sublime, one can therefore discern a thread of influence leading from Leibniz's account of the subliminality of monadic perception to the modern equation of sublimity and lyric obscurity.

References to "arcane" elements, to unconscious perception, to secrecy, to sublime harmony, all suggest that Leibniz's system is little more than some kind of esoteric philosophy. Yet one must always bear in mind that Leibniz considered the methodologies of metaphysics and logic to be identical: "J'ay reconnu que la vray Métaphysique n'est guère différent de la vray Logique, c'est à dire, de l'art d'inventer en général" (I realized that true metaphysics is no different from real logic, that is to say, from the art of discovery in general).[76] Indeed, Leibniz's attempt to revise the premises and the implications of the concept of obscurity within his metaphysical system—what may be described as the enigma of the "Monadology"—is an important contribution to a broader, historical revision of the concept of obscurity precipitated by the rise of modern science and shaped, more specifically, by the development of logical analysis.

Adherents, including Leibniz, of the new physics and metaphysics (known as "mechanical philosophy") sought to eliminate the notion of occult—and insoluble—properties in nature. In essence, attempts by Leibniz and other theorists of mechanical philosophy to reform the Renaissance doctrine of nature's secrets amounted to a *rationalization,* or materialization, of secrecy. Catherine Wilson, for example, finds a distinct continuity between Renaissance nature philosophy, with its occult properties, and the invisible, material world of seventeenth-century physics:

74. Burke, *Philosophical Enquiry into the Origin of Our Ideas of the Sublime and the Beautiful,* 170.

75. G. H. Lessing, *Laocoön: An Essay on the Limits of Painting and Poetry* (1766), trans. Edward Allen McCormick (Baltimore, MD: Johns Hopkins University Press, 1984), 88. Concerning the question of Burke's influence on Lessing, it should be noted that Lessing began a translation of Burke's treatise in 1758, although he never completed it.

76. Leibniz, *Die philosophischen Schriften von Gottfried Wilhelm Leibniz,* ed. C. J. Gerhardt, 7 vols. (1875–1890; repr., Hildesheim: Olms, 1965), 4:292. The verb *inventer* is essential of course—and problematic—to the meaning of Leibniz's observation here. I take the verb to mean, in this context, the revelation of entities, or relations, not previously evident—a usage in keeping with the Latin term *inventio*. This term is consistent with Leibniz's notion of "inventive logic." One might also take into account that *inventio* was used in the Middle Ages to denote the "discovery" of religious relics.

> It is easy to imagine philosophical rationalism, manifested in methodologies employing new and stringent canons of evidence, driving out irrationalism. . . . It is less easy to see how, in terms of choices actually available, certain modes of practice and language came to authority over others. One way to understand this is by looking at how the belief in hidden powers, in the subtlety of nature in Cardano's sense, and in the mandate of occult philosophy to seek them out, was demystified and attached to concrete and specific procedures of inquiry.[77]

In other words, from the Renaissance doctrine of nature's secrets, mechanical philosophy produced modern conceptions of a material, or metaphysical, occult—that is, the realm of atoms. In addition, the figurative model of *reading* nature's secrets, or signatures, was gradually displaced—under Leibniz's influence—by a rhetoric of logical analysis: a *rationalized* means of penetrating the subtlety of matter, or substance.

Obscurity in its modern aspect thus became a procedural, or methodological, principle, concerned with the perspectival, or subliminal, aspect of knowledge (or substance). More narrowly, the monad survives as a *modern* enigma, a *mechanical* model of obscurity precipitated by the invention of logic and science—a conception of obscurity that would eventually contribute (via the writers of the Jena Circle) to formulations of modern poetry and poetics. For the procedural and even technical disposition of modern obscurity helps to explain its rapid migration as a concept from the context of "real logic" and metaphysics to the emerging discourse of aesthetics.

It is a remarkable fact—indicative of the dialectical relation between the sublime and the subliminal—that the jargon of the criminal underworld (cant) could be invoked disparagingly as an analogy for the esoteric doctrine of nature's secrets, but also sympathetically (by Leibniz himself) as a useful illustration of the unavoidable obscurity of modern systems of logical notation. On the one hand, Renaissance nature philosophy, with its "theory of signatures" and occult properties, was condemned by the seventeenth-century bishop John Wilkins as "that *canting* Discourse about the language of Nature."[78] Yet, on the other hand, cant, notorious for its obscurity, could also serve as an analogy, according to Leibniz, for the kind of synthetic languages conceived by himself and others—designed to supersede the antiquated doctrine of signatures and *arcana*. In a discussion of "the Signification of Words," Leibniz observes:

77. Catherine Wilson, *The Invisible World: Early Modern Philosophy and the Invention of the Microscope* (Princeton, NJ: Princeton University Press, 1995), 43.

78. John Wilkins and Seth Ward, *Vindiciae academiarum* (1654), cited in Catherine Wilson, *The Invisible World: Early Modern Philosophy and the Invention of the Microscope* (Princeton, NJ: Princeton University Press, 1995), 42 (emphasis added).

Perhaps there are some artificial languages wholly chosen and completely arbitrary, as that of China is believed to have been, or like those of George Dalgorno and the late Bishop Wilkins of Chester. But those which we know to have been made up out of already known languages involve a mixture of chosen features and natural and chance features of the languages upon which they are built. It is like that with the languages which robbers have made up so as not to be understood except by those of their band, which the Germans call *Rotwelsch*.[79]

Although Leibniz fails here to note the disparate *intentions* of his examples (cant deliberately cultivates obscurity, while the new systems of logical notation seek to eliminate it), there can be little doubt that both of these synthetic languages are inaccessible to outsiders—and hence united by the problem of obscurity.

Attempts to find analogies for the mechanism of modern obscurity extended, as these references to cant indicate, well beyond the terms of scientific discourse as it existed in the seventeenth century. Descartes, for example, claims that the development of a universal language of concepts "presupposes great mutations in the order of things . . . as one can suggest only in novels."[80] Descartes seems to be saying that a logical inscription of the world would change "the order of things" in a manner resembling the changes wrought by literary inscription. Indeed, these "great mutations" could, by implication, obscure the world as we know it—even render it unrecognizable. The idea of a world encrypted by logic or literature—by language, in both cases—recalls Leibniz's comparison of synthetic languages to the languages of robbers, a jargon that seals off the demimonde from the lawful world. Given these correspondences between logical and literary formations of obscurity, it is not hard to understand why Novalis and Friedrich Schlegel later found the expression of logical obscurity that is implicit in the "Monadology" to be a compelling platform for a doctrine of modern, *lyric* obscurity. Hölderlin even goes so far as to adopt Leibniz's terminology of logical expression in referring to the "lawful Calculus" of poetry and to the emerging Romantic doctrine of "poetic logic."[81]

79. Leibniz, *New Essays on Human Understanding*, 3.2.1.

80. Descartes cited in Rossi, "Twisted Roots of Leibniz' Characteristic," 271.

81. Commenting on Hölderlin's reception of Leibniz, Peter Fenves writes: "From its call for a 'lawful calculus' in the opening paragraphs of the 'Remarks on *Oedipus*,' to its exploration of the 'perspective' from which the infinite can be grasped in the last paragraphs of the 'Remarks on *Antigone*,' Hölderlin's final poetological reflections appropriate and transform Leibnizian terminology—and never so clearly as when he proposes the development of a 'poetic logic' [*poetischer Logik*]." Fenves, *Arresting Language*, 6.

Logic, Expression, Harmony

The solution to the riddle of solipsistic perception, to what Peter Fenves calls "the paradox of unaffected receptivity," can be found in the basic premises of "real logic" espoused by Leibniz and in his theory of *expression* (which recast logic—for modernity—as an instrument of expressionism).[82] Furthermore, the principle of expression allowing for the possibility of monadic relations (that is, relations between hermetic substances) also holds the key to understanding the relational structure of solipsistic communities (that is, cultures composed of solipsistic beings). Leibniz equates "real metaphysics," we have already seen, with "inventive logic," an assertion prompting Bertrand Russell to claim that "Leibniz's metaphysic was derived by him from the subject-predicate logic"—that is, from his conception of a logical proposition, which holds that every predicate of a given subject inheres within that subject.[83]

By extrapolation from logical to metaphysical truth, the implicative autonomy of the grammatical subject therefore mirrors the infinite self-sufficiency of individual substances—of monads. Hence, "the relation between a substance and a property is such that the complete cause and explanation of a property is supposed to be discoverable in the nature of the substance to which it belongs."[84] In other words, every external denomination of a monad—ranging from the properties of the physical universe to its relations with other monads—can be deduced from the substance of the monad itself. No extrinsic relations are necessary to obtain knowledge of things external to the monad.

The logical self-sufficiency of the monad therefore supplies the grounds for the principle of solipsistic perception, which holds that knowledge of exterior conditions can be deduced from knowledge of interior conditions: the monad "perceives" the world (that is, its relation to other monads) by "perceiving" itself—without sensation or awareness. Leibniz writes, "this correspondence of the internal and the external, or representation of what is external in what is internal, or what is compounded

82. Fenves, *Arresting Language,* 186.

83. Russell, *Critical Exposition of the Philosophy of Leibniz,* v. More precisely, Russell observes that "all the main doctrines of the 'Monadology' are deduced, with terse logical rigor, from the premise: *'Semper igitur praedicatum seu consequens inest subjecto seu antecedenti, et in hoc ipso consistit natura veritatis in universum'*" (v). In this statement, one finds the kernel of Leibniz's conception of "the subject-predicate logic" and its correlation to metaphysical truth: "Always therefore the predicate or consequent inheres in the subject or antecedent, and in this fact consists the nature of truth in general."

84. Christia Mercer and R. C. Sleigh Jr., "Metaphysics: The Early Period to the *Discourse on Metaphysics,*" in *Cambridge Companion to Leibniz,* 94.

in what is simple, of multiplicity in unity, constitutes perception."[85] The rationale, according to Leibniz, for the correspondence between the order of monadic perception and the order of the universe—an isomorphic relation—lies in the concept of *expression:* "one thing expresses another, in my usage, when there is a constant and regular relation between what can be said about one and about the other. . . . Now this expression takes place everywhere, because every substance sympathizes with all the others and receives a proportional change corresponding to the slightest change which occurs in the whole world."[86] Each monadic perception therefore constitutes an *expression* of the world—a medium—insofar as expression is understood as a purely structural relation, implying concordance between an expression and what it expresses.[87]

Leibniz explains that all forms of expression are united by a common assumption:

> That is said to express a thing in which there are relations [*habitudines*] which correspond to the relations of the thing expressed. But there are various kinds of expression; for example, the model of a machine expresses the machine itself, the projective delineation on a plane expresses a solid, speech expresses thoughts and truths, characters express numbers, and an algebraic equation expresses a circle or some other figure. What is common to all these expressions is that we can pass from a consideration of the relations in the expression to a knowledge of the corresponding properties of the thing expressed. Hence it is not necessary for that which expresses to be similar to the thing expressed, provided that a certain analogy is maintained between the relations.[88]

Thus, the principle of the *analogon* (replicating relations, or ratios, across different structures and media) ensures the integrity of expression. More broadly, Gilles Deleuze explains that expression functions at once as a mode of *production* (in its ontological aspect), as a mode of *knowledge* (in its logical aspect), and as a mode of *action* (in its social aspect): "Being, knowing, and acting are the three forms of expression."[89]

85. Leibniz, *Philosophischen Schriften*, 7:529. Cited in Mondadori, "Solipsistic Perception," 34.

86. Leibniz, *Philosophical Papers and Letters,* 339 (from a letter to Arnauld, 1687).

87. One must bear in mind, however, as Margaret D. Wilson points out, that "every monad expresses the whole world from its own point of view, but Leibniz does not suppose that a human or animal mind has knowledge or sensation of everything in its world." Wilson, "The Phenomenalisms of Leibniz and Berkeley," in *Essays on the Philosophy of George Berkeley,* ed. Ernest Sosa (Dordrecht: Reidel, 1987), 9.

88. Leibniz, *Philosophical Papers and Letters,* 207–208.

89. Deleuze, *Expressionism in Philosophy,* 321. Summarizing these correspondences, Deleuze writes: "The knowledge of things bears the same relation to the knowledge of God as the things themselves to God" (14).

Although "perception," "representation," and "expression" appear to be interchangeable terms in the "Monadology," Leibniz emphasizes that "expression is common to all forms, and is a genus of which natural perception, animal feeling, and intellectual knowledge are species."[90] Thus, since expression does not rely on causal interaction (and indeed proscribes it in the case of the monad), the extrinsic and causal relations associated with *representation* must be viewed, in the context of Leibnizian metaphysics, as a subcategory of the immanent and acausal correspondences of expression. Deleuze explains how the subordination of representation (and sensory perception) to expression emphasizes the role of what he calls "the logic of sense": "Representation is thus located in a certain extrinsic relation of idea and object, where each enjoys an expressivity over and above representation. In short, what is expressed everywhere intervenes as a third term that transforms dualities. . . . What is expressed is sense: deeper than the relation of causality, deeper than the relation of representation." Conversely, "the supposition of causality" regarding relations between substances, or between substance and phenomenon, "overlooks the rich and deep world of *acausal correspondences*. It is possible, moreover, that real causality is established and reigns only in certain regions of this world of acausal correspondences, and actually presupposes it. Real causality might be merely a particular case of some more general principle." In other words, "Real causality is a species of expression."[91]

The lyric implications of Leibniz's doctrine of expression radiate from the monadic texts of Novalis, later recovered by Walter Benjamin in his account of the poetics of German Romanticism. Emphasizing the solipsism of the reflective medium (a Leibnizian compound of thinking and perceiving), Benjamin, adopting a "proposition" by Novalis, asks, "Do we perhaps see each body only insofar as it sees itself and insofar as we see ourselves?" Turning to another Novalis fragment, he declares, "All the capacity to be known on the part of a thinking being presupposes that being's self-knowledge: 'Everything that one can think, itself thinks—is a problem for thinking.'" Deriving human reflection from the self-knowledge of objects (from the *petites perceptions* of bare monads), Benjamin develops the foundation for a reciprocal knowledge (resembling Keats's "negative capability") of object and mind: "the thing, to the extent that it intensifies reflection within itself and includes other beings in its self-knowledge, radiates its original self-knowledge onto these other beings.

90. Leibniz, *Philosophical Papers and Letters,* 359.

91. Deleuze, *Expressionism in Philosophy,* 335, 326 (emphasis in original), 327.

In this way, too, the human being can participate in this self-knowledge of other beings."[92] Appropriating, via Novalis, Leibniz's doctrine of solipsistic perception (and perception without awareness), Benjamin therefore aligns "the basic law of the reflective medium" with an expressive task: think like an object!

Anticipating the requirements of modernism, Benjamin weighs "the designation of this method as experiment"—as a lyrical science—and declares, "Experiment consists in the evocation of self-consciousness and self-knowledge in the things observed." Further, the monadic "method" relies on "magical observation, which is itself an experiment": "observation fixes in its view only the self-knowledge nascent in the object; or rather it, the observation, *is* the nascent consciousness of the object itself."[93] Deleuze cultivates a similar model of expressionism, evoking the solipsistic perception—that is, the lyrical expression—of insensible objects: "Expression in general involves and implicates what it expresses, while also explicating and evolving it"; hence, "it is now the object that expresses itself, the thing itself that explicates itself."[94]

Leibniz's theory of expression, rooted in the combinatorial logic of inscription—of encipherment—thus allows for the concentration, or involvement, "of what is external in what is internal, of what is compounded in what is simple, of multiplicity in unity."[95] The qualities of the thing are encrypted in its name; the predicate inheres in the subject; the universe appears miraculously—like *writings on the wall*—within the monad. The basic premises of Leibniz's theory of expression ensure, moreover, that obscurity, confusion, and equivocation are intrinsic features of monadic substance and, by implication, of all corporeal phenomena (including language itself).

Leibniz's doctrine of expression, or expressive relations, appears in its most comprehensive form in his conception of the *harmony* of monadic perception and, by extension, of aesthetic form. With its emphasis on self-containment and the absence of causal relations, the theory of monadic perception fails to account, on its own, for the *conformity* of perceptions of infinite numbers of monads. Monads express the universe in diverse ways (each from its own perspective), yet the premise that all monadic perceptions pertain to a single universe common to all can be guaranteed—in the absence of causal relations between monads--only if all perceptions occur in concert, so to speak, with one another. Otherwise, the percep-

92. Benjamin, "Concept of Criticism in German Romanticism," 145, 146.

93. Benjamin, "Concept of Criticism in German Romanticism," 148 (emphasis in original).

94. Deleuze, *Expressionism in Philosophy,* 16, 22.

95. Leibniz cited in Mondadori, "Solipsistic Perception," 34.

tions of each monad would constitute a separate and singular universe. Furthermore, in addition to being universal, the "harmony" of monadic perceptions must, in the absence of causal interaction, be established *in advance, for all time,* in order to coordinate the "continuous modifications" of monadic perceptions. Between monads and bodies, according to Bertrand Russell, "there is no real interaction, but the appearance of it results from the pre-established harmony."[96]

The theories of monadic perception and preestablished harmony are, as Leibniz reminds his reader, mutually contingent: "Since it is the nature of the soul to represent the universe in a very exact way . . . the sequence of representations which the soul produces will correspond naturally to the sequence of changes in the universe itself." The concordance pertains to the solipsistic relations between monads, but also to the monad's "blind" knowledge of material bodies: "There is a perfect harmony between the perceptions of the monad and the motions of the body, pre-established from the beginning between the system of efficient causes and that of final causes." In a famous analogy borrowed from the rhetoric of mechanical philosophy, Leibniz describes the preestablished harmony between monad and body, substance and phenomenon, as possessing the regularity, the lawfulness, of machines: "these two beings of entirely different kind meet together and correspond like two clocks perfectly regulated to the same time."[97] Thus, preestablished harmony secures the complementarity of the "blind thoughts" of conscious monads, yet complete harmony among all things remains contingent on the theory of *petites perceptions* (unconscious perception) to regulate the substance of insensible objects (at the level of bare monads). For the perceptions of a stone, a word, or a doorknob must be harmonized, according to the premises of the "Monadology," with those of rational souls.

Michel Serres reminds us that *"pre-established* harmony is, in its strictest sense, the *establishment* of analogical *tables"* finding equivalence, and calculating relations, between God, substance, body, and world.[98] Harmony, conceived as a *table,* functions at once as a book (of combinations) and, in its lawfulness, as a *machine:* "the alphabet is, by itself, really a machine, the pre-establishment in an ensemble of tangible signs of an ensemble

96. Russell, *Critical Exposition of the Philosophy of Leibniz,* 140.

97. Leibniz, *Philosophical Papers and Letters,* 458, 637, 587.

98. Serres, *Système de Leibniz,* 1:105 (emphasis in original). Articulating Leibniz's analogy of music, Peter Fenves emphasizes the *tonality* of monadic correspondences within the sublime mechanism of preestablished harmony: "truth is the harmonious tone among those 'things'—monads, ideas, *Wesenheiten,* paradisal names—that have *de jure* and *de facto* nothing to do with one another." Fenves, *Arresting Language,* 10.

of combinatory relations."[99] Ultimately, the *table* of harmonic relations may be regarded as a *tableau*: a complete logical "image," or mapping, of all being at all times. Yet this correlation of tangible signs and intangible relations evokes as well the role of obscurity, or secrecy, in Leibniz's philosophy. For, as Serres observes, "secrecy, really, is the harmony of the visible and the invisible"—or, one might add, of the mechanical and the infinite, the legible and the illegible, body and substance.[100]

The harmony among all things and their continuous modifications is preestablished, according to Leibniz, by God. Yet the foundational role of linguistic concepts in his theory of substance implies that his metaphysical system inevitably reverts, in a pragmatic sense, from theological to linguistic determinism, yielding a model of expression which later reveals its secular disposition in Romantic and modern linguistic theories. For the structure of preestablished harmony is, by nature, symbolic: the expressive correspondences extending from God to rational souls to the phenomena "resulting" from the harmony of monadic perceptions never escape the "logic" of encrypting and deciphering. God's design for the universe becomes an ornament of the medium in which it is expressed: human language. The equivalence of God's will and human language finds expression moreover in the genetic priority of language, as Leibniz sees it, in human existence: "if characters were absent, we could neither think of anything distinctly nor reason about it."[101]

Leibniz's theory of the innate harmony of languages becomes fully articulated only with the emergence of Noam Chomsky's theory of generative, or transformational, grammar in the 1960s (a line of influence leading directly, Chomsky acknowledges, through the German Romantics). Chomsky grounds his theories in what he calls "Cartesian linguistics," a discursive constellation of ideas and thinkers associated, he contends, with the Port-Royal Grammar of 1660. Some critics complain, however, that Chomsky places undue emphasis on Descartes and that the philosophical premises of generative grammar can be described more accurately as Leibnizian; Chomsky does indeed cite Leibniz in his survey of historical precedents.[102] Chomsky's rationalist orientation is fully evident

99. Serres, *Système de Leibniz*, 2:498.

100. Serres, *Système de Leibniz*, 2:506 n. 2.

101. Leibniz, from an untitled dialogue of 1677, cited in Fenves, *Arresting Language*, 38.

102. In his essay "Leibniz and Generative Grammar," Marcelo Dascal writes that "my comments support the view that there is an analogy between generativism and Leibniz, who is placed by Chomsky in the tradition of 'Cartesian linguistics.'" Dascal, *Leibniz: Language, Signs, and Thought* (Amsterdam: John Benjamins Publishing, 1987), 141 n. 1. Aarsleff is more sharply critical of Chomsky's version of the history of linguistic theory (as it pertains to "universal grammar"), contending that Chomsky

in his famous hypothesis of the innate, or "deep," structures of language and in his emphasis on the "discovery" of these structures by theoretical or logical analysis rather than by empirical observation. Chomsky's affinity with Leibniz becomes evident more specifically in his emphasis on the principle of *expression:* "human language is free from stimulus control [the criterion of animal languages] and does not serve a merely communicative function, but is rather an instrument for the free expression of thought."[103] Further, Chomsky contends, "the 'poetical' quality of ordinary language" derives from its expressive orientation—that is, "its freedom from practical ends" and from the task of communication.[104] The focus on grammar—on formal structures—in Chomsky's linguistic theory becomes explicable in light of the emphasis on expression, just as Leibniz's theory of expression pertains, in essence to *formal* correspondences. Chomsky even evokes the idea of *"la métaphysique grammaticale":* a notion of substance contingent on what Chomsky calls "the fundamental correspondence of human languages."[105]

Clockwork of the Infidel

The problematic of obscurity in the "Monadology" stems at once from its linguistic determinism and from the enigmatic structure of monadic substance (including its solipsistic relations). Leibniz resolves the paradox of solipsistic perception—the discontinuity of monadic relations—by introducing, as I have indicated, the theological principle of "preestablished harmony," which ensures the coherence of monadic being by regulating and synchronizing the immanent "perceptions" of its hermetic elements.[106] In this scenario, God ensures the expressive, yet acausal, correspondences between monads (which determine the massing of individual elements) by treating monads, according to Leibniz, like clocks—each separate, yet harmonized with all other clocks. Every monad possesses a unique, perspectival (hence obscure), and internalized "view" of the entire universe—a potential anarchy of countless, disparate

pays insufficient attention to the writings of Leibniz. Aarsleff, "The History of Linguistics and Professor Chomsky," in *From Locke to Saussure,* 116.

103. Noam Chomsky, *Cartesian Linguistics: A Chapter in the History of Rationalist Thought* (New York: Harper and Row, 1966), 13.

104. Chomsky, *Cartesian Linguistics,* 17.

105. Chomsky, *Cartesian Linguistics,* 109 n. 112, 64.

106. Leibniz, "Monadology," 219–220.

perspectives—yet God regulates the radical perspectivism of the monadology like an infinite machine: a clockwork anarchy.[107]

Absent the figure of God, however (the fate of Leibniz's system in a secular context), monads revert to the condition of absolute solipsism (the hypothesis of Peter Strawson, the preeminent Analytic philosopher of social being and individuality)—to what may be described as the clockwork of the infidel, the faithless, the isolate.[108] Alternately, some force other than God must regulate the potential anarchy of hermetic substances, accounting for expressive relations between entities that are otherwise radically self-contained. In the latter scenario, a secular model of expression would need to account for the transmissibility of discontinuous substances and, by implication, to supply a rigorous explanation of the labyrinthine topologies of nightlife and lyric obscurity.

Jacques Derrida, for example, who regards the "Monadology" essentially as a theory of *secrets,* characterizes his own philosophy of radical difference as "Leibnizianism without God."[109] One might suppose then that the linguistic fundamentalism of Leibniz's metaphysic would resonate with the linguistic, and even literary, bias of Derrida's theory of deconstruction to produce a rather-obvious hypothesis: once an expression of God, language now looms as an expression of the *absence* of God, regulating and synthesizing the hermeticism of individual elements. The idea that social being—or metaphysical substance—is structured like a language does indeed inform Giorgio Agamben's conception of "the coming community." Curiously, however, one finds no mention of Leibniz in Agamben's text, no intimation of the monadological (or lyrical) nature of what he calls "linguistic being" or "*being-in-language.*"[110]

Much like his conception of the poetic "stanza" as a phantasmatic topos, the "being-in-language" of the "coming community" is a topology, a "taking place," that finds no place in the world as such; that is, in Agamben's vocabulary, it is a "utopia."[111] In my view, this placeless place can

107. On the sociological correspondences between anarchy and Leibniz's monadology, see Daniel Colson, *Anarchies* (Paris: Lignes/Manifeste, 2005); also Daniel Colson, *Petite lexique philosophique de l'anarchisme* (Paris: Livre de Poche, 2001).

108. P. F. Strawson, *Individuals: An Essay in Descriptive Metaphysics* (London: Methuen, 1964), 123–124.

109. Jacques Derrida and Maurizio Ferraris, *A Taste for the Secret,* trans. Giacomo Doris (Cambridge, UK: Polity Press, 2001), 58–59, 71.

110. Giorgio Agamben, *The Coming Community,* trans. Michael Hardt (Minneapolis: University of Minnesota Press, 1993), 9, 73 (emphasis in original).

111. Agamben, *The Coming Community,* 13–15, 19, 103. Agamben's earlier theorization of lyrical topologies appears in his *Stanzas: Word and Phantasm in Western Culture,* trans. Ronald L. Martinez (Minneapolis: University of Minnesota Press, 1993).

be understood, or imagined, more fully as a lyrical demimonde, a social monadology, an orphic underworld. Further, the topology of "linguistic being" comprises, according to Agamben, entities "without name," innumerable "singularities without identity."[112] Clearly, the linguistic being of the coming community is founded, in Agamben's view, on secrecy and, more pertinently, on *anonymity,* though he never mentions the lyric occasion and identity of Anon (much less the word "anonymity"), just as he makes no reference to the "Monadology" (though he introduces the principle of "singularity" in a chapter called *"Principium Individuationis"*).

Agamben does, however, refer indirectly to the phantasmagorical nature of "linguistic being" by equating it with "the whatever body, whose *physis* is resemblance": "the incommunicable foreignness of the singular *physis* has been abolished by its mediatization or spectacle," yet "this is the good that humanity must learn how to wrest from commodities."[113] Ultimately, "being-in-language" (which must be understood, in my view, as the expressive substance of obscurity) is indistinguishable from the perceptivity of the fetish: Agamben declares simply that "the spectacle is language"; and further, "in the spectacle our own linguistic nature comes back to us inverted."[114]

The principle of "substitutability" (associated with the "nameless") and the transvalued substance of fetish (embodied in the verbal figure of the halo) lead Agamben to characterize the substance of the coming community as "whatever being." Yet the principle of "whatever"—central to Agamben's thesis—collides all at once with the "taking place," the topology, of social being, with its metaphysical intimations, and with its linguistic character. For the essential modalities of the topical, the metaphysical, and the linguistic are all rigidly deterministic—the farthest thing from *whatever.* The monadological community envisioned by Agamben, composed of countless, anonymous singularities, becomes possible only with the imposition of a radically deterministic force (such as God or language) to regulate and harmonize the disparate elements. In a secular world—or underworld—infidel relations are conditioned by fatality, by the binding powers of language. Determinism and infidelity are indeed the two, basic axes of all monadic relations (devoid of content or causal interaction) between hermetic substances.

112. Agamben, *The Coming Community,* 76, 65, 67.
113. Agamben, *The Coming Community,* 50.
114. Agamben, *The Coming Community,* 78.

Infinity, Inc.

Starting from the foundational premise of the "Monadology," which holds that only monads (i.e., incorporeal entities) exist, one would presume that material bodies must be viewed as nothing more than the harmonized representations of monads: "I believe that there are only monads in nature, the rest being only phenomena which result from them."[115] Thus, in the most extreme interpretation of the idealism of the "Monadology," material bodies are little more than "regulated dreams" common to all monads: "Material things and their movements are only phenomena. Their reality is only in the agreement of the appearances of monads. If the dreams of the same person were exactly connected and the dreams of all souls concurred, nothing more would be needed in order to make body and matter."[116] To grasp the mundane character of these conditions, one need only acknowledge that the regulated unreality of the material world, as Leibniz conceives it, has already been fully realized in contemporary culture through the regulated consumption of the modern technical media. The "science" of media will perhaps one day formulate a new metaphysics based on the "Monadology"—a metaphysics already anticipated by the lyric monadologies of the riddle and the canting song.

Despite the evidence supporting a phenomenalistic reading of Leibniz's conception of material bodies, most philosophers now agree that Leibniz ultimately abandoned the view that bodies are nothing more than appearances (and hence unreal). Instead, he asserts that bodies are what he calls "well-founded phenomena" *resulting* from true substances (monads); he therefore refers to bodies as "*substantiata*" (semi-beings), a category of beings that are neither fully real nor entirely unreal.[117] The

115. Leibniz cited in Rutherford, "Phenomenalism and the Reality of the Body," 12 n. 3.

116. Leibniz, *Philosophischen Schriften*, 3:567. Cited in Rutherford, "Phenomenalism and the Reality of the Body," 13 n. 3. Peter Strawson, one of Leibniz's most forceful interpreters in the postwar Analytic tradition, takes precisely this position: "the literal-seeming world is not Leibniz's picture of reality. We obtain the Leibniz picture . . . only by eliminating the single common world of spatially extended objects. All that is real in the Leibnizian system is just the monads, i.e., consciousnesses or potential or quasi-consciousnesses, and their states. There is no common spatial world for them to mirror; there is just a certain correspondence between their states of consciousness. . . . Space is internal to the monad. The *views* remain, as it were, and correspond to each other . . . but there is nothing of which they are views." P. F. Strawson, *Individuals: An Essay in Descriptive Metaphysics* (London: Methuen, 1964), 123–124 (emphasis in original). Leibniz's reference to bodies as "regulated dreams" is cited by Daniel Garber in his essay "Leibniz and the Foundation of Physics: The Middle Years," in *The Natural Philosophy of Leibniz*, ed. Kathleen Okruhlik and James Robert Brown (Dordrecht: D. Reidel, 1970), 67.

117. Leibniz cited in Rutherford, "Phenomenalism and the Reality of the Body," 17–19.

notion of "*real* phenomena"—a contradiction in terms—follows from Leibniz's thesis that bodies are "beings through aggregation" (*ens per aggregationem*) or, in Bertrand Russell's colorful phrase, "families of tiny souls."[118] Leibniz explains, "We can therefore conclude that a mass of matter is not truly a substance, that its unity is only ideal, and that (leaving aside the understanding) it is only an aggregate, a collection, a multitude of an infinity of substances, a well-founded phenomenon."[119] Hence, material bodies must be understood as incorporating the infinite, harmonized perception of monads.

Leibniz is careful to emphasize that bodies are not aggregates of monads (material things composed of immaterial substances), but aggregates which *result* from monads, in the sense that aggregates can only exist as things which are perceived or thought (since relations, in monadic terms, are "beings of reason," supplied by a mind). Leibniz thus secures the reality of the body—an equivocal reality—by claiming that monads "do not constitute *parts* of its matter, but are immediate *requisites* of it."[120] Further, the monad's "requisite" status does not imply a physical or causal relation to the body. Rather, as Donald Rutherford explains, "It is instead best understood as a relation of ontological determination. To say that a given being 'results' from certain other beings is to say that its existence can be conceived as being immediately determined by the existence of those prior beings."[121] According to the premises of the "Monadology," then, the individual substances (monads) determining the material word are real, yet relations between monads, which establish the continuum of appearances, are only "modes of conceiving," or modulations of true substances.

Sleeper Cells and Slumbering Monads

Leibniz's iconography of aggregate *phenomena*—of material bodies—indicates that his conception of *mass* as a physical substance evokes in certain basic respects his understanding of substance as expressive, or

118. Leibniz cited in Rutherford, "Phenomenalism and the Reality of the Body," 16, 18–19. Bertrand Russell, *A History of Western Philosophy* (New York: Simon and Schuster, 1945), 583.

119. Leibniz, *Philosophischen Schriften*, 7:564. Cited in Rutherford, "Phenomenalism and the Reality of the Body," 17.

120. Leibniz, *Philosophischen Schriften*, 2:252 (emphasis in original). Cited in George MacDonald Ross, "Are There Real Infinitesimals in Leibniz's Metaphysics?" in *L'infinito in Leibniz*, ed. Antonio Lamarra (Rome: Edizione Ateneo, 1990), 135.

121. Donald Rutherford, "Metaphysics: The Late Period," in *Cambridge Companion to Leibniz*, 149.

sympathetic, as well as the subliminal domain of collective experience.[122] Physical mass, insofar as it consists of imaginary relations (according to Leibniz) always evokes the massing of individuals into a crowd, into collective formations that are mere "beings of reason": "An aggregate is nothing save all those things considered at once, from which it results; and these naturally have their unity only from the mind, on account of the things they have in common, like a herd of sheep."[123] As this example indicates, Leibniz's analogies for aggregate phenomena—for material bodies—often evoke some form of mass psychology (not surprising, given the psychological inflection of monadic substance), yet he also sometimes borrows analogies from the iconography of matter: "I think *parhelia* and other such things can be called 'real phenomena,' as can beings through aggregation, like a pile of stones or an army; for a rainbow is an aggregate of drops which jointly produce certain colors that are apparent to us."[124] In this passage, he compares bodies—"real phenomena"—to *parhelia* (multiple suns appearing on the horizon, produced by atmospheric conditions), to rainbows, and to "other such things" (i.e., other meteoric phenomena). The idea that material bodies—and matter itself—are like rainbows can be found in numerous texts treating the nature of matter in the seventeenth century, yet the trope of meteoric bodies also belongs to the iconography of the lyric "air," to modern poetry and poetics. Thus, Leibniz's trope of the rainbow-body (one of his favorite analogies for aggregate phenomena) alludes to the convergence of materialism and his own conception of monadic substance (illustrated by the composite "roar of the sea" or the teeming "pond of fish").

Leibniz compares the "semi-being" of material objects to the lyric substance of meteoric bodies, yet he also contends that the relational substance of an object is like a "herd of sheep" or an "army," analogies which clearly invoke varieties of mass formation. The two basic modes of the aggregate (the meteoric body and the body of the crowd) find common expression, ultimately, in a single trope: a material body, Leibniz claims, is like "the Dutch East India Company"—like a corporation.[125] All monads, one could therefore argue, are *incorporated;* and all bodies are corporations, or phantasmic bodies, comprising countless, disparate elements.

122. Concerning the "imaginary" relations that unify the disparate elements of material bodies, Leibniz writes: "A body is not a true unity, it is only an aggregate, which Scholastics call a being per accidens, a collection, like a herd. Its unity comes from our perception. It is a being of reason or, rather, of imagination, a phenomenon." Leibniz, *Philosophical Papers and Letters,* 623.

123. Leibniz, *Philosophischen Schriften,* 2:256. Cited in Rutherford, "Phenomenalism and the Reality of the Body," 20.

124. Leibniz cited in Rutherford, "Phenomenalism and the Reality of the Body," 16 n. 15.

125. Leibniz cited in Montgomery Furth, "Monadology," *Philosophical Review* 76 (1967): 188.

This trope pertains to imaginary formations but also to a mode of social being evoking the subliminal disposition of monadic substance. More specifically, the mass psychology of the corporation (a phantom formation of social relations) may be compared to the unconscious perception of *bare monads*—that is, to the psychology of *objects* but also to the aggregation of social underworlds. The incorporation of the monad thus becomes the common ground unifying the self-knowledge, or perceptiveness, of objects and the objecthood of negative sociability—of underground culture. Hence, the "slumbering monads" of nature become conversant with the "sleeper cells" of infidel culture.[126]

Leibniz understood the mindless perception of objects, which ensures the universality of preestablished harmony, as one of "the secrets of the sublime." Walter Benjamin, in turn, saw the unconscious perception of bare monads, which Leibniz describes as a kind of "stupor" or "dizziness" in rational souls, as a model for the modernist psychology of *shock*.[127] Informed by Husserl's phenomenological *epoché,* whose "primary fiction," according to Peter Fenves, is "the annihilation of the world of objects," Benjamin's writings continually return to the anatomy of "monadological structures—crystallized by shock, evacuated of everything natural, including consciousness, and thus made into historical objects for the first time."[128]

Looming behind Benjamin's elaboration of shock, which forms one of the basic components of his apocalyptic vision of mass culture, is the theorization of crowd psychology by Gustav Le Bon and Gabriel Tarde in the late nineteenth century. At the same time, we must recall that shock, as an emblem of modernity, finds its most cogent verbal expression, according to Benjamin, in Baudelaire's lyric sensibility. Thus, the psychology of ontological substance, which describes the material body as a rainbow or as a crowd, at once nebulous and atavistic, also bears within it the contours of a modern poetic sensibility that is ostentatiously neutral, at once windowless and untouchable—an agent of lyric fatality and modern sublimity. Insofar as this lyric posture (or imposture) may be described as obscure, it would appear to be linked to the riddle of the material object (its partial reality), to the objecthood of crowds, and to the *social ontol-*

126. The phrase "slumbering monad" is Friedrich Schlegel's, from Athenaeum frag. 361.

127. Concerning the stupefaction of bare monads, Leibniz writes that, "when there is a great multitude of *petites perceptions* in which nothing is distinct, we are stupefied. This is similar to when we continually spin in the same direction several times in succession, from which arises a dizziness that can make us faint and does not allow us to distinguish anything." Leibniz, "Monadology," 216.

128. Fenves, *Arresting Language,* 12. Fenves offers a superb reading of the monadological ground of Husserl's "paradisal *epoché*" (191–195).

ogy of objects, insofar as all objects are aggregates, or mass phenomena, unified by imaginary relations. In this regard, all social configurations or societies—all crowds—are rhapsodic and fateful objects, susceptible to lyric expression. Ultimately, like Ariadne's thread, the genetic obscurity of lyric poetry guides the reader through correspondences extending from a metaphysics of equivocal expression, through the meteoric substance of mass phenomena, to the windowless poetic sensibility of the modern allegorist—that is, ultimately, to the lyrical company of zombies, infidels, and mind readers.

FIVE

Infidel Lyric: The Rhymes of the Canting Crew

Stow your whids & plant, and whid no more of that,
Budg a beak the crackmas & tip lowr with thy prat.
If treyning thou dost feare, thou ner wilt foist a Jan
Then mill, and wap and treine for me,
A gere peck in thy gan . . .

SAMUEL ROWLANDS, "THE MAUNDER'S WOOING" (1610)

Leibniz, as I indicated in the previous chapter, saw a link between synthetic languages of logical inscription (so closely aligned with his theory of metaphysics) and the patois of canting speech (what he called "the language which robbers have made up so as not to be understood except by those of their band").[1] In addition, based on his thinking about aesthetic experience, one may compare the subliminality of cant to the manifest secrecy—the *arcana*—of sublime expression. For the dappled obscurities of cant, sublime expression, and Leibniz's *charactéristique* all derive in part from the "mixture of chosen features and chance or natural features of the languages upon which they are built" (3.2.1)—yet another illustration of the "clear but confused" perception of monadic substance. We also know that the equivocation of monadic substance—resembling the inscrutable roar of the sea—finds itself replicated in the imaginary

1. Leibniz, *New Essays on Human Understanding*, ed. and trans. Peter Remnant and Jonathan Bennett (Cambridge: Cambridge University Press, 1996), 3.2.1.

bonds of social being. Hence, these correspondences suggest that the inaccessibility of songs written in cant, like the ontological obscurity of the riddle, serves to model a kind of abject sociability, as well as the discontinuous substance of the monadology. The verbal underworld of vernacular poetry and the sociological obscurity of the demimonde therefore give palpable expression to the radical infidelity of monadic substance.

The anonymous lyric, including the riddle and the metrical charm, appears to have been gradually eclipsed by the emergence of an elite and self-consciously literary tradition of poetry, but these ancient modes and forms did not vanish altogether, nor are they absent from the dominant tradition. Rather, as these poetic models slipped into the shadows, they became part of a vital and complex vernacular tradition: spells, oaths, lullabies, and nursery rhymes; yet also curses, toasts, tongue twisters, namings, recipes, work songs, vendors' cries, and beggars' chants; in addition to counting and alphabet songs, love tokens, spitting words, insults, and the like. The ragged ontology of infidel poetry and its curious "genres" throws into relief the resources of obscurity (the use of rhyming slang, for example, or repetition and nonsense, misspellings, and inversion) available to the vernacular tradition of poetry. In addition, the subversive edge of vernacular poetry which depends in part on its repertoire of obscurity, exposes the sociological occasion of lyric substance, even as it revises our understanding of the *uses* of obscurity: concealment, defiance, deception, conservation, mockery, consolation, seduction, and so on. The infidel lyric thus defines in distinctive ways the history, purpose, and methods of poetic obscurity, which discloses its powers and the range of its effects in part through exchanges of lyric malfeasance between vernacular and self-consciously literary traditions.

The historical transmission of vernacular forms remains, in many cases, inscrutable, yielding at best a genealogy of "curious" publication. Riddles, for example, have survived for centuries largely through so-called novelty publications: magazines and anthologies for children, party manuals, "puzzle corners" in newspapers, public contests, encyclopedias of nonsense, toy books, and other popular media. Supplementing these eccentric forms of publication, one also finds a continuous, though often unacknowledged or disguised, history of thievery—appropriately enough—by poets associated with the dominant literary tradition: from Chaucer's elevation of the poetics of vagrancy in *The Canterbury Tales,* to "Gascoigne's Lullaby," to Elizabeth Bishop's "tom o' bedlam" song about Ezra Pound in the asylum. More generally, symptoms of the infidel lyric (lexical, prosodic, thematic, rhetorical) can often be found in the songs or carols of the dominant tradition (and more specifically in the refrain or "burden" of these lyrics)—forms that tend to preserve certain elements of obscurity common to vernacular poetic practice.

My aim in this chapter is to focus on a particular genre in the vernacular tradition of poetry: songs written in the jargon of the criminal underworld. As a literary phenomenon, the inscrutability of this jargon to outsiders is itself worthy of attention, yet it also serves as an index of the broader spectrum of lyric obscurity in the vernacular tradition. Some passages in these infidel songs are perfectly opaque—unintelligible—to an outsider. A great deal of historical information and insight lies embedded in such poems (indeed, I will emphasize the correlation between lyric and sociological obscurities), yet I am principally concerned with the literary properties of infidel poetry, especially the unavoidable obscurity introduced by the element of slang, which links the songs of various social underworlds to the productive obscurity of vernacular lyric in general.[2] Further, through an analysis of the correspondences between slang and lyric poetry, I want to consider whether lyric obscurity—that is, the substance of lyric expression—may be viewed, not as an obstacle to fashioning social relations, as it is conventionally regarded, but rather as an element essential to the formation of communities marked at once by secrecy and transmissibility.

Insofar as a poem written in cant may be described as literary, it involves some element of appropriation or commodification; hence, the canting song becomes—one must emphasize from the start—unavoidably *sentimental* once it enters the domain of literary culture. Indeed, although the canting song appears, in terms of Friedrich Schiller's famous dichotomy, to be a *naïve* artifact—the secret of its false allure—it can never, as a result of the mediation required for its appearance in society, refer directly to sensible experience, thereby revealing its innate sentimentality. Thus, the canting song must always, because it is removed from its sources, refer principally to feelings evoked by the *idea* of infidel society.

Schiller makes the correlation between sentimentality and abstraction one of the basic criteria of his typology: "Sentimental poetry differs from naive poetry in that it relates the real state at which the latter stops to ideas and applies ideas to that reality." Elsewhere, he writes: "The sentimental genius on the other hand [in contrast to the naïve poet] aban-

2. In her *Vagrancy, Homelessness, and English Renaissance Literature* (Chicago: University of Illinois Press, 2001), Linda Woodbridge attends to the historical value of canting songs but shows little interest in the literary dimension of cant.

dons reality in order to ascend to ideas."[3] Hence, the sentimental object is always abstracted, or infused, by its own reflections—by verbal reflection—and by rational feeling. The material ambiguity of the sentimental object or place calls to mind Giorgio Agamben's definition of poetry as "a topology of the unreal."[4] The enigma of sentimentality thus offers a way of remapping (in modern terms) the dematerialized sites of infidel poetry and, as we shall discover, the precincts of modern nightlife.

If sentimentality, as an index of the reverberation of sensuous phenomena, displays certain pragmatic tendencies, one might then also speak of a *pornographic* dimension of lyric poetry, not as it pertains to any particular content or even to obscenity, but regarding its powers of evocation and arousal. Poetry's capacity to evoke and even produce the tonality of certain unreal material environments pertains to the alluring—and binding—aspect of the beggar's chant (a recognizable topos in the vernacular tradition of flash poetry). That is to say, the pornographic aspect of lyric pertains to its efficacy as a speech act and to its capacity to bind or possess the listener, apart from its meaningfulness or content. As a verbal snare designed to captivate and disorient its listener, a certain kind of lyric poetry—in full possession of its powers of material persuasion—has periodically, and controversially, supplied the aesthetic and ethical codes for a submerged tradition of vernacular forms (including riddles, charms, nursery rhymes, work songs, oaths, and curses), a subject well beyond the scope of the present chapter but relevant to the genealogy of the canting song.

Access to the infidel songs of the demimonde often depends, in part, on popular "treatment" of these rough wares and their inscrutable milieu. Anyone familiar, for example, with John Gay's *The Beggar's Opera* (or its modern adaptations) will recall that much of the play is set in the criminal underworld of the early eighteenth century. One is perhaps less likely to recall, however, that the play—including its many songs—is said to be *written by a beggar*. Certainly, this fanciful attribution of anonymous authorship is in keeping with the emphasis given to English popular music in the play, including forty-one "broadside ballads." The anti-

3. Friedrich Schiller, *On the Naive and Sentimental in Literature,* trans. Helen Watanabe-O'Kelly (Manchester: Carcanet Press, 1981), 103 n. 60, 42. Elsewhere, using Ossian (the counterfeit Gaelic bard) as an example of the elegiac poet (elegy being the primary genre of sentimentality), Schiller declares: "The content of a poetic lament can consequently never be an outward but always an inner ideal object. . . . The elegiac poet is in search of nature but as an idea and in a perfection in which it never existed" (49). From this perspective, one could argue that the general tone of the canting song is one of lamentation.

4. Giorgio Agamben, *Stanzas: Word and Phantasm in Western Culture,* trans. Ronald L. Martinez (Minneapolis: University of Minnesota Press, 1993), xviii.

quarian disposition of the play's revival of these ballads, along with the abject figure of the beggar/poet, is essential to the innovation (that is, the modernity) of the ballad-opera form developed by Gay.[5]

At the same time, however, the comments exchanged between a "Beggar" and a "Player" in the play's introduction and again at its conclusion suggest that the vagrant poet may be the anonymous representative of a vibrant, historical countertradition. The play opens with the Beggar declaring, "If poverty be a title to poetry, I am sure nobody can dispute mine. I own myself of the company of beggars; and I make one at their weekly festivals at St. Giles."[6] He goes on to reveal the origin of the play about to be performed: "This piece I own was originally writ for the celebrating the marriage of James Chanter and Moll Lay, two most excellent ballad-singers."[7] The reader or spectator is left to wonder whether the beggar/poet is merely a fanciful persona or whether he may possess some historical authenticity. Is the beggar/poet no more than a colorful figure in the play's ensemble of stock characters (with names like "Filch" and "Matt of the Mint" and "Mrs. Vixen"); or does the Beggar belong to an actual, though submerged, genealogy of infidel poetry? References to the historical reality of St. Giles (a precinct in London associated with thieves and vagrants) and the "ragged" diction of the Beggar's speech suggest that the derelict poet is something more than a figure of fancy. In addition, many of the sixty-nine tunes in *The Beggar's Opera*—the form of expression most relevant to the "company of beggars"—contain elements of slang that point to a coherent and originally clandestine formation of underworld speech.

Flash, etc.

"Slang" is a word of slang origin—a "cant" word, to be completely accurate, a term in the "canting" vocabulary of criminals and vagrants. In its original context, "slang," according to onc early "librarian" of cant,

5. *The Beggar's Opera* has been well received by modern audiences, with celebrated adaptations by Bertolt Brecht and others. Edgar V. Roberts, in his introduction to the text of Gay's play, contends: "*The Beggar's Opera* has thus reached a wide modern audience, wider perhaps than that of any other eighteenth-century play." John Gay, *Beggar's Opera*, ed. Edgar V. Roberts (Lincoln: University of Nebraska Press, 1969), xxvii–xxviii.

6. A note to the text states: "Named after the patron saint of beggars and lepers, the parish of St. Giles-in-the-Fields, 'has passed into a byword as the synonym of squalor and filth' (Thornbury III, 206). It was a notorious haunt of beggars, thieves, and prostitutes." Gay, *Beggar's Opera,* 5.

7. Gay, *Beggar's Opera*, 5.

meant "to exhibit anything in a fair or market, such as a tall man, or a cow with two heads; that's called *slanging,* and the exhibitor is called the *slang cull.*"[8] "Slanging" thus referred to the marketing of something freakish or shocking. At the same time, shock and display—the elements of profanity—appear to be linked here, somewhat perplexingly, to the secretive nature of slang. Once the term "slang" had acquired the sense it possesses today, however (of "colloquial speech" in a broader sense), and moved into general use (by about 1800), it subsumed the earlier and more narrowly defined term "canting," which referred solely to the "jargon" of thieves, vagabonds, and beggars. Prior to the eighteenth century, terms used to designate what we now call slang (including expressions such as "pedlar's french," "thieves' latin," and "flash," as well as "jargon" or "cant") referred to the verbal inventions of a particular (closed) community. Slang—as we know it today—was for centuries then not a general phenomenon, according to the evidence of the lexicon, but the "canting" of social and criminal underworlds.[9] Canting, a signifying practice marked at once by secrecy and by intense communal responsibilities, may be described as a perverse element lodged in the broader spectrum of colloquial speech and standard English. The *Oxford English Dictionary*'s practice of including separate entries for certain cant words (while refusing consideration of ordinary slang) attests to the anomalous status of canting jargon. (The word "queer," for example, has two separate entries in the *Oxford English Dictionary,* one pertaining to cant and one to its counterpart in standard English—which derives from the cant term.)

The appearance of cant in the European vernacular languages (as the illegitimate speech of beggars and vagabonds) evokes the social texture of religious pilgrimage and, more broadly, the conditions of itinerancy and homelessness.[10] "Pedlar's french," one of the earliest synonymous expressions in English for "canting," testifies to the itinerant circumstances of

8. George Parker cited in Eric Partridge, *Slang, Today and Yesterday* (New York: Macmillan, 1960), 75.

9. The *Oxford English Dictionary,* after noting that the basic sense of "cant" is "singing, or musical sound," defines it as "the speech or phraseology of beggars."

10. Eric Partridge writes: "The history of European slang begins in the thirteenth century, when we find the word *Rotwalsh,* now *Rotwelsch,* the name for the slang of vagabonds. It is a significant fact that the earliest records, whether for Germany, France, or England, are of thieves, not of general slang. A glossary of *Rotwelsch* appeared about 1490; about twenty years later we come on the famous *Liber Vagatorum,* in which Martin Luther had a hand." Partridge, *Slang, Today and Yesterday,* 41. For an excellent overview of canting literature (and its critical apparatus), see Lee Beier's essay "Anti-language or Jargon: Canting in the English Underworld in the Sixteenth and Seventeenth Centuries," in *Languages and Jargons,* ed. Peter Burke and Roy Porter (Cambridge, UK: Polity Press, 1995), 64–101.

cant, to the adoption of an alien tongue, and perhaps to the petty "trades" (often illicit) associated with vagrancy. The "peddling" nature of cant may refer as well, however, to a certain aimlessness in the language itself, in the "rhymes" produced by these underground communities. Robert Copland, the author/printer of the earliest treatise on canting speech, in 1536, ridicules (even as he recites) the "babbling" speech of peddlers in a poem called "Rhymes of the Canting Crew": "And thus they ["these peddlers"] babble tyll their thryft is thin / I wote not what with their pedlyng frenche."[11] The "canting crew" is the band of vagrants whose "thryft"—their secret livelihood—is worn "thin" by their wandering speech. And the errant nature of this babbling is of course the essential cause, or condition, of its inscrutability. Thus, the itinerant (and collective) vocation of the canting crew, which blurs the distinction between vagabond, peddler, and thief, finds expression in its anonymous productions as a language collective. The rhymes of the canting crew may, with the help of a glossary, become more or less intelligible, but they remain, in a more critical sense, irretrievable—a persistent enigma awaiting a pragmatic, and persistently lyrical, solution.

The etymology of the term "canting" (from the Latin word for "song") raises important questions about the relation between slang and the historical vicissitudes of incantation, as well as the literary status of the song form.[12] The infidel lyric draws attention, for example, to the functions of obscurity and illegitimacy in poetic language and to the correlation between lyric obscurity and social cohesion. It also reveals the powerful role of class identity in the formation of divergent poetic traditions, as well as the complex interdependence between literary and vernacular traditions. In addition, at the level of stylistics, the verbal fashioning of cant is quite explicitly lyrical in a conventional sense. For example, Julian Franklyn documents a phenomenon called "rhyming slang," which reaches back to the origins of canting speech. Among the expressions of "vagabonds who converse in rhyme and talk poetry," Franklyn lists "sugar and honey" for "money"; "snake in the grass" for "looking

11. Robert Copland, *The Hye-way to the Spyttel-hous* (1536), reprinted in John S. Farmer, ed., *Musa Pedestris: Three Centuries of Canting Songs and Slang Rhymes* (London: privately printed, 1896), 2. See also A. V. Judges, ed., *The Elizabethan Underworld* (1930; New York: Octagon Books, 1965), 24.

12. In his treatise on cant, *Lanthorne and Candlelight* (1608), Thomas Dekker writes: "And very aptly may *canting* take his derivation from *a cantando,* from singing, because amongst these beggarly consorts that can play upon no better instruments, the language of *canting* is a kind of musicke." Cited in Bryan Reynolds, *Becoming Criminal: Transversal Performance and Cultural Dissidence in Early Modern England* (Baltimore, MD: Johns Hopkins University Press, 2004), 72. Reynolds's book offers a lively consideration of the cultural politics of canting speech.

glass"; "apple pips" for "lips"; "April fools" for "tools"; and countless other examples.[13]

Linguists and writers alike commonly assert the close correspondence between poetry and slang, though usually without providing substantial evidence of how the two actually converge and interact.[14] Walt Whitman, for example, pungently states his convictions about the affinity of poetry and slang: "Slang, profoundly consider'd, is the lawless germinal element, below all words and sentences, and behind all poetry, and proves a certain perennial rankness and protestation in speech. . . . Such is slang, or indirection, an attempt of common humanity to escape from bald literalism, and express itself illimitably, which in the highest walks produces poets and poetry."[15] Given Whitman's predilection for the vernacular and his emphasis on the lawless and elemental qualities of slang, it is surprising here that he insists on poetry's elevation, in contrast to slang's base nature.[16] His reluctance to cite particular poems as evidence of his general thesis about the poetic nature of slang is common to many casual comparisons of poetry and slang.

Canting offers a specific example of slang's influence on the history of

13. Julian Franklyn, *A Dictionary of Rhyming Slang* (London: Routledge, 1960), 9. In addition to an extensive glossary, Franklyn offers several examples of poetry written in rhyming slang, including a ballad containing the following stanza:

> And he laid there, weighing out prayers for me,
> Without hearing the plates of meat
> Of a slop who had pinched him for d. and d.
> And disturbing a peaceful beat.
> And I smiled as I closed my two mince pies,
> In my insect promenade;
> For out of his nibs I had taken a rise,
> And his stay on the spot was barred. (164)

The poem was written in the late nineteenth century by "Doss Chiderdoss" (a pseudonym of A. R. Marshall).

14. Partridge, in his chapter "Slang Characteristics," cites a number of writers who draw comparisons, either directly or indirectly, between poetry and slang, including G. K. Chesterton's colorful views on the subject: "the one stream of poetry which is constantly flowing is slang. . . . The world of slang is a kind of topsy-turvydom of poetry, full of blue moons and white elephants, of men losing their heads, and men whose tongues run away with them—a whole chaos of fairy tales." Chesterton cited in Partridge, *Slang, Today and Yesterday,* 24.

15. Walt Whitman, "Slang in America," in *Complete Poetry and Prose,* by Walt Whitman, ed. Justin Kaplan (New York: Library of America, 1982), 165–166.

16. Zora Neale Hurston, on the other hand, avoids the misguided division between the "germinal element" of slang and the "highest walks" of poetry—though she too falls prey to a binary model, viewing the correlation of poetry and slang (or the lack of it) as a function of racial identities. For Hurston, the principal characteristics of slang—the "will to adorn" and "the use of metaphor and simile"—are intrinsic to "negro expression." Thus, she claims, "the negro thinks in hieroglyphics" and "descriptive pictures," in contrast to "the written language" of "the white man." She does, however, correct the lack of specificity in Whitman's manifesto by providing a glossary of "negro expression." Zora Neal Hurston, "Characteristics of Negro Expression," in *Folklore, Memoire, and Other Writings,* ed. Cheryl A. Wall (New York: Library of America, 1995), 830–832.

English poetry in diverse periods. This influence is especially evident in the early modern period (beginning with John Skelton's infatuation with vagrancy and tavern life in "Colin Clout" and other poems) and in periods when literary antiquarianism betrays the effects of social upheaval (in the years 1750–1850, for example). One can trace these influences through certain lyric forms or genres which slip back and forth between the literary and vernacular traditions: tom o' bedlam songs (Blake's "Mad Song," for example), testament poems (Isabella Whitney's version is a pleasant surprise), songs documenting the experience of itinerant labor (John Clare and Ivor Gurney come to mind), and other transactional forms. One also finds polemical lyrics (such as Ben Jonson's "A Fit of Rhyme Against Rhyme") directed—homeopathically—against certain features of the vernacular tradition.[17]

Aside from sporadic (and tantalizing) appearances in court records (preserving the lingo of petty crooks), the earliest examples of beggars' songs and peddlers' chants were recorded, collected, and inevitably formalized by writers who had some familiarity with the infidel society of rogues and vagabonds. Though the tavern or public house—the precursor of modern nightlife—would become the enduring topos of the poet's rendezvous with the clandestine society of the canting crew, the titles of many of the earliest examples of cant (surviving, for the most part, as songs in Elizabethan prose treatises or dramas) recall its mendicant origins.

Copland's "Rhymes of the Canting Crew" is simply the first of many coarse—but fashionable—beggars' chants and oaths, such as "The Beggar's Curse," from Thomas Dekker's *Lanthorne and Candlelight* (1608); "The Maunder's [Beggar's] Wooing," from Samuel Rowland's *Martin Markall* (1610); and "The Maunder's Initiation," from John Fletcher's *The Beggar's Bush* (1625). As these titles suggest, the genre of the beggar's chant comprises a number of different types, some of which are restricted to the vernacular tradition of the canting song—that is, forms not common to the history of conventional lyric. Among the subgenres of the infidel lyric, one notes, for example, the oaths sworn by individuals upon joining the secret society of the canting crew:

I, Crank Cuffin [a rogue], swear to be
True to this fraternity;
That I will in all obey

17. The poems I have mentioned by Skelton, Jonson, and Whitney, along with a superb example of an anonymous "tom o'bedlam" song, can be found in Margaret W. Ferguson, Mary Jo Salter, and Jon Stallworthy, eds., *The Norton Anthology of Poetry*, 4th ed. (New York: Norton, 1996).

Rule and order of the lay.
Never blow the gab or squeak;
Never snitch to bum or beak.[18]

One also finds many drinking songs (set in the "bousy ken," the tavern), curses (against the constable or judge), and genealogical lists:

A Craver my Father, a Maunder my Mother,
A Filer my Sister, a Filcher my Brother,
A Canter my Uncle, that car'd not for Pelf.
A Lifter my Aunt, and a Beggar myself.[19]

The listing of "trades" can become more technical and comprehensive, as in "The Black Procession" (1712), which records "twenty black craftsmen" of the underworld: coiner, adder, mill-ken, gamester, beau-trap, bubber, angler, dunaker, and others.[20] In this same vein are ballads describing in detail the stratagems and techniques of begging, or "cadging."[21] Finally, there are more eccentric subgenres, such as the spate of ballads (early in the nineteenth century) dealing with pugilism and boxing. One finds as well the occasional oddity, such as "The Milling-Match" (1819), an account in canting verse of the combat between Entellus and Dares, "translated from the Fifth Book of the Aeneid by One of the Fancy."[22]

All of the "flash" songs I have cited here contain a high percentage of cant words, setting them in bold contrast to the language of more conventional lyrics—especially if they appear in a conventional, dramatic text—and making it difficult for a lay audience to follow the meaning, often obscene, of these rude songs. The obscurity of these poems (to the uninitiated) demonstrates the correlation between song and nonsense in the term "cant": cant sounds like gibberish to the outsider. It keeps the

18. "The Oath of the Canting Crew" (1749), from *The Life of Bampfylde Carew* by Robert Goadby; reprinted in Farmer, *Musa Pedestris,* 50–51. Another example of this type is "The Maunder's Initiation," reprinted in Farmer, *Musa Pedestris,* 19–20.

19. "A Beggar I'll Be" (anonymous broadside ballad), reprinted in Farmer, *Musa Pedestris,* 26. Among the many drinking songs are "The High Pad's Boast" and "The Mort's Drinking Song," reprinted in Farmer, *Musa Pedestris,* 132, 25. This type of ballad is among the most obscene in the canting tradition, as it often describes the sexual carousing that accompanies the drinking bout.

20. "The Black Procession," from *The Triumph of Wit* (1712) by J. Shirley; reprinted in Farmer, *Musa Pedestris,* 37–39.

21. The most lengthy and explicit of these ballads celebrating the beggar's "craft" is "The Song of the Beggar" (Anon, 1610); reprinted in Farmer, *Musa Pedestris,* 14–18.

22. "The Milling-Match" by Thomas Moore in *Tom Crib's Memorial to Congress;* reprinted in Farmer, *Musa Pedestris,* 84–87.

authorities in the dark and signals the perilous boundaries of class identity with a profane—and weirdly melodic—verbal ruse.

This troubled yet binding relation between poet and audience borrows its essential dynamic from a typical scene, a chance encounter, familiar to any city dweller. To the uninitiated—to the stranger in the street—the beggar's chant resonates with alluring, yet also disturbing, pragmatic and tonal effects. The pronounced obscurity of the chant—its "thrifty" meaning—throws into relief its rudimentary acoustic platform, its aural textures. Moreover, the crudity of the song, in a material sense, confirms the lexicographical thesis (in the *Oxford English Dictionary*) that cant derives its power and allure from certain verbal qualities *preceding* speech, insofar as cant is said to be "the whining sound of beggars' speech; a whine." Conceived in a manner that is more explicitly eroticized—and perhaps more threatening—the beggar's chant operates according to what may be called "the logic of the lure."[23] Anomalous, itinerant, promiscuous, the beggar's chant, as well as the space it engenders, calls forth an erotics of social anonymity.

The canting songs of beggars and peddlers offer a compelling and, one could even say, unique perspective on the desperate measures available to poetry in fashioning public space and anonymous relations. The street cries of peddlers and vendors, for example, function as verbal and often metrical charms, diverting the listener and binding him or her—for an instant—to the chanter: "Cherries a hapenny a stick / Come and pick! Come and pick!" "Maids I mend old pans and kettles / mend old pans and kettles O!" "Long and strong, two / yards long, cotton laces."[24] Akin to these vendors' cries are "rhymes" employed as a ruse in a crime (a pickpocket's stunt or the feint of a cutpurse). And at the root of these deliberate forms of solicitation lie the songs of the abject, which sound to an elite audience like nothing more than the whining complaint of a beggar. The beggar's call—the barest form of the canting song—randomly hails a passing stranger. Whether it calls forth some buried source of charity in the listener or whether it asks for nothing, the beggar's chant—a vexing, foreign sound—is a prelude to captivation, aiming to lure the stranger off course, to cull the anonymous mark.

23. John Paul Ricco's conception of the "logic of the lure" pertains to what he calls "the affects of the secret" in queer identity: "imperceptible visuality, anonymous sociality, and itinerant spatiality." Ricco, *The Logic of the Lure* (Chicago: University of Chicago Press, 2002), 82.

24. John Kirk, *Cries of London* (c. 1754), a pack of fifty-two playing cards; reprinted in facsimile (Kent, UK: Harry Margary, 1978). A selection of vendors' cries can be found in Tom Paulin, ed., *The Faber Book of Vernacular Literature* (London: Faber, 1990), 367.

Strange Navigation

Though one may not immediately detect in the beggar's chant an echo of the Sirens' song, there can be little doubt, on closer inspection, that the correspondences between the two are deeply instructive. From the perspective of those outside the company of beggars, the foreignness of the canting song—its whining, almost inhuman sound (as the elite audience perceives it)—calls to mind the captivating strangeness, the wailing, of the Sirens' song. The pedigree of the Sirens, who are part human and part animal (and who are themselves a kind of canting crew), mirrors the social depravity of the beggar and vagabond: the Sirens, too, are outcasts, marooned on an island, calling indiscriminately on those who are fully human.

Though the animal blood of the Sirens is anathema—the very sign of otherness—it is also the substance of their demonic talent and authority over human nature. The complex relation of the human and bestial elements of the Sirens' song accounts for its binding power (its medusal property) and, by implication, for its notorious eroticism. The etymology of the Sirens' name (from the Greek verb *seirazein,* "to bind with a cord") suggests that the special potency of their song, like the riddle of the Sphinx (another human/animal hybrid), belongs to the larger phenomenon of verbal charms, or binding spells, in antiquity.[25] Yet the binding power of the riddle/song should be attributed not simply to its inhuman origin but rather, according to Maurice Blanchot, to the Sirens' vexing capacity "to reproduce the ordinary singing of mankind"; hence, "it created in anyone who heard it a suspicion that all human singing was really inhuman." As a result, "there was something marvelous about the song . . . it was ordinary and at the same time secret."[26] The same could be said as well about the alluring features of the canting song, which confronts the uninitiated listener with its demotic spell, thereby evoking the social underworld in which it flourishes.

The Sirens, we must remember, sang to sailors, a circumstance that calls to mind, though it also reverses, the itinerary of the beggar's chant (which is sung by wanderers and vagabonds). Blanchot calls the Sirens'

25. In his discussion of erotic charms and binding spells in antiquity, Christopher Faraone notes that "Socrates calls the Sirens' song an incantation (*epoide*) that they used to attract and bind men, precisely like a love charm." Faraone, *Ancient Greek Love Magic* (Cambridge, MA: Harvard University Press, 1999), 6 n. 15. The Sphinx's name (from a verb meaning "to choke" or "to trap") suggests that her riddle possesses as well the binding power of the Sirens' song.

26. Maurice Blanchot, "The Song of the Sirens," in *The Gaze of Orpheus and Other Literary Essays,* by Maurice Blanchot, ed. P. Adams Sitney, trans. Lydia Davis (Barrytown, NY: Station Hill Press, 1981), 105, 106.

song "a form of navigation," with the implication that it negotiates, or in some sense produces, an erotic space characterized by itinerant relations, or skewed itineraries, a *queer* space, one could argue, according to several recent theorizations of the topographies of queer sociality.[27] The "strange navigation" afforded by the Sirens' song, or by the rhymes of the canting crew, is at once anonymous (the Sirens have no proper names) and promiscuous. Further, the lurking anonymity of the Sirens' song intimates, even as it disguises, its hazardous effects. The call of the Sirens, like the canting song of the beggar, opens up a space of unmappable promiscuities, which exemplify a poetics of solipsistic expression. The open secret of the canting song therefore defines a queer space of aimless and hazardous gains, which, distilling the inhuman allure of the common song, become the basis for a poetry of subliminal and predetermined effects, a New Pornography: flawed, secretive, binding, senseless, sublime.

In many canting songs, the beggar's chant serves as a pretext for uttering curses and swearing oaths against the "harmanbecke" (the cop or the judge), or other adversaries. Hence the pragmatic and irrational effects of the beggar's song may be said to feed upon the binding (and malicious) powers of the oath or curse. Indeed, given cant's deliberate obscurity, the beggar's garbled solicitation may well conceal, even as it formulates, a curse against its anonymous prospect, at once enchanting and disabling its "mark." The same could be said for the experience of the audience in the theatrical presentation of cant songs, since cant may be regarded, in a fundamental sense, as a generalized form of profanity.

The secrecy, profanity, and pragmatic force of the canting song hold profound implications for a theory of poetry oriented toward questions of expression and social being. The binding power of vernacular obscurity (upon both the initiate and the uninitiate) radiates from the *solipsistic expression* of the canting song—from its capacity to achieve its ends without making sense, to find its mark without losing its hermetic composure. That is to say, by demonstrating the paradox of lyric expression, the beggar's chant invents a form of anonymity and a means of captivation founded on the principle of the open secret, a structure related to the *petites perceptions* of monadic substance, to the spectacle of lyric obscurity, and to the history of anonymous publication.

The community established (or preestablished) by poetry depends

27. Blanchot, "Song of the Sirens," 106. Ricco characterizes the anonymous aspect of queer sociality as "a non-communicative, incomprehensible audibility." Ricco, *Logic of the Lure,* 7–8, 81–82, passim. See also William Haver, *The Body of This Death* (Stanford, CA: Stanford University Press, 1996). One should note that the word "queer" is originally a canting term meaning "bad" or "base," as in the phrase "queer cove" (bad guy or wise guy).

neither on meaningfulness nor on external relations—indeed, it may be described as an *impossible* community. To be sure, the canting language of beggars and thieves is founded on secrecy, which in turn helps the demimonde of the canting crew to do business in public without getting busted, yet the jargon of "thieves' latin" resounds in the world and thus compels various expressive relations among disparate social classes, especially as it becomes markedly literary in form. Furthermore, cant's function as a means of clandestine communication within the closed society of vagrants and crooks is exceeded by its capacity to shock and seduce individuals and social classes on the other side of the law, thereby establishing liaisons which are as enigmatic as they are binding, at once untenable and inescapable.

Sparrow Language

The correlation of song and slang inscribed in the word "cant" governs as well the strange economy of the word "jargon." The range of meaning of the two terms is nearly synonymous, as the *Oxford English Dictionary* indicates when it defines "cant" as "any jargon used for the purpose of secrecy." "Jargon," one of the oldest terms in continuous use in English for the verbal phenomenon of slang, no longer betrays, however, its original association with music and singing. For the first meaning of "jargon" in the *Oxford English Dictionary* is "birdsong." Thus, Chaucer, for example, describing a man who "sang ful loude and cleere," writes: "He was al coltissh, ful of ragerye, / And ful of jargon as a flekked pye."[28]

To the constellation of song, slang, and nonsense in the term "cant," "jargon" thus introduces the sense of the language of *animals*—a characteristic already noted in the identity of the Sirens. In addition, the vernacular gives us "sparrow language," which is yet another synonym for "cant," related to "pedlar's french" and "thieves' latin."[29] It is not at all clear, however, what significance we should attribute to the analogy of birdsong and canting speech—though, as I mentioned earlier, the animal trait of jargon must be viewed as anathematic. That is to say, the bestial features of the chant impress the elite audience as being both abject (ostensibly beneath human nature) and totemic (symbolic of a higher collective identity). The depravity of the song—its pathetic character—is

28. Geoffrey Chaucer, "The Merchant's Tale," *The Canterbury Tales,* in *The Works of Geoffrey Chaucer,* ed. F. N. Robinson, 2nd ed. (Boston: Houghton, 1961), 1845–1848.

29. Eric Partridge notes the phrase "sparrow language" in his survey of the history of slang. Partridge, *Slang, Today and Yesterday*, 35.

thus the key to its social efficacy, to its power to create binding (magically binding) social ties.

From a purely literary perspective, however, if we understand birdsong to be a figure for poetry, and to be akin as well to the anomalous—and perhaps vaguely menacing—chatter of "flash" language, then we must surely leave aside many clichés and props cluttering the topos of the Romantic bird poem. The canting bird is no elf or sprite, though it may well stand "amid the alien corn," beside Keats's nightingale, or be part of the "crew" loitering in Blake's "Mad Song": "the rustling birds of dawn / The earth do scorn." And it has the dour look, most certainly, of Hardy's "darkling thrush"—a punk at a cadger's ball.

Birdsong is, by definition, anonymous, a condition essential as well to "thieves' latin" and to the authorship of canting songs. Yet the anonymity of birdsong, understood as a trope for poetry, is unavoidably tautological, since the word "anonymous" itself derives from the history of poetry's publication, from its appearance in print as a form of nameless expression. In a posthumously published essay entitled "Anon," Virginia Woolf argues that the human imitation of birdsong in verse marks the origin of the figure of the anonymous poet.[30] Woolf's suggestive tale of poetic origins reminds us that the term "anonymity"—an idea that is central to modern conceptions of subjectivity and urban experience—is a very recent (mid-nineteenth century) backformation of the original, adjectival form of the word "anonymous." This word, shortened to "Anon," first appeared in poetry anthologies in the early seventeenth century as a means of designating the work of nameless authors—including the "flash" songs I have been discussing.[31] Hence, for nearly four centuries, the principle of the *anonymous* pertained quite specifically and narrowly to formations of lyric identity and authorship. The modern sociological and psychological concept of *anonymity* can be fully understood therefore only in reference to its historical association with writing, authorship, and lyric poetry.

Citing an early, anonymous lyric that makes reference to "a birdes voice," Woolf states: "The voice that broke the silence of the forest was the voice of Anon."[32] Anonymity as a human (and lyrical) condition has its origin therefore in the transference of a bird's "voice"—an alien tongue—into human language. The character of birdsong thus prefig-

30. Virginia Woolf, "Anon," *Twentieth Century Literature* 25, no. 4 (1979): 382. This short essay on the anonymous voice in literature was composed shortly before her death.

31. Herbert F. Tucker discusses the history of the term "anonymous" in his introduction to a special issue of *New Literary History* 33, no. 2 (2002), devoted to the topic of anonymity (190–193).

32. Woolf, "Anon," 382.

ures the nature of lyric anonymity: a bird's song is a proper name of sorts, an impersonal signature expressing the singular fact of existence ad infinitum. Indeed, the bird sings its tune again and again, like an automaton, unto death. Pleasure, for both the singer and the listener, appears to be an effect of the boundless repetition of "cant," conditioned by anonymity.

The lyrical incorporation of nonhuman sources calls to mind, though it also inverts, the Sirens' flawed imitation of the human voice. In addition, anonymity, understood as a condition that is precipitated by *poesis,* unites the singing of birds, Sirens, and beggars. One might therefore regard the *obscurity* of lyric poetry in general (and of the infidel song in particular) as a distant expression, or recollection, of the inhuman voice. Further, because it is difficult to place, the sound of a bird jargoning in the woods, like the Sirens' song on the open sea, commands even as it disorients the space it inhabits. The very placelessness and aimlessness of the song engenders a space characterized by uncertainty and promiscuity. As a result of these correspondences between human jargon and the inhuman voice of the anonymous lyric, one must view the "sweetness" of birdsong as a symptom of its predetermined and solipsistic nature.

The Spy's Lexicon

The canting speech of beggars and thieves is deliberately obscure. One of its pragmatic aims, in contrast to its role in soliciting strangers (or perhaps these tasks are related), is to shield the criminal activities of the canting crew from scrutiny by outsiders. The members of this secret society are not about to supply a glossary of their puzzling jargon. So how do we know what the canting speech of the underworld means? How have we acquired a knowledge of its vocabulary, and what hermeneutic implications does cant possess for lyric poetry in general? One must begin by acknowledging that the meaning of many cant words remains uncertain and will probably never be fully known. As a result, the meaning of numerous passages in the canting literature is largely a matter of guesswork. The barriers to communication originally built into canting speech have therefore proved to be effective and enduring over time, as have the allure and the unaccountable transitivity of cant.

The history of the retrieval and partial decipherment of cant holds special significance not only for the poetics of the canting song but for poetry in general. The earliest glossaries of cant were compiled by the police, for use in trials of suspected criminals.[33] The court records from which these hasty lexicons can be retrieved remind us not only that cant was a means of communication used by thieves and scoundrels but also that it was considered a material accessory to crime. Thus, the earliest translations of cant—the moment when the language of the underworld first became intelligible—coincided with a demonstration, in the most pragmatic terms, of the tension between the lyrical resources of cant and the exercise of legal authority.

The police could not personally gain access to the jargon of the demimonde; an intermediary was required to penetrate the society of thieves and vagabonds. Hence, the foundation of our knowledge of canting vocabulary was produced by spies, or informants, working on behalf of police authorities. The first deciphering of cant—and perhaps *every* instance of reading "flash" thereafter—relied on a form of espionage. One of the earliest court records of this practice involves the canting speech of the Coquillards, a loose affiliation of criminals in medieval France, whose secret tongue François Villon employed to compose his notorious *Ballades en jargon* (c. 1460). The Coquillards took their name from the emblem of the seashell (*coquille*) associated with the famous shrine at Santiago de Compostella in Spain, the destination of a steady stream of pilgrims in the Middle Ages. The Coquillards were thieves, dice players, mountebanks, and beggars, as well as "false pilgrims," trafficking in dubious relics and souvenirs.[34]

Spies, acting on behalf of the authorities, were not alone in revealing and bringing to public attention the secret language of vagrants and thieves. They were aided by the minstrels and balladeers who formed part of the itinerant society of the Coquillards, as well as by poets such as Villon, who, though not part of the sect, circulated among its members and favored their positions. Educated poets, like spies, made intelligible a phenomenon that was by necessity clandestine; they revealed the secret tongue of those who wished to remain inscrutable. These poets must therefore be viewed, however sympathetic their intentions may have been, as outsiders, as unwitting allies of the police.

The same poets and dramatists who appropriated the tantalizing dic-

33. Concerning the reading apparatus—the means of decipherment—spawned by the secrecy of cant, Julian Franklyn observes: "Rhyming slang, having thus been adopted by thieves, became a subject of study by the 'Officers of the Law,' and grist to the mill of lexicographers." Franklyn, *Dictionary of Rhyming Slang,* 7.

34. My knowledge of Coquillard society and of Villon's knowledge of their idiom and culture depends on Andre Lanly's edition (including translations into modern French and annotations) of François Villon, *Ballades en jargon* (Paris: Champion, 1971), 11–15.

tion of cant for their own work sometimes published haphazard anthologies of canting songs, usually and necessarily accompanied by a lexicon, albeit desultory, of canting words. Like their counterparts working for the police, early anthologists and grammarians of cant often had one foot in the criminal underworld. Indeed, there is a distinctly ethnographic orientation to the earliest treatise on cant, Copland's *The Hye-way to the Spyttelhous*. John Farmer, the modern editor who reprinted several of Copland's examples, describes the narrative frame that Copland provided for the anthology:

> The plan of *The Hye-way* is simplicity itself. Copland, taking refuge near St. Bartholomew's Hospital during a passing shower, engages the porter in conversation concerning the "losels, mighty beggars and vagabonds, the michers, hedge-creepers, fylloks and lusks" that "ask lodging for Our Lord's sake." Thereupon is drawn a vivid and vigorous picture of the seamy side of social life of the times. All grades of "vagrom men," with their frauds and shifts, are passed in review.[35]

Thus, Copland's strategy is to interview the many "false pilgrims" as a way of "slanging" (displaying) their colorful speech and disreputable activities.

We know that the spy's lexicon of Coquillard speech in court records offers reliable definitions of cant terms used by Villon in the *Ballades en jargon* because the glossary was compiled in the same year (1455) that Villon was exiled from Paris for the murder of a priest and about the same time that he wrote these poems. But this synchronicity does not explain how Villon came to be familiar with Coquillard speech. Though we may surmise that Villon's peripatetic existence between 1455 and 1461 placed him in direct contact with the itinerant society of "false pilgrims" and petty criminals, the poems themselves identify the usual site of the poet's encounter with the canting crew: the tavern. Many of the ballads are set in "*la gauldruse gaudye*" (the gaudy joint), as in the opening stanza of ballad 9:

> Un gier coys de la vergne Cygault
> Lué l'autreyer en brouant à la Loirre
> . . . .
> Ung maquonceau a tous deux gruppelins
> Brouant au bay, a tout deux walequins,
> Pour avancer au solliceur de pye.

35. Farmer, *Musa Pedestris*, 200.

[Scrambling for some swag the other day,
I saw in one of the taverns of our fair city
a little pimp with two apprentice thieves
up to no good with two poor dupes,
scamming to pay the wine merchant.][36]

In these tavern scenes, the poet betrays, however, the distance between himself and his "brothers" by warning them not to be careless or go too far in their exploits, lest they be "married" to the hangman:

Seekers after money, make-believe cripples,
Thieves too and cutpurses,
Beggars perpetually on foot
who on the road have demanded in jargon
hand-outs of food, where you've been
out in the fields to hunt for coins
and who, to support your girls,
have reached for bread—and handcuffs—
For all that, they make themselves feared,
the cops, crooked, tough, and cruel.[37]

Even as Villon leaves himself out of this vivid portrait of the canting crew, the adopted jargon of his ballad echoes the jargoning solicitation of the beggar in this stanza.

In addition to providing documentation of an underground culture that is all but irretrievable, Villon's poems preserve significant elements of a secret language, a jargon, that possessed innate lyrical resources. Furthermore, these ballads help to identify the tavern as a site where the language, the anonymity, and the itinerancy of the canting crew became intelligible—and available—to society at large. In poems such as Villon's *Ballades en jargon,* the tavern begins moreover to reveal itself as a literary topos in which the obscurity of canting speech echoes or models, so to speak, the sociological obscurity of the demimonde: a queering of material substance under the sway of the lyric vernacular. The promiscuity

36. Villon, *Ballades*, 122 (my translation of Lanly's modern-French version). It is interesting to note that several terms in the Coquillard jargon used by Villon in this passage are similar to words found in English cant: *Loirre* for "lure" (swag, stolen goods) and *gruppelins* for "gripper" (thief, swindler). The appearance of these terms in Villon's poem predates by nearly a century the publication of Copland's text, *The Hye-way to the Spyttel-hous,* in 1536.

37. François Villon, *Complete Poems,* trans. Barbara N. Sargent-Baur (Toronto: University of Toronto Press, 1994), 315.

of the beggar's chant and the inhuman aspect of the Sirens' song converge in the illicit space of the tavern to suggest ways that lyric expression always implies—and betrays—a model of social being. These sorts of poems, at once abject and alluring, function like verbal charms or spells (like the binding nomenclature of the law that threatens the canting crew) in drafting a community founded in part on the obscurity of its counterfeit tongue.

Ragpicker, Dandy, Apache

The verbal spring of the canting song passes through literary history like a river in a desert, running beneath ground for long stretches, then transforming the landscape briefly in colorful and unexpected ways. I have already mentioned the dramatic topos of the tavern scene—the nightspot—peppered with the jargon of the underworld. But one also detects the rude charm, if not an echo, of the canting song in the materials of literary antiquarianism. What Nick Groom calls "the forger's shadow" almost certainly harbors the obscurity of canting speech. Adapting Groom's model of forgery's influence over the literary canon, we could say that Thomas Chatterton's forgery of poems by a fictitious medieval cleric, Thomas Rowley, renews—indirectly—the resources of the canting crew, as does James Macpherson's spectacular forgery of the epic poetry of Ossian, said to be a third-century (and preliterary) Celtic bard.[38] These early-eighteenth-century forgeries, which fed the wellspring of modern kitsch, also helped prepare the ground for publication of Bishop Percy's *Reliques of English Literature* in 1765, the year that saw the earliest edition of nursery rhymes: *Mother Goose's Melody: or Sonnets for the Cradle.* Combined with a garbled selection of Shakespeare's songs, this diminutive edition of Mother Goose (2.25 by 3.5 inches), with its mock introduction and facetious notes, preserved the gibberish and the incantatory charm of thieves' latin.

The canting song underwent a more substantial revival, abetted by

38. Chatterton's forgery lends an orthographic flourish—a material sheen—to the doggerel of "pedlar's french," converting obscurity into a literary commodity. Here's a scrap from Rowley's (i.e., Chatterton's) unfinished drama "Goddwyn":

> To the Skyes
> The dailie contekes of the Londe ascende,
> The Wyddowe, Fahdrelesse, and Bondmennes Cries,
> Acheke the mokie Aire, and Heaven astende.

Keats called Chatterton "the purest writer in the English Language." Nick Groom, *The Forger's Shadow* (London: Picador, 2002), 176, 174.

pockets of radicalism in the literary underground of postrevolutionary London, during the period of the Regency in England (1820–1840). These manifestations of abject political forces coincided historically with the emergence of the figure of the dandy in England (quickly appropriated and revised on the Continent), a dialectical relation that is already present in John Gay's *The Beggar's Opera* (1728), whose depiction of the criminal underworld was seen as a satire of the beau monde.[39] Indeed, one could argue that this dialectic is intrinsic to the poetics of the canting song, since the word "fancy" (as a noun) can refer to the sporting crowd (the canting crew)—as in Pierce Egan's nineteenth-century cant "Sonnets for the Fancy." This dialectic, a permanent feature of the modernity of the canting song, makes its most substantial appearance in Baudelaire's poetry and criticism (and, for a time, in his personal dandyism).

In *Les fleurs du mal,* Baudelaire sharpened modern poetry's taste for the demimonde, assembling a gallery of abject figures—beggars, ragpickers, whores, murderers, pimps, thieves—who evoke the milieu of the canting crew, bathed in the "fitful and garish luster" of the gas lamp and transported to the back rooms of elegant society. Famously, "Le crépuscule du soir" begins:

Voici le soir charmant, ami du criminel;
Il vient comme un complice, à pas de loup; le ciel
Se ferme lentement comme une grande alcôve,
Et l'homme impatient se change en bête fauve.

. . . .

Les tables d'hôte, dont le jeu fait des délices,
S'emplissent de catins et d'escrocs, leurs complices,
Et les voleurs, qui n'ont ni trêve ni merci,
Vont bientôt commencer leur travail, eux aussi,
Et forcer doucement les portes et les caisses
Pour vivre quelques jours et vêtir leurs maîtresses.

[It comes as an accomplice, in stealth,
the lovely hour that is the felon's friend;
the sky, like curtains round a bed, draws close,
and man prepares to become a beast of prey.

. . . .

39. In the final scene of the play, the "Beggar" declares, "Through the whole piece you may observe such a similitude of manners in high and low life, that it is difficult to determine whether (in the fashionable vices) the fine gentleman imitates the gentleman of the road, or the gentleman of the road the fine gentleman." Gay, *Beggar's Opera,* 82.

The dens that specialize in gambling fill
with trollops and their vague confederates,
and thieves untroubled by a second thought
will soon be hard at work (they also serve)
softly forcing doors and secret drawers
to dress their sluts and live a few days more.][40]

While these lines sustain a tradition of infidelity stretching from Villon to Genet, Baudelaire conspicuously avoids (unlike Genet) using the jargon of the demimonde. Yet the milieu of Baudelaire's poems has sometimes tempted English translators to convert the relative purity of his diction into the rude charm of "flash" language. Tom Scott, for example, uses a mixture of Scots dialect and cant words to produce a translation of "Le crépuscule du soir" that makes audible the secret tongue of Baudelaire's canting lyric:

Comes the gloamin hour, the cut-throat's freend;
Comes on sleekit fuit wi wowfish mien.
The lift like an auditorium dims doun,
And man waits till his change to beast comes roun.

. . . .

Mirklan cafes, spivs' haunts and their ilk,
Fill up wi pimps and whures in crepe and silk,
And picklocks, saikless o guid sense or thocht
Cantilie gang ti the yae darg they're aucht,
Cannilie forsin windae, safe and lock
For daily breid—and cled some doxie's dock.[41]

Translation in this context amounts to an act of conjuring the "permanent midnight" of canting speech from Baudelaire's oblivious text. The fastidious diction and prosody of the original poem submit to the hazards of "pedlying French," to the allure of the rude song lining the dandy's habit.

Walter Benjamin identified Baudelaire's abject lyrics as the origin of "the poetry of apachedom . . . a genre that has not disappeared in more than eighty years. Baudelaire was the first to tap this vein." Benjamin goes on to explain: "The apache abjures virtues and laws; he terminates

40. Charles Baudelaire, "Le crépuscule du soir," in *Les fleurs du mal,* by Charles Baudelaire, ed. Claude Pichois (Paris: Gallimard, 1972), 128–129. For the English translation, see "Twilight: Evening," in *Flowers of Evil,* by Charles Baudelaire, trans. Richard Howard (Boston: Godine, 1982), 99–100.

41. Tom Scott, *The Shorter Poems of Tom Scott* (London: Chapman Press, 1993), 36.

the *contrat social* forever."[42] The lyrical and hybrid figure of the "apache," signifying the moment when the canting crew discovered its rhetorical affiliation with the ethnicity of the New World, was born from certain historical incidents in London in the early eighteenth century: bands of upper-class youths, calling themselves "Mohocks," committed random acts of vandalism and violence against citizens. John Gay, who later saw fashionable society reflected in the company of beggars, based his first play, *The Mohocks* (1712), on these incidents in London. In one scene, the "Mohocks" swear an oath that will one day resound in the libertinage of Baudelaire's apache, even as it echoes the "beggar's curse" of the canting crew:

> We'll to virtue bear invet'rate hate,
> Renounce humanity, defy religion;
> That villainy, and all outrageous crimes
> Shall ever be our glory and our pleasure.[43]

The elegant vandals speak in prose for the most part, rather than blank verse, a vulgar affectation which surely anticipates Gay's superimposition of poet and beggar in *The Beggar's Opera*.

Like the rude songs of the canting tradition, the modern poetry of apachedom, which extends at least as far as the Beat poets and perhaps even to the punk and hip-hop cultures of our own era, sustains the countertradition of the infidel lyric. Yet the poetry of apachedom also elaborates what may be called the enigma of sentimentality, an aesthetic ideology of solipsistic transgressions sustained by class difference and by the masked rendezvous between literary and vernacular traditions of poetry. Baudelaire's complex relation to the demimonde, for example, resembles that of the police informant or lexicographer in the history of cant's decipherment and transmission—though the uneasy rapport between the dandy (or the flaneur) and the criminal is at once more explicit and less pragmatic in modern poetry.

The urban apache is at once a lawless nomad and an inspired detective, a profile evoking the renegade intelligence of the canting crew and of the spy who betrays the demimonde. Further, the lyric resistance concentrated in the apache calls to mind the alluring, but also menacing, effects

42. Walter Benjamin, *Charles Baudelaire: A Lyric Poet in the Era of High Capitalism* (London: Verso, 1970), 79. Benjamin made the comment about the durability of the "poetry of apachedom" in the 1930s. In fact, use of the term "apache" persisted until well after World War II. In Paris in the early 1950s, white aficionados of American jazz, especially bebop, were known as "*les apaches.*"

43. John Gay, *The Mohocks*, in *The Plays of John Gay* (London: Chapman, 1923), 1:47.

of the beggar's chant. Baudelaire revives for modernity the rhetoric, if not the diction, of the infidel lyric by placing the poet at the center of a constellation that includes the ragpicker, the apache, the dandy, and the flaneur. Indeed, Baudelaire regards the constellation of the infidel as central to the modernity of the poet. The solitariness and stealth of these figures mark as well the moment when the features of the anonymous lyric, exemplified by the canting song, begin to assume the aspect of *anonymity* as it pertains specifically to modern identity and urban experience. Less obviously, the formulation of modern anonymity from the specifically lyrical condition of a nameless speaker—located in the historical underworld—bears directly on the social implications of lyric expression.

SIX

Flash Crib: A Genealogy of Modern Nightlife

The Infidel Sublime

The tradition of English poetry harbors, as I indicated in the previous chapter, a kind of rude song—a fugitive lyric—written in the jargon of the demimonde, garbled and misplaced by design, which draws the reader into a historical underworld of taverns and nightclubs. Placing poetry in this particular way—tracing lyric to one of its hidden sources—helps to recover a little-known genre of infidel songs, yet it also raises, more generally, certain theoretical questions about configurations of place, or placelessness, in language and about the topology of poetic form. The labyrinth of the historical underworld may be described as a social and cultural *monadology* expressing, or compounding, the verbal obscurity of infidel poetry. Just as Leibniz found in the category of the sublime an expression of the subliminality and the dappled obscurity of monadic substance, so does the senseless topology of infidel poetry evoke the *topography* of underground culture. More pointedly, the historical construction and elite consumption of infidel culture reveals a sociological mode of the sublime—indeed, a dialectical inversion of the sublime (a *subliminal* sublime)—magnetized by the abject, by the labyrinthine topography of the so-called dangerous classes.

The question of how lyric obscurity might be understood topographically arises directly in a line of Hölderlin's poem "The Rhine": "Ein Rätsel ist Reinentsprungenes" (Pure of source is the riddle).[1] The purity of the river's source is not, according to this statement, a mystery—a mode of obscurity that is unresolvable—but a riddle: "a device of language," according to Paul de Man, "that can, in turn, be deciphered only by another operation of language."[2] Thus, the river's enigmatic source appears to be defined by the "operation" of a verbal figure. At the same time, however, the principle of verbal obscurity, conventionally defined as a failure of meaning or communication, appears in Hölderlin's poem as a topographical phenomenon. Places characterized by obscurity appear objectively in the world, though their exact location may be unmarked or unknown. Whether marked or unmarked, however, the place of the riddle (or the riddle of the place) resists discovery. Verbal obscurity (the place of the riddle) therefore expresses the condition of that which is neither lost nor found but *undiscovered,* or unanswered.

Setting aside the standard view of obscurity as a failure of meaning or communication clears the way as well for a more pragmatic conception of verbal obscurity. Just as the rhetoric of topography reconfigures obscurity in productive ways, so does the shift away from a preoccupation with meaning (or its lack) allow one to view lyric obscurity, in particular, principally as an event or speech act: a remedial charm capable of affecting the reader or listener in various ways. Combining this pragmatic model of verbal obscurity with a topology of lyric form provides a theoretical platform from which one might begin to develop a substantive correlation between infidel culture and the vernacular poems evoking that fugitive milieu.

As a *form* of secrecy, nightlife (or the history of nightlife) describes a topology, a study of lyrical sites, in language and in correspondingly anomalous material environments. One must distinguish, however, between topology and *topography,* a physical mapping of the city, which Walter Benjamin identified as the matrix of its many forms of solicitation and pleasure:

> There is no doubt, at any rate, that a feeling of crossing the threshold of one's class for the first time had a part in the almost unequalled fascination of publicly accosting a whore in the street. At the beginning, however, this was a crossing of frontiers not only social but *topographical.* . . . But is it really a crossing, is it not, rather, an obstinate and voluptuous hovering on the brink, a hesitation that has as its most cogent

1. Friedrich Hölderlin, *Poems and Fragments,* trans. Michael Hamburger (London: Kegan Paul, 1966), 73.

2. Paul de Man, "The Riddle of Hölderlin," in *Critical Writings, 1953–1978,* by Paul de Man, ed. Lindsay Waters (Minneapolis: University of Minnesota Press, 1989), 206.

motive in the circumstance that beyond this frontier lies nothingness? But the places are countless in great cities where one stands on the edge of the void.[3]

Benjamin is referring here, ostensibly, to the physical precincts of the metropolis and to the topographical boundaries of one's class, yet he also veers toward a mapping of topological space: wherever he, or the city dweller, senses "the void," the "nothingness" across the frontier, he ventures into what I am calling the *topology* of nightlife.

Giorgio Agamben follows Benjamin over the brink into the void and discovers in the principle of the topos a model for understanding the lyrical chamber of the *stanza*. Providing evidence for Schlegel's Romantic hypothesis of lyric form, the Italian word *stanza* indicates that we may think of the poetic stanza as a topos, according to Agamben, if we "accustom ourselves to think of 'place' not as something spatial, but as something more original than space. . . . Only a philosophical topology, analogous to what in mathematics is defined as *analysis situ* (analysis of site), in opposition to *analysis magnitudinis* (analysis of magnitude), would be adequate to the *topos outopos*, the placeless place."[4] Like the monad, the poetic topos of the stanza exists, under these terms, without material extension (or "magnitude"). Further, as a matrix of social obscurity, the lyric substance of the nightspot approximates, insofar as the actual sites of nocturnal culture continually elude material and pragmatic definition, the ambiguous substance of verbal reality. Reading the stanza into the topos (and vice versa) allows Agamben to define poetry generally as "a topology of the unreal," a phrase that aptly describes as well the partial world (demimonde) of nightlife.[5] Agamben traces the problematic of obscurity (and the lure of "enjoyment") inherent in these unreal forms to the Provençal model of the *trobar clus,* yet we must not forget that the pleasures of the "closed lyric" (or "close" lyric) are associated with the emergence in Europe of the vernacular tongue as a medium for poetry (in the *langue d'Oc* and the Italian *stil nuovo*).

Taverns and nightclubs are places where casual social interaction, business, and even crime coexist in a place governed ostensibly by pleasure. They are also sites where the illicit and often subversive habits (or "trades") of the demimonde become intelligible—and available—to members of lawful society. As a verbal site, a place in poetry, the topol-

3. Walter Benjamin, "A Berlin Chronicle," in *Reflections*, by Walter Benjamin, ed. Peter Demetz, trans. Edmund Jephcott (New York: Harcourt Brace Jovanovich, 1978), 11 (emphasis added).

4. Giorgio Agamben, *Stanzas*: *Word and Phantasm in Western Culture,* trans. Ronald L. Martinez (Minneapolis: University of Minnesota Press, 1993), xviii–xix.

5. Agamben, *Stanzas,* xviii.

ogy of the nightspot has its origins in the drinking songs of the canting tradition. In this respect, cant should be viewed as the idiom of a vernacular culture located in the "flash crib," the place where flash talk, or cant, is spoken. The history of nightlife and the riddling speech of cant illuminate one another, blindly and reciprocally, disclosing the labyrinth of infidel society. In this sense, the rhymes of the canting crew (embedded in a variety of literary texts) function as sources of historical—and profane—illumination, fitfully and haphazardly lighting the topography of nightlife.

Many canting songs refer to, or take place in, the "bousy ken" (the boozy place, or alehouse), which is frequented by the "bousy coves" (vagabonds and thieves) of the demimonde; and the medium of these songs is the "bousy speche / Jagged and ragged" of the canting crew. "Bousy" can mean "intoxicated," of course, yet the use of the term in these phrases also conveys the more general sense of dissolution or rhapsodic expression. Hence, a fundamental correspondence obtains between the rhapsodic tongue of thieves' latin and the monadic place—the nightspot—to which it lends its substance.

The reference to "bousy speche" comes from Robert Copland's cant song "Rhymes of the Canting Crew," a dialogue between the author and the night porter of a hospice for the indigent (the "spyttel-hous"):

Copland. Come none of these pedlars this way also
With pak on bak with their bousy speche
Jagged and ragged with broken hose and breche?
Porter. Inow, ynow; with bousy cove maimed nace,
Teare the patrying cove in the darkeman cace
Docked the dell for a coper meke.[6]

The base substance of the nightspot (the "darkeman cace") becomes evident through the porter's "bousy speche" in response to the poet's inquiry: "Come none of these pedlars this way also"? The porter says, "Inow, ynow" (the plural form of "enough," repeated twice, each with a variant spelling), as if to say, there are "enough"—and more than enough—of the "pedlars" who come that way. He then gives the poet a sordid picture of what is more than enough in the netherworld of the "bousy ken": take a look ("Teare"), he says, at the guy talking trash (the "patrying cove") in the night-house (the "darkeman cace"), who, with

6. Robert Copland, "Rhymes of the Canting Crew" (1536), reprinted in John S. Farmer, ed., *Musa Pedestris: Three Centuries of Canting Songs and Slang Rhymes* (London: privately printed, 1896), 1.

a pal as drunk as a cripple ("bousy cove maimed nace"), deflowered the virgin ("docked the dell") for half a penny (for a "coper meke"). We glimpse the rough trade taking place in the darkeman cace (the nightspot) through this compelling and excessive tongue—excessive and unstable from the start, as the word for "enough" (for what is too much) changes its spelling capriciously, not to mention the cant words whose meaning remains undefined. And, if the phrase "patrying cove" refers to a "strolling priest," the general atmosphere of inebriation and violation in the poem would also contain a note of blasphemy. The "priest" reference requires the word "patrying" (pattering) to mean both "strolling" and the mumbling of the *pater noster* recited by clergy—hence, perhaps, the origin of "thieves' latin" as a synonym for "cant." The low, jargoning sound of these verses would thus supply the auditory platform—and the particular atmosphere—of the darkeman cace.

The correlation between the society, the jargon, and the place of nightlife (all combined in the concept of the topos) that is embedded in the word "bousy" finds expression as well in another cant word, "quire," meaning "base" or "roguish," which gives us the common English word "queer," meaning "strange," "eccentric," or "abnormal."[7] Hence, we have, for example, the following expression from Samuel Rowlands's cant song "Towre Out Ben Morts" (1610): "The quire coves are budgd to the bowsing ken" (The bad guys sneaked away to the alehouse).[8] The "bowsing ken" (nightspot) can also be referred to as the "quier ken" (or "quirken"), and "to cutte quyre whiddes" means to talk "flash" or to use profanity or "queer words" ("whiddes" being a cant term for "words").[9] These various expressions (and variant spellings) suggest that the "queer words" of the canting crew lend their substance to the topography of nightlife and to the forms of social identity inscribed in the bousy ken.

The queerness of nightlife possesses, however, a dialectical twist: the word "queer" in cant refers not only to the substance of the "fancy" (the sporting life), as I have indicated, but also to its antithesis, the punitive character and apparatus of the law. Hence, the term "quier-ken" can mean "prison" as well as "alehouse," and the word "queer" frequently appears in compound with words designating phenomena that threaten to dispel

7. The *Oxford English Dictionary* indicates that the currently conventional meaning of "queer" (meaning "strange" or "eccentric") comes into use about 1700, considerably later than the earliest recorded evidence of the cant word "queer," which appears in the mid-sixteenth century.

8. Samuel Rowlands, "Towre Out Ben Morts," from *Martin Mark-all* (1610), reprinted in Farmer, *Musa Pedestris,* 5.

9. The phrase "to cutte quyre whiddes" (and its definition) appear in the cant glossary *Caveat for Common Cursetours* (i.e., vagabonds), compiled by Thomas Harman in 1566.

the "queer" (that is, lyric) substance of the canting crew. The promiscuity of the term, as in the following stanza, suggests an erotic polarity between the excessive authority of the law and the excessive substance, or jargon, of nightlife:

Till Cramprings quier, tip cove his hire,
and quier-kens doe them catch;
A canniken, mill quier cuffen,
so quier to ben cove's watch.[10]

In these lines, the "quyre whiddes" of the canting song lend material substance, perversely, to the "Cramprings quier" (shackles) associated with the "quier cuffen" (the magistrate). Hence, the queer topology of nightlife can be entered, and negotiated, through the binding eroticism of the law.

Tavern Talk

The queer space of the nightspot, as it appears in canting songs, gradually develops into a literary, or poetic, topos, with recognizable contours. Not surprisingly, these infidel songs often preserve historical features of the demimonde. Voices, never entirely real, rise out of the historical night, scant evidence of a culture lying just below the threshold of verisimilitude. The anonymous measures of the canting song contribute not only to our knowledge of places where history is made at night but also to a literary topos, a place made of words, a placeless place, where history and poetry converge in the proverbial dark.

Among the works of the dominant literary tradition that might serve as a *locus classicus* of the poetics of nightlife (John Skelton's "Colin Clout" or François Villon's *Ballades en jargon*, for example), the most memorable are the tavern scenes in Shakespeare's *Henry IV*, parts 1 and 2 (and in *Henry V* as well). These rude *tableaux de nuit* offer what is essentially a prehistory of modern nightlife. Not simply a place of intoxication and illicit, or even criminal, activities, the tavern in these scenes is a refuge where people of different social classes, vocations, and sexual persuasions mingle apart from the stratification of the world in daytime. In the tavern, a prince rubs shoulders with thieves, whores, and pimps;

10. Thomas Dekker, "Bing Out, Bien Morts" (1612), reprinted in Farmer, *Musa Pedestris*, 13.

the world encounters the demimonde. As a site of social experiment and dissolution (as a model of lyric expression), the tavern or club proves to be an enigma to the rationalized and productive world from which it is deliberately concealed by its nocturnal hours and often unfamiliar location.

From the text of the tavern scenes in *Henry IV*, one learns, at the very least, a great deal about the material culture of nightlife in the Elizabethan period: the kinds of food and beverages consumed; the cost of such items (one scene ends with a tally of Falstaff's bill); the availability of credit to customers; the tradespeople involved in the business (hostess, vintner, "drawer," etc.); the role of itinerant musicians; the naming of private rooms within the tavern (such as the "dolphin" or "half-moon" rooms); the use of "links" for street lighting; the hours of operation (often very late—several scenes do not begin until after midnight and end with breakfast being served shortly before dawn).

As rich as this material may be, the most substantial and memorable insights gained from these scenes concern the types of individuals apt to be found in a tavern late at night, the nature of their social bonds, and—of course—the way people talk in such places. Indeed, because language happens to be, in this case, the very medium of the profane dream of nightlife, it is not surprising that the way people talk comprehends the hermetic world of the tavern. Inevitably, the reader (or spectator) is both amused and puzzled by the tavern talk of Falstaff, Pistol, Bardolph, Mistress Quickly, Doll Tearsheet, and other pseudonymous figures of the demimonde in the chronicle plays. For the queer language of the tavern is distinguished by its general obscurity, by wordplay of all kinds, by the rhetoric of cursing and malediction, and by performative display. In this regard, tavern talk recalls (and employs) many features of the canting song, even as it anticipates the riddling speech of Shakespeare's later plays. One could even say that the intense lyricism of tavern talk brings to mind a kind of *poèsie pure* associated with literary modernity.

The tavern scenes in Shakespeare raise important questions about the context of the riddling speech of nightlife. Could we say, for example, that the *profanity* of tavern talk—perhaps its most common feature in Shakespearean nightlife—somehow renders the social, topographical, and even architectural obscurity of the tavern? To put it another way, should we understand the "pattering flash" of Pistol, Falstaff, and Doll Tearsheet as an expression of the illegitimacy of nocturnal culture? How do the "ragged" properties of nightlife find expression in Falstaff's riddling description of Prince Hal in the social underworld of the tavern? One detects a hint of virtuosity in Falstaff's rude encomium:

a' plays at quoits well, and eats conger and fennel, and drinks off candles' ends for flapdragons, and rides the wild-mare with the boys, and jumps upon joined-stools, and swears with a good grace, and wears his boots very smooth, like unto the sign of the leg, and breeds no bate with telling of discreet stories. (*Henry IV*, part 2, 2.4. 204–210)

The diction in this passage veers from idiomatic phrases (to breed no bate) to rhyming slang (conger and fennel) to cant words (flapdragon, quoits), the meaning of which may be recovered (or not) with the help of specialized glossaries. Yet, aside from the specific meaning of these squibs, Falstaff clearly revels in his ability to talk trash, which generates a halo of "obscurity effects." In general, then, we might say that the insular nature of Falstaff's flash talk somehow models the inscrutability—the material secrecy—of the nightclub.

We can be certain that Prince Hal views his association with "the good lads of Eastcheap" as something resembling an honorary membership in the fraternity of the canting crew, for he says:

I have sounded the very base-string of humility. Sirrah, I am sworn brother to a leash of drawers [tapsters]. . . . They call drinking deep "dying scarlet"; and when you breathe in your watering, they cry "ahem!" and bid you play it off. To conclude, I am so good a proficient in one quarter of an hour, that I can drink with any tinker in his own language during my life. (*Henry IV*, part 1, 2.4.5–19)

The prince refers here not only to a drinking game called "dying scarlet" but to the oaths and cant songs accompanying the game: "I can drink with any tinker in his own language." He claims to be a quick study, and the colorful nature of his speech throughout the scene bears him out. It is no mystery where the prince learned so well to swear and boast in canting speech; one need only attend to the "pattering flash" of the rogues around him. Here, for example, is Doll Tearsheet abusing poor Pistol: "Away, you cut-purse rascal! you filthy bung, away! by this wine, I'll thrust my knife in your mouldy chaps, an you play the saucy cuttle with me. Away you bottle-ale rascal! you basket-hilt stale juggler, you!" (*Henry IV*, part 2, 2.4.126–129). Doll belongs to the marginal world of the canting crew, and her speech, as this passage reveals, contains a higher percentage of cant vocabulary than that of any other character. But all of the characters, including the prince, are familiar with thieves' latin to varying degrees.

In one tavern scene, the sociological and verbal habits of this degraded yet lyrical precinct, which represent a queering of material substance, are captured in the trope of a particular, physical phenomenon: pitch. At one point, Hal asks Falstaff to play-act the role of his father, the king, in order to interrogate him (the prince) concerning his association with the canting crew and his wayward habits. Falstaff holds forth:

Shall the blessed son of heaven prove a micher and eat blackberries?—a question not to be asked. Shall the son of England prove a thief and take purses?—a question not to be asked. There is a thing, Harry, which thou hast often heard of and it is known to many in our land by the name of pitch: this pitch, as ancient writers do report, doth defile; so doth the company thou keepest. (*Henry IV,* part 1, 2.4.404–411)

The tone, or dark substance, of pitch represents here the various kinds of obscurity associated with the tavern: its nocturnal hours and notorious location; the derelict company of harlots and thieves; the verbal filth of thieves' latin ("the *name* of pitch"). The pitch of each of these phenomena defiles the prince, which is precisely why one must not pose the question "Shall the blessed son of heaven prove a micher and eat blackberries?" In this form, the question itself is defiled by canting speech: "micher" is a cant word for "thief," and "to eat blackberries" means to do nothing, to waste one's time. Evidently, the inky substance of the blackberry incorporates a trifling matter into the metaphor of "pitch," so that the blue-black substance of cant defiling the mouth appears to be evidence of petty theft: "Shall the son of England prove a thief and take purses?" Only several lines earlier, Falstaff refuses to explain his ridiculous behavior in a bungled theft by declaring, "Give you a reason on compulsion! if reasons were as plenty as blackberries, I would give no man a reason under compulsion, I" (*Henry IV,* part 1, 2.4.236–238). Certainly, the contaminating verbal substance of the blackberry, like the defiling "pitch," has its "reasons," however difficult they may be to extract from the queer speech of the canting crew.

Judging from the texts I have examined here, the poetry of the topos of nightlife is not uniformly obscure; rather, it is variable and heterogeneous—a verbal chiaroscuro. In Shakespeare's tavern scenes, different characters use varying amounts of slang and speak with various degrees of clarity or intelligibility, ranging from the color and profanity of Doll Tearsheet's speech to Prince Hal's occasional show of courtly diction. Even the expression of individual characters is variable and unstable, sliding easily between different registers of jargon and colloquial and conventional speech. One finds the same variability of tone in the canting song, which can incorporate different voices and modulate the thickness of its "pedlyng french."

In Shakespeare's tavern scenes, Falstaff is the most volatile figure verbally, capable one moment of speaking like a gentleman and, at the next, of cursing like a rogue. Prince Hal, too, as he himself likes to boast, can talk like one of the canting crew when he wishes—though his tone is less erratic than Falstaff's. This variability suggests that, for many of these characters (and indeed for the anonymous authors of canting songs), jargon or canting speech is never unadulterated and can be easily adopted or discarded, once it is learned, like a mask. Indeed, impersonation and role-playing are common features of the conduct in the tavern scenes, suggesting that verbal—or poetic—obscurity involves elements of craft, artifice, and transformation.

In addition, the heterogeneity of tone evident among (and within) different voices betrays verbally the principal social function of the club as a rendezvous for disparate, often notorious, elements of society. Although the club may be concealed from society at large, it is nevertheless the place where one finds individuals who may be otherwise difficult or impossible to find—either because they have no stable residence or because they are obliged to conceal their whereabouts. Hence, though the club may be a place to do business in public without getting busted or a place to rob and cheat—all in the name of pleasure—it is also, for these reasons, a magnet for the police. In Shakespeare, the sheriff and his deputies, "Fang" and "Snare," repeatedly descend on the Boar's Head Tavern, trolling for suspects. From its origins as a topos in canting literature, the tavern has always been a refuge of sorts, a place to which the "quire coves" retire (to party) after a night of burgling houses or picking pockets. Such is the case in *Henry IV,* part 1, when Falstaff and his crew retire to the Boar's Head after bungling a robbery, where the prince is waiting for him.

As a social space, the tavern is fluid, promiscuous, and highly contingent: the sheriff drops by, looking for suspects in a robbery; the prince waits for Falstaff to show up; and representatives of the king come by periodically, searching for the prince, to remind him of his duties. In this respect, the social space of the tavern, like its verbal substance, is at once open and closed, flagrant and secretive: an open secret. The social contingencies and heterogeneity of nightlife reflect back to us the nature of poetic expression. Within the queer ken of the nightspot—within its jargon and within poetic language—the speaker always seems to lie just beyond the reach of the world and its appointments, its duties, its certainty. The monadic relations characterizing the nightspot therefore compound the queering of material substance encrypted in the canting song.

One may present evidence evoking a *history* of nightlife, yet one must always bear in mind that the nightlife of the past survives for the most part in transcriptions of the vernacular: a place finding its tempo, its economy, its afterlife—its charm—in language. Since much of the evidence comes from songs, plays, or ballads, the historical place of the tavern depends on literature—on poetry in particular—for its specific qualities and its enduring substance. The chiaroscuro of the canting song, its dappled sense and senselessness (what Hopkins would call its "pied beauty"), its rude but alluring textures: these verbal qualities constitute the queer substance of the nightspot and its clandestine society.

One should not presume, however, that the inescapably verbal substance of nightlife under these conditions is somehow secondary to the physical reality of nightlife, either in the past or in the present. For that reality is fundamentally dissolute, its very existence placed in question by the obscurity of its material conditions: its unmarked facades and inaccessible locations; its late hours and tardy timetable; its nameless (or nicknamed) and promiscuous society. That is to say, the external conditions of nightlife continually revert to the material ambiguity of verbal reality, thereby betraying the essential inwardness, the incommensurability, of its primary substance. The appearance of nocturnal culture thus always follows the logic of disappearance, dissolving into the material and social fabric of the world, in order to secure a location which betrays no outward aspect—an impossible place—an open secret in the facade of the city. From this perspective, the lyrical topos of nightlife (in writing) is the primary form of that which takes place, secondarily, in the world: the secretive and senseless charm of the canting song would thus be the truest form of nightlife, in contrast to the more explicit—and therefore compromised—version of it taking place in the streets.

The material ambiguity of the nightspot, which must be viewed as evidence of its topological nature, becomes an issue as well when one deploys the principle of sentimentality—a concept originally developed in relation to poetry—as an index of the sensuous properties of nightlife. Indeed, the modern spectacle of underground culture, voiding experience and reverberating with that loss, falls generally under the logic of sentimentality. The culture of nightlife becomes, as we shall discover, more brazenly sentimental as it employs the modern technical media to publicize obscurity, an orientation recalling the innate sentimentality of the canting song.

The Brands of Cupid

The history of nightlife cannot be separated from the history of illumination and the technology of lighting. These phenomena spawned an evolving vocabulary of lighting, which can be recovered from various textual sources (mostly literary), and which now casts a faulty and often symbolic glow on the nocturnal side of things. History at night becomes evident, though not really visible, through literature. Poetry, especially dramatic verse, therefore plays a substantial role in the tenuous archaeology of nightlife. By implication, the vocabulary of lighting helps to reveal the terra incognita shared by the culture of nightlife and the criminal—but also lyrical—practice of the canting crew.

Prior to the development of wick lamps and reflective illumination in the late seventeenth century, one negotiated the city at night with the aid of torches and "links"—that is, "brands" saturated with pitch or wax (the root of the modern term for trademarks or "brand" names).[11] "Links" and "brands" tend to function interchangeably in the literal, and sometimes figurative, realms of nocturnal life, so that the torches for hire in the hands of "link-boys" evoke the "brands of Cupid" (cf. Shakespeare's *Cymbeline,* 2.4.91: "Two winking Cupids, nicely depending on their brands"). The link-boy appears then, more suggestively, to be a puerile and nocturnal guide for hire, a figure of erotic assignation: "This is the page, love's link-boy, that must light me the way" (Farquhar, *Love and Battle,* 3.1). For one did not, of course, carry one's own torch but rather called on the services of link-boys posted on street corners—in every muddy lane—until the light of day chased them from the streets.

The erotic overtones of this transaction are drawn habitually in terms of class difference. Even as late as the mid–nineteenth century, long after the link had become a nostalgic feature of the Jacobean night, Thackeray, for example, like Baudelaire, could distill the late-night habits of the sporting life into a courtly dance between young prigs and swells, flunkies and dandies: "Link-boys with their torches lighted the beaux over the mud" (*The Newcomes,* 1.17.161). In any case, the cost of hiring links was an expense that had to be reckoned into the price of doing business (or pleasure) at night. In *Henry IV,* part 1, for example, Falstaff jokingly refers to

11. In his cultural history of lighting and illumination, Wolfgang Schivelbusch writes: "London and Paris had possessed 'mobile' public lighting in the form of linkmen since the seventeenth century. Pedestrians could hire them like cabs to light the way home. . . . linkmen remained part of the nocturnal street scene until the early nineteenth century." Schivelbusch, *Disenchanted Night: The Industrialization of Light in the Nineteenth Century,* trans. Angela Davies (Berkeley and Los Angeles: University of California Press, 1988), 89, 96.

Bardolph's nose as "an ignis-fatuus or a ball of wildfire" floating above the muddy lanes of Eastcheap in London: "O, thou art a perpetual triumph, an everlasting bonfire-light! Thou has saved me a thousand marks in links and torches, walking with thee in the night betwixt tavern and tavern" (*Henry IV,* part 1, 3.3).

The role of the link-boys (or link-men) in nocturnal culture was subject, as one might imagine, to a variety of permutations, often overlapping the ambiguous, or frankly illicit, "trades" of the canting crew. Because link-boys inevitably witnessed activities taking place under the cover of night, it was not unusual for them to be employed as spies by the police. One eighteenth-century observer of Parisian nightlife explains this phenomenon: "The nocturnal wanderers with their torches are in the service of the police and see everything that happens; thieves who want to force open locks in the back streets can never be sure that their unexpected lights will not turn up. . . . The torch-bearer goes to bed very late and the next day reports everything to the police."[12] As the eyes of the night, especially in the service of the law, link-boys played a role similar to that of the police informants and shady lexicographers who first penetrated—and deciphered—the obscurity of canting speech.

At the same time, however, the link-boys' proximity to criminal persuasion—their status as a medium between lawful society and the demimonde—inevitably drew them across the frontier of illegality as messengers, lookouts, procurers, shills, and worse. One historian, for example, writes: "It was well known that London's linkmen . . . had close contacts with, or even belonged to, the criminal underworld: 'Far more often than not, these "servants of the public" were hand in glove with footpads or highwaymen, and would rarely think twice on receiving a signal from such accomplices of extinguishing the link and slipping away.'"[13] Being a crook, in addition to being a torchbearer, did not of course preclude the possibility of being a spy. Indeed, the anonymous aspect of the link-boy appears to have been predisposed to games of confidence and impersonation. Intelligence always becomes "intelligence" in the streets at night.

The combination of roles gathered under the figure of the link-boy (guide, hustler, criminal, spy, medium) closely resembles the typology of the canting crew and may be distilled to yield a portrait of the infidel poet. Indeed, the link-boy appears in a number of canting songs, some-

12. Schivelbusch, *Disenchanted Night,* 89, citing Louis Sebastian-Mercier.

13. Schivelbusch, *Disenchanted Night,* 89, citing William C. Sidney, a historian of eighteenth-century England.

times in the first person, as in the following stanzas from an anonymous ballad called "The Potato Man":

I am a saucy rolling blade,
I fear not wet nor dry,
I keep a jack ass for my trade,
And thro' the streets do cry

. . . .

A link boy once I stood the gag,
At Charing Cross did ply,
Here's light your honor for a mag,
But now my potatoes cry.[14]

The link-boy for hire ("for a mag," a halfpenny) has grown into a "saucy rolling blade," a wise guy, who cries "potatoes" only to hide his real business on the street. ("I'm up to all your knowing rigs / Whilst I my potatoes cry.") Another "dashing" link-boy appears in one of Pierce Egan's cant "Sonnets for the Fancy" (said to be "After the Manner of Petrarch"):

A link-boy once, Dick Hellfinch stood the grin,
At Charing Cross he long his toil apply'd;
"Here light, here light! your honours for a win,"
To every cull and drab he loudly cried.

. . . .

In Smithfield, too, where graziers' flats resort,
He loiter'd there to take in men of cash,
With cards and dice was up to ev'ry sport,
And at Saltpetre Bank would cut a dash;
A very knowing rig in ev'ry gang,
Dick Hellfinch was the pick of the slang.[15]

Once again, as in the earlier poem, being a link-boy appears to be a stage of incubation—historicizing the incubus—from which emerges the "saucy rolling blade" or the "Dick Hellfinch" who is "the pick of the slang" and who "cuts a dash" (a showy appearance). The link-boy incubates the dandy and the cheat, a conversion that activates the dialectic of "the fancy" (the society of the canting crew).

14. "The Potato Man," reprinted in Farmer, *Musa Pedestris*, 54–55.
15. Pierce Egan, "Sonnets for the Fancy," reprinted in Farmer, *Musa Pedestris*, 90–91.

One of the remarkable things about these sketches of nightlife (before cities were lit by streetlamps) is that they allow us to hear the lyrical cries of the link-boys in the street. For these and other canting songs preserve the actual calls of these "night birds," which resemble the solicitations of beggars and therefore prove the barest element of the canting song. "The Potato Man" gives us "Here's light your honor for a mag," and Egan cites a variation of this cry: "Here light, here light! your honors for a win [a penny]." In Thomas Heywood's *Rape of Lucrece* (1641), we find the lines "Lanthorn and Candlelight here, / Maid ha' light here, Thus go the cries"; and the same call resounds in Thomas Dekker's *Satiromastix* (1609): "dost roar? thou hast a good rouncival voice to cry lantern and candlelight."

Significantly, Dekker, a well-known Elizabethan pamphleteer and dramatist (and one of the earliest anthologists of canting songs), used the phrase "Lanthorne and Candlelight" (the call of the link-boy) as the title for a popular collection of flash songs (first published in 1608). The title was lengthened in a second edition (1612) to *A New Cryer of Lanthorne and Candlelight, Being an Addition or Lengthening of the Belman's Second Night Walke*. (The reference here to "the Belman," a night watchman, indicates that *Lanthorne and Candlelight* was, in its first edition, the second part of a larger miscellany entitled *The Belman of London Bringing to Light the Most Notorious Villainies that are now practiced in the Kingdome.*) All of these references point to Dekker's judgment that the "rum-cove pattering flash" (the busker "spitting" cant) resembles the link-boy and the belman. For each of these figures bears witness to nightlife—to history at night—hence Dekker's choice to name his collection of cant songs *Lanthorne and Candlelight*. The nocturnal call of the link-boy is itself an iconic element of the canting song—a cry of solicitation—and makes evident the fundamental correlation between the linguistic obscurity of the canting song and the sociological or topographical sublimity of nightlife.

The Politics of Nightlife

The sociological sublime enveloping the nightclub provides cover for practices judged to be improper, indecent, or illegal by ordinary society. These forms of transgression have historically often amounted to little more than intimate transactions between disparate social classes and races—events that would be impossible in the light of day. The fact that these transgressions have political significance becomes evident only when they are identified as elements in a larger field of cultural experimentation. Under these circumstances, the nightclub becomes a social and political laboratory, a theater, but also, more surprisingly, an early site for the implementation of the new technical media—a media lab. Transmission becomes a form of transgression in the sociological half-light of the tavern.

The advent of modern nightlife, the moment of historical self-awakening, coincides with a general expansion of court records of infidel culture. The portrayals of the demimonde encrypted in the canting song begin to appear in the records of the political state, as witnessed, for example, by these dossiers on subversive individuals from the archives of the Parisian police, 1781–1785:

GORSAS: proper for all kinds of vile jobs. Run out of Versailles and put in Bicêtre [a jail for especially dangerous criminals] by personal order of the king for having corrupted children whom he had taken in as lodgers. . . . Gorsas produces *libelles* [slander sheets]. He has an arrangement with an apprentice printer who has been fired from other printing shops. He [Gorsas] is suspected of having printed obscene works there. He peddles prohibited books.

AUDOUIN: calls himself a lawyer, writes *nouvelles à la main* [seditious pamphlets], peddler of forbidden books; he is connected with Prudhomme, Manuel, and other disreputable authors and book peddlers. He does all kinds of work; he will be a spy when one wants.

DELACROIX: lawyer, writer, expelled from the bar. He produces [judicial] *mémoires* for shady cases; and when he has no *mémoires* to write, he writes scurrilous works.[16]

These shadowy figures participated in the formation of *la basse littérature,* a new kind of literary community shaped in part by radical politics but also by a revolution in the media of the demimonde, which began to take shape in the waning years of the Old Regime in France. Though we have some evidence of the ephemera produced by this community of authors and printers (pamphlets, scandal sheets, squibs, broadside ballads), a detailed picture of this clandestine milieu—from the lower depths of the Enlightenment—depends largely on reports filed by government spies. As comments in the files I have cited indicate, many of these individuals served the Jacobin revolutionary cause by participating in the burgeoning democratization of print media at the time. They were authors

16. Excerpts from dossiers compiled by government spies, 1781–1785, in the archives of the police in Paris. Cited in Robert Darnton, *The Literary Underground of the Old Regime* (Cambridge, MA: Harvard University Press, 1982), 26.

(and so-called *philosophes*) but also booksellers, smugglers of forbidden texts, and radical pressmen; they had no choice but to operate underground, apart from the monopolistic and government-protected guild of printers.

This clandestine society of ultraradicals made its headquarters in what had been the domain of the canting crew: taverns, night cellars, and coffeehouses. In Paris, a constellation of "counter-academies and anti-salons" emerged prior to 1789, as Robert Darnton explains: "While the great names gathered in the Procope or La Régence [celebrated Parisian cafés], lesser figures congregated in the notorious Caveau of the Palais-Royal, and the humblest hacks frequented the cafés of the boulevards, blending into an underworld of 'swindlers, recruiting agents, spies, and pickpockets; here one finds only pimps, buggers, and *bardaches*.'"[17] Darnton emphasizes that one could not easily distinguish between the radical and criminal elements of the demimonde: "Many writers lived on the fringes of the law. . . . Some, at the bottom of the literary underworld, sank into criminality."[18] At the same time, however, the pamphleteers and radical pressmen who occasionally turned to crime to make ends meet could also be recruited as government spies, in order to protect themselves from prosecution for their criminal pursuits. Darnton claims that many spies were "underworld writers themselves with their own dossiers in the archives of the police."[19]

Evidently, the manifold, queer identities of the canting crew extended to the formation of a radical underground, yet the topology of nightlife was permanently and fundamentally altered by its increasingly political orientation, by its incorporation of new technical media (print, at this stage), and by the industrialization of light in the mid-nineteenth century. With these changes, the latent, though by no means guaranteed, affinities between nightlife and radical politics became more discernible, as did certain topologies of pleasure (such as the emergence of the modern *beauty salon*, a sequestered place related by its liberatory aspect—for women—to the evolving political space of the tavern).[20] Through this historical revision of nightlife, the dissolute and adversarial nature of the canting crew became more explicit, more agitational, and more

17. Darnton, *Literary Underground of the Old Regime*, 23–24. In the latter part of this passage, Darnton is citing a pamphlet of 1784 by one of the most notorious and violent pamphleteers in Paris at that time, Charles Théveneau de Morande.

18. Darnton, *Literary Underground of the Old Regime*, 25.

19. Darnton, *Literary Underground of the Old Regime*, 26.

20. On the beauty salon as a form of Enlightenment praxis, see Susan Ossman, *Three Faces of Beauty: Casablanca, Paris, Cairo* (Durham, NC: Duke University Press, 2002).

organized—though still largely improvised and ephemeral. In addition, the *class implications* integral to the violence and dissolute pleasures of the "dangerous classes" became far more distinct and overt in the newly politicized topos of the tavern. The new "rhymes" of the canting crew (songs, slogans, sermons) adapted the rough trade of the nightspot to the social and sexual libertinage of insurrection, contributing to the anomalous genre of the night-book, *le livre philosophique,* which is at once pornographic and politically seditious. In many respects, the social, textual, and political experimentation informing the fluid topology of nightlife at this time established the groundwork for what would become the modern avant-garde.

The incorporation of a technical medium (print) into the newly politicized topology of nightlife represents an exceedingly complex and ambiguous development in the history of infidel society. One could argue that the dissemination of the libertine rhetoric and praxis of the demimonde—facilitating revolution via the technical medium of print—caused an irreparable breach in the hermeticism (and integrity) of the topos, or stanza, of the nightspot. Yet the secrecy of the canting crew, as I indicated earlier, had already been compromised by the dissemination of anonymous lyrics written in the canting speech of vagrants and thieves. Hence, breaking the secrecy of the nightspot—its conversion into an *open* secret—is an inherently lyrical event, recapitulated in the technical dissemination of its abruptly politicized habits and judgments. Integrating print (a technical medium) into the topology of nightlife thus renewed its lyrical economy, demonstrating as well the transmissibility of its substance. For if it is true that the canting song, with its inscrutable jargon, may be understood as the truest form of nightlife (precisely because of its ambiguous verbal substance), then the dissemination through the press of a radicalized (but also newly mediated and derealized) form of nightlife offers historical evidence of the reciprocity between the substance of a verbal medium and the improvised substance of the nightspot. Furthermore, any traditional society undone, or dissolved, by this transfusion of substance, so to speak, can be refashioned in the image of the demimonde, becoming its own underworld: a means of queering the world that deprives it, happily, of material certainty and continuity.

Insofar as the transfusion of substance (via the medium of print) can be viewed as an *abstraction* of physical circumstances and events, then one must acknowledge the increasing *sentimentality* of nightlife—that is, its progressive derealization, or removal from its physical settings. In other words, the evolving sentimentality of nightlife coincides with the increasing role of the technical media in its articulation. Furthermore, this process of mediation (in a revolutionary context), this depletion of the purely sensual aspect of nightlife, can be seen as advancing the hidden teleology of its primary, verbal substance, as a restoration (and a revision) of the elemental correspondence between the lyric stanza and the topos of nightlife. One could therefore claim that the essential inwardness of nightlife, its resistance to appearing openly in the world, finds renewed expression (and political significance) in the tenuous substance of the new media.

Infidel Culture

The French expatriate colony of radical pamphleteers, offshore printers, and smugglers active in London prior to 1789 spawned cadres of native revolutionaries operating out of a confederation of Jacobin clubs, radical public houses, and dissenting chapels in the 1790s. Analyzing the social composition of this "tavern political underworld," historian Iain McCalman writes that "the London democratic movements of the 1790s comprised three separate but related elements: the mainly artisan proponents of French Jacobin-republicanism; overlapping groups of infidels, or political freethinkers, dedicated to moral and political subversion; and an 'auxiliary' force of lower-class religious enthusiasts with a similar passion to overthrow the established order." Further, as was the case in the milieu of *la basse littérature* in Paris, according to McCalman, "many of these ultras were also connected with London's notorious underworld of crime and profligacy. Through activities such as theft, pimping, rape, blackmail, and pornography they introduce us to a region where popular politics intersected with lumpen and organized crime." As a result, McCalman speculates, this marginal society of artisan revolutionaries, infidel poets, and plebeian social prophets helped to preserve cultural forms associated with the criminal underworld—that is, the vernacular productions of the canting crew: "Some elements of this ultra underworld act also as long-term carriers of 'rough' political and cultural traditions which are thought to have perished at the end of the Regency [1820–1830]."[21] Evidence of the radical underworld's affinity for the canting tradition can be found, for example, in the career of William West, author and infidel printer, who published not only seditious and pornographic texts but anthologies such as *The Rambler's Flash Songster* and *The Flash Chaunter*.

21. Iain McCalman, *Radical Underworld: Prophets, Revolutionaries, and Pornographers in London, 1795–1840* (Cambridge: Cambridge University Press, 1988), 1, 2, 3.

As an author, West published *Tavern Anecdotes and Reminiscences of the Origins of Signs, Clubs, Coffeehouses . . .* (1825), one of the few contemporaneous sources documenting the tavern culture of the radical underworld.[22]

The significance of the term "infidel" as a general rubric for these underground activities can be traced to the appearance in London (after the 1790s) of seditious "chapels" devoted to the proliferation of various "outlaw discourses" supporting the "ultraradical" cause (i.e., those advocating physical force, in contrast to "reform" radicals). More remotely, this term would have reverberated with the atavistic threat of the alien disbeliever, the Muslim infidel. Taking advantage of laws permitting public assembly for religious purposes, these abject meeting places functioned as "a public forum in which the discourse of the emergent could be grafted over the discourse of the dominant. . . . Religion could be read as an allegory of politics."[23] That is to say, these heretical "chapels" spawned a generation of political "prophets" and "infidels," cultivating a revolutionary theater of "mock worship."[24] Such "worship" included the circulation of "fugitive literature" and "infidel publications": tracts by Voltaire, Paine, and Volney, chapbooks of infidel poetry, and halfpenny pamphlets such as *Every Man His Own Pike Maker*.[25]

Although we have the rare autobiographical or historiographical text (such as *The Polemic Fleet of 1816*, a lengthy, satirical broadsheet), our knowledge of this clandestine milieu, like our picture of the Parisian literary underground, depends largely on reports of government spies, whose testimony was periodically compiled in the parliamentary *Report from the Committee of Secrecy*. Many of the surviving pamphlets and broadsheets of the radical underworld exist only in copies confiscated by informants (along with their scribbled notes) and deposited in the archives of the British Home Office. Further, the various infidel societies meeting in taverns, coffeehouses, and dissenting chapels were thoroughly infiltrated by informants and spies (hence the common practice of "No Names" at meetings), including a type known as "engraver-spies," who were trained

22. I should note that there is some uncertainty as to whether the publisher William West is the same person as the author William West—an indication of the challenges facing a historian of this milieu.

23. David Worrall, *Radical Culture: Discourse, Resistance, and Surveillance, 1790–1820* (Detroit: Wayne State University Press, 1992), 178–179. Robert Wedderburn, the most notorious of the dissenting "preachers," declared of himself (and his kind): "we might call him an Infidel, true he once professed Christianity but now he was an Infidel, Ignorance was better than knowledge, Barbarism better than Christianity" (129).

24. See Worrall's chapter "The 'Temple of Sedition' of Hopkins Street," in *Radical Culture*, 165–186. See also Iain McCalman, "The Infidel as Prophet: William Reid and Blakean Radicalism," in *Historicizing Blake*, ed. Steve Clark and David Worrall (London: St. Martin's Press, 1994), 24–42.

25. Worrall, *Radical Culture*, 143, 196.

to produce *visual* records of clandestine events. William Blake called government spies "Satans Watch-fiends." Indeed, so pervasive was the surveillance that David Worrall contends: "Britain 1790–1820 was a spy culture. Even the surveillers were surveilled." Jeremy Bentham, for example, came under surveillance for funding conspirators seeking to assassinate the British cabinet: "the inventor of the Panopticon had already been fixed in the Government's panoptic gaze."[26]

Emphasizing the correlation between the unreliability of the evidence in these reports and the need for secrecy among the ultras (and citing the example of the infidel Robert Wedderburn), McCalman writes:

> Such people usually escape the historian's notice because they leave few traces. That we are able to reconstruct something of Wedderburn's mentality and milieu is thanks in large part to the labours of government spies and informers. Needless to say this is partial evidence in every sense; scholars such as Edward Thompson and Richard Cobb have warned how carefully we must fumigate every fact that comes from police and intelligence records. Yet, allowing with Ben Jonson that most spies are "of base stuff," the early nineteenth-century variants offer a surprising diversity of testimony and perspective: they include casual observers of all classes, nosey clergymen, anonymous informers, professional shorthand writers, stolid police undercover men, self-appointed sensation seekers, needy, greedy, or fearful radicals and their disgruntled relatives, and a few schizoid individuals with loyalties to both government employers and radical colleagues.[27]

Taking into account McCalman's observations, we find, once again, a basic correspondence between the hermetic nature of the communities under consideration in this chapter (the radical/infidel underground, the demimonde of the canting crew, the topology of nightlife) and the obscurity of the verbal elements disclosing (or substantiating) these communities (spies' reports, canting songs, tavern talk). In the particular circumstance of the London radical underground, the correlation between verbal and sociological obscurities became more acute with the rise of counterrevolutionary sentiment and government repression in the late 1790s, a development, as Bryan Palmer explains, requiring the infidel community to withdraw more effectively into the back rooms of taverns and brothels: "Forced into darkness by state repression, the Jacobinism of the late 1790s withdrew into the shadows of political culture and the last of the decade's revolutionaries, their democratic, public agitation outlawed, nurtured

26. Worrall, *Radical Culture,* 72–73, 6 (Blake), 7.
27. McCalman, *Radical Underworld,* 3.

the radicalism of the clandestine cell."[28] These developments suggest that the dissemination of infidel culture (via print) waxed and waned, periodically withdrawing into the social monad of the tavern, the archetype of the clandestine political cell.

Bearing in mind McCalman's revelation of the intricate motivations of spy testimony, which contribute to its status as "partial evidence," one would want to emphasize its lack of objectivity, its variegated tone, and, hence, inadvertent *literary* effects. In this sense, one should identify the writing of spies, despite its official task, as one of the principal productions of the world of radical-infidel letters.[29] Indeed, from a purely stylistic perspective, some attention might be given to the curious innovations in prose resulting from the spies' efforts to record verbatim, coupled with their own interpolations, the oaths sworn by infidels in boisterous taverns.[30]

The clandestine society of writers and "hacks" made its headquarters, as I have indicated, in seedy alehouses, backroom chapels, and low coffeehouses. The *Report from the Committee of Secrecy* of 1817 describes the freethinking literati who attended the secret meetings of the London Corresponding Society (LCS), a seminal organization in radical politics: "the minds of those who attend their meetings are tainted and depraved; they are taught contempt for all Decency, Law, all Religion and Morality, and are thus prepared for the most atrocious scenes of outrage and violence."[31] Thomas Spence, the founder of the LCS and author of an agrarian reform plan which became the basis of ultraradical doctrine, maintained a bookstore called the Hive of Liberty, a clearinghouse of "seditious publications." A spy's report from 1794 describes the setting: "Another shop is Spence's in Little Turnstile where a periodical work called Pigs' Meat is published. This man lives in dirtiest poverty, but his shop is decorated with lines in prose and verse, expressing a determination to carry on his traffic in spite of Laws and Magistrates. This is one of the houses where they train to arms."[32] In addition to training men "to arms"—an act of

28. Bryan D. Palmer, *Cultures of Darkness: Night Travels in the Histories of Transgression* (New York: Monthly Review Press, 2000), 111–112.

29. Although Iain McCalman's scholarship in *Radical Underworld* is based on extensive archival research, he does not generally cite the actual testimony of spies in the dossiers he has examined. Hence, to see these materials, one would have no choice but to visit the pertinent archives in London: the Home Office Papers, the Privy Council Papers, the Treasury Solicitor's Papers, the King's Bench Records, and the Records of the Metropolitan Police Office.

30. See, for example, Worrall's citations of informants' records of songs and speeches presented by various infidels. Worrall, *Radical Culture,* 136–138.

31. Parliamentary *Report from the Committee of Secrecy* (1817), cited in McCalman, *Radical Underworld,* 120.

32. Cited in Worrall, *Radical Culture,* 20.

high treason—Spence developed what he called a "New Alphabet," a curious phonetic system designed to "enable the inarticulate."[33]

For a number of years (between 1801 and 1814), Spence also conducted political "free-and-easies" (the preferred mode of ultraradical debate) every Wednesday night at "a low alehouse called the Cock at the corner of Lumber Court and Grafton Street, Soho."[34] There, according to McCalman, "no one was too poor or unrespectable to be excluded from Spence's utopia; it embraced 'every man, woman, or child, whether born in wedlock or not,' as well as immigrants, foreigners, blacks and even criminals—'all those who have no Helpers.'"[35] In addition, Worrall claims, "Radical debating clubs (and perhaps radical politics in general) may have been socially important in providing the opportunity for people with disabilities to fully realize their own potential: Thomas Preston and Thomas Hazard, the post-war Spenceans, were both lame while the more famous Samuel Waddington was 4 feet 2 inches tall."[36]

The Spencean underworld harbored, in one spy's words, "disciples of the wildest wickedst theories," intending to "inflame the unthinking."[37] A detailed description of a typical free-and-easy appears in a spy's report of 1817:

> It wanted about 10 minutes to 7 when they got there—they went first into the tap room then up stairs—The room upstairs is two Rooms made into one, it is a cosy room. They waited in the tap Room till the Company became very numerous, then they went up. . . . Then Porter [Thomas Porter, associate of Spence] called Silence and gave the first Song—It was a song against the Prince Regent, about the fat pig in Hyde Park, and the King gone to St. Paul's—then others sang a great many Songs all against the Government and after each Man had done singing he gave a toast—One was given by Porter and was this "May the Skin of the tyrants be burnt into Parchment and the Rights of Man written on it."[38]

Besides making a succession of songs and "toasts," the infidels at a free-and-easy (sometimes as many as 150) wore what one informant called

33. Worrall, *Radical Culture*, 78. McCalman notes that Spence, who was representative of "a vital autodidact culture," produced pioneering works in the field of phonetics, including his *Grand Repository of the English Language* (1775), which, "along with his other contributions to English orthography and language, are now acknowledged as significant works of scholarship as well as agents of linguistic levelling." McCalman, *Radical Underworld*, 92.

34. McCalman, *Radical Underworld*, 7.

35. McCalman, *Radical Underworld*, 46.

36. Worrall, *Radical Culture*, 36–37.

37. Cited in Worrall, *Radical Culture*, 95.

38. Cited in Worrall, *Radical Culture*, 93.

a kind of "radical millenary," that is, items of clothing and accessories signifying radical sympathies: white hats, for example, or "a green silk umbrella with a hooked yellow stick."[39] What's more, the "mechanicks," sailors, and others present could order a "glass of Radical": "'Radical' was a beverage drunk as an alternative to heavily taxed tea, coffee, and alcohol: to order and drink a 'glass of Radical' was to take part in an economic boycott. Like a white hat, it was a badge recognized by others."[40]

The range of signifying practices and experimental media extended to infidel print culture: "In much of his propaganda, Spence deliberately sought to use the language and literary forms of the vulgar, the poor, and semi-literate (including chapbooks, ballads, posters, and almanacs)."[41] Not surprisingly, elements of canting speech surfaced in these ephemeral media and in the incendiary "wall-chalkings" that appeared on walls overnight—a practice reflected, perhaps, in the mottoes and lines of verse covering the walls of Spence's bookshop.[42] Experimentation in new—and traditional—media thus ranged from handbills to graffiti to small metal tokens stamped with revolutionary slogans and mottoes (sometimes on existing coinage).[43]

A notable, strategic variation of subversive "wall-chalkings" occurred through the agency of so-called cell-wall poets: political detainees slated for execution who scribbled their final poems on the walls of their cells. One of the Cato Street conspirators, for example, inscribed several quatrains against the government, one of whose spies (anticipated in the poem) dutifully recorded these lines:

Written in the tower by J T Brunt

The home Departments Secretaire
His Orders they would make you Stare
An hour a Day Consigned to Walk
But mind they neither Wink nor talk

For those Are Gifts of human reason
And they Are Adepts At high Treason

39. Worrall, *Radical Culture,* 58, 159. Worrall indicates that a short-lived journal entitled *The White Hat* was published in 1819.

40. Worrall, *Radical Culture,* 188.

41. McCalman, *Radical Underworld,* 46–47.

42. McCalman, *Radical Underworld,* 22.

43. See Worrall's discussion of Spence's "tokens" in *Radical Culture,* 26–28. See also R. H. Thomas, "The Dies of Thomas Spence (1750–1814)," *British Numismatics Journal* 38 (1969–70): 126–162.

No biger rogues on earth they be on
For so Saith edwards the espion

You may Let them eat drink And sleep
But Knives and forks must from them keep
or theyll Comit Assassination
The rogues would Overturn the nation.[44]

Concerning the transitivity of this speech act, Worrall notes: "Brunt's declaration of authorship is interesting and probably an attempt to circulate his thoughts to a wider audience after his execution and subsequent to some Home Office leakage."[45] And, indeed, since our knowledge of this poem depends on the spy's preservation of it, Brunt's strategy has apparently achieved a kind of success.

In addition, however, to the emerging vernacular "genres" of slogans, mottoes, toasts, and cell-wall "testaments," Spence appropriated and published excerpts of canonical British poetry in his radical journal *Pigs' Meat.* Accordingly, Worrall notes the efforts of "house-to-house booksellers who 'recommended' Spence's pamphlets while they sold Pope's poetry in part-works." More specifically, in *Pigs' Meat,* one finds "Examples of Safe Printing," where Spence introduces a garbled passage from "Spencer's" *Faerie Queen* (punning on the spelling of the poet's name) with an apology of the most devious kind: "To prevent misrepresentation in these prosecuting times, it seems necessary to *publish* everything relating to tyranny and Oppression, though only among the brutes, in the most guarded manner. The following are meant as Specimens." He then proceeds to demonstrate how sixteenth-century Elizabethan poetry might be turned to the ends of radical politics in the 1790s:

That tyger, or that other salvage wight
Is so exceeding furious and fell,
As WRONG,
(*Not meaning our most gracious sovereign Lord*
the King or the Government of the country)
when it has arm'd himself with might;
Not fit 'mong men that do with reason mell
But 'mong wild beasts and salvage woods to dwell,
Where still the stronger

44. Cited in Worrall, *Radical Culture,* 195.
45. Worrall, *Radical Culture,* 195.

(Not meaning the Great Men of this country)
doth the weak devour.

In a "most guarded manner"—in a gesture of ironic deflection—the interpolated lines in italics convert "Spencer's" allegory into an "Example of Safe Printing": one curious "Specimen" of infidel poetry. Less ambiguously, the slogan for the Spa Fields Rising (the closest the ultraradicals came to armed insurrection) was a fragment from Shakespeare's *Tempest:* "like the baseless fabric of a Vision leaving not a wrack behind."[46]

Poetry and singing, as the spy's report cited above indicates, were essential to the conviviality and revolutionary praxis of the tavern political underworld:

> Songs and ballads—one of the oldest expressions of the English poor—also featured prominently at Spencean debating club meetings, just as they had done in Jacobin taverns during the 1790s and at Spencean free-and-easies during the war years. This kind of singing alarmed the establishment almost as much as plebeian debating. . . . The *Report from the Committee of Secrecy* of 1817 cited the Spenceans' "profane and seditious songs" as one of the chief justifications for suppressing the society.[47]

More concisely, Thomas Evans, in his manifesto of the Spencean free-and-easy, exhorts the infidel: "Sing and meet and meet and sing, and your Chains will drop off like burnt Thread."[48] Elaborating on the subversive measures of oral poetry, Worrall comments: "A populace who 'sing their rights' and instruct each other in song eluded surveillance in their chorus of members. Though there were spies in the tavern, they could sing Spencean songs 'in their Families.' The music of the 'free and easy' is the music of carnival, harlequin with an apocalyptic dagger."[49]

Many poets of "unrespectable" origin, including Spence himself (whose poems were collected in *Spence's Songs* of 1811), helped to record scenes from an underworld in the making. Here, for example, "burly stonecutter-thief, Thomas Porter" recalls (in a ballad of 1807) meeting Spence at the sign of the Swan:

To the Swan I took my flight,
Down in the New Street Square, Sir,

46. Cited in Worrall, *Radical Culture,* 101, 23, 24, 107.
47. McCalman, *Radical Underworld,* 118.
48. Thomas Evans, "Address to All Mankind" (1817), cited in Worrall, *Radical Culture,* 91.
49. Worrall, *Radical Culture,* 91.

Where every Monday night,
Friend Tommy Spence comes there, Sir.[50]

Another portrait of Spence appears in a tavern ballad of 1811 by Thomas Evans (a leading activist):

At the sign of the Fleece
For a trifle apiece
Spence treats all the swine with a Book
But not for vile pelf,
'Tis all wrote by himself
To instruct by Hook or by Crook.[51]

The reference to "swine" alludes to Spence's radical journal *Pig's Meat*, a title appropriating Burke's reference to the "swinish multitudes" in *Reflections on the Revolution in France*. ("Pelf" is a cant word meaning "spoils" or "booty," which gives us the verb "to pilfer.") The appearance of cant in some of these poems can be explained by the class origin of many of the participants at these meetings: "bakers' boys, mechanics and artisans, the backbone of London's drunken free-and-easies, cider cellars, cock and hen clubs, and blackguard taverns. . . . many of whom also exercised their literary bent by composing tracts, elegies, odes and songs."[52] These comments point to the influence of the militant drinking songs of the canting crew (which often abuse the authorities) on the writing of poetry in freethinking circles and clubs.

Shoemaker-Poets

The laboring poor and indigent classes appropriated and revised the critical philosophy of the Enlightenment in myriad ways. In France, where

50. Porter's ballad appears, according to McCalman, in a paper appended to an 1807 account of Spence's trial. McCalman, *Radical Underworld*, 47.

51. The 1811 edition of *Spence's Songs* includes several examples of Evans's poetry. McCalman describes Evans as "a restless, marginal artisan, an incorrigible revolutionary, a tavern *bon vivant* and balladeer, a radical blackmailer and a smut-pedlar." McCalman, *Radical Underworld*, 47, 49. Quite a résumé.

52. McCalman, *Radical Underworld*, 83. Worrall indicates that "bakers' boys," along with shoemakers, were among the most radicalized tradesmen in London. One government spy wrote in 1819 that many bakers were prepared, in a call to arms, to convert their underground ovens into weapons—into improvised bombs that could ignite the underground gas lines of London: "their [*sic*] is a Great number of Bakers Ovens that runs under the street which can be easy Blown up, and best of all the

this volatile amalgam of social and "philosophical" elements first began to coalesce prior to 1789, the descent of rationalism from the salon to the street, from Voltaire to Marat, provided the most immediate intellectual framework for the Jacobin revolution. The figure of the *philosophe,* the Enlightenment intellectual, gave birth to "the Rousseau of the gutter" (*le Rousseau du ruisseau*): "the revolutionary spirit passed to the lean and hungry men of Grub Street, to the cultural pariahs who, through poverty and humiliation, produced the Jacobin version of Rousseauism."[53] In this context, the word "philosophical" (or *philosophique*) could be applied to a work of scholarship but also to a pornographic novel, a scatological ballad, or a seditious political tract.[54]

A similar phenomenon, with a more pronounced literary orientation, developed in the tavern political underworld of London: "The legendary eighteenth-century Grub Street milieux of London and Paris had been partly created by influxes of educated provincial artisans who burned to become *philosophes.* By the early nineteenth century the trend was being facilitated by the rapid increase in elementary popular literacy and the rising status of the professional man of letters, particularly the young Romantic poet-philosopher made fashionable by Byron, Shelley, and Keats."[55] The vocation of the infidel poet-philosopher found its most eccentric and forceful initiates, according to McCalman, at the lowest levels of society: "workers from what were seen as 'contemptible' trades such as shoemaking and tailoring frequently manifested disgust at the poor and demeaning nature of their trades by involving themselves in literary and intellectual activities."[56] Hence, the "embattled and traditionally militant trade" of shoemakers supplied to the radical underground a remarkable number of its leading activists and poets, including Robert Fair, the mulatto William "Black" Davidson (who became the leader of the New Union of Shoemakers in 1819), activist and organizer Thomas Preston, author Allen Davenport, and many others who eked out a living from their "dishonorable" trade.[57]

Bakers are almost to a Man Radicals and Spenceans. London stands upon nothing." Worrall, *Radical Culture,* 175.

53. Darnton, *Literary Underground of the Old Regime,* 40.

54. Darnton cites a letter of 1772 from a bookseller in Poitiers to his supplier in Switzerland, in which the phrase "philosophical books" (*livres philosophiques*) refers to a range of outlawed texts (hence the Swiss publishing house): "Here is a short list of philosophical books that I want. Please send the invoice in advance: *Venus in the Cloister or the Nun in a Nightgown, Christianity Unveiled, Memoir of Mme la Marquise de Pompadour, Inquiry on the Origin of Oriental Despotism, The System of Nature, Theresa the Philosopher, Margot the Campfollower.*" Darnton, *Literary Underground of the Old Regime,* 1–2.

55. McCalman, *Radical Underworld,* 156.

56. McCalman, *Radical Underworld,* 48.

57. In the history of the novel, the figure of the infidel shoemaker-philosopher is memorialized in the character of Doctor Manette in Dickens's novel *A Tale of Two Cities.*

From his shoemaking shop on Edgware Road in London, Davenport rose to become a wide-ranging author and activist: "Davenport's testimony forms one of the most complete records of how an artisan entered and acquired his contemporary symbolic culture of literacy, literary aspiration, and ultra-radical politics."[58] Davenport's autobiography, *The Life and Literary Pursuits of Allen Davenport,* remains a seminal account of "the obscure tavern world of London radical culture."[59] In addition, Davenport's most successful poem, *The Kings, or Legitimacy Unmasked,* was printed on the Oxford Street press of the Spencean activist Samuel Waddington—a milieu, Davenport complained, where "instead of the errors of the author being corrected, in passing through the press, they were doubled by typographical errors and blunders."[60] A spy purchased a copy of Davenport's poem at Robert Wedderburn's dissenting "chapel" and sent it to the Home Office—the sole surviving copy of Davenport's pamphlet.[61]

Some of Davenport's poems betray his advocacy of physical force, as do, more provocatively, the goading—and sometimes philosophical—poems of the ultraradical E. J. Blandsford. A musician and a barber, Blandsford published poems regularly in Thomas Davison's pro-Spencean journal, *Medusa: or, Penny Politician* (masthead motto: "Let's Die like Men, and not be Sold as Slaves").[62] The physical-force sympathies of *Medusa* provided a ready outlet for Blandsford's "chauvinist taunting" (of his comrades in arms):

I dreamed a real dream awake
And told those sleepers what to do!
But they, too DULL to understand
Or else their *nerves* too *weak* and *loose,*
Are with the weapon in hand
Too COWARDLY to try its use.[63]

In addition to exasperated polemic, Blandsford, along with Davenport and Robert Wedderburn, played a critical role in developing the Spen-

58. Worrall, *Radical Culture,* 83. On Davenport's formation, Worrall comments: "By comparison, Davenport's contemporary, the field-labourer poet John Clare in the village of Helpston, Northamptonshire, was much more advantaged in educational opportunities. It took initiative, independence, labour and careful planning to learn to read and write. The result, in adulthood, was that Davenport 'could not shake off the ruling passion' of poetry" (81).

59. Worrall, *Radical Culture,* 83. See Allen Davenport, *The Life and Literary Pursuits of Allen Davenport* (London: G. Hancock, 1845).

60. Davenport cited in Worrall, *Radical Culture,* 83.

61. Davenport's *The Kings* was reprinted in his poetry collection of 1827, *The Muses' Wreath.*

62. Cited in Worrall, *Radical Culture,* 151.

63. Blandsford, "AN EX POST FACTO HINT" (referring to the title of his earlier poem "A Real Dream"), cited in Worrall, *Radical Culture,* 158.

cean equation of the radicalized laborer and the surplus of *nature*. On this point, Worrall explains that, "enigmatically, the battle-cry of revolution is the battle-cry of 'Nature.' Those who read only a Romanticist metaphysic of 'Nature' would miss the call to the populace to arm."[64]

These autodidact literati aspired to become not only artisan-*philosophes* and poets but radical pressman as well. They saw the burgeoning medium of print as a revolutionary tool—the technical counterpart of their infidel "philosophies" and poetic vocation. Though too poor to own presses or cover costs of printing, they sought out patrons with radical sympathies to underwrite the production of "poetry as cannon shot," to fund printing of radical materials: song sheets, broadsides, chapbooks. In addition, these artisan-*philosophes* produced, and often wrote, the first generation of underground journals and newspapers, including Thomas Spence's *Pig's Meat,* Robert Wedderburn's ephemeral *Forlorn Hope* and *Axe Laid to the Root* (1817), Thomas Davison's *Medusa,* James Griffins's *Cap of Liberty,* and Jonathan Wooler's *Black Dwarf* (1817–1824).[65]

Among the unlawful materials issuing from underground printshops were pirate editions of libertine texts. Such items circulating in the underground book trade of London in the first quarter of the nineteenth century included *Les nuits de Paris* (originally published 1788–1794, in sixteen volumes) and *Nocturnal Revels* (1779), set in London, both works by the French novelist and reformer Restif de la Bretonne; as well as *The Voluptuous Night: or, Ne Plus Ultra of Pleasure* (1777) by Baron Vivant. As these titles indicate, the earliest libertine (and sometimes pornographic) novels laid the foundation for what might be called a *literature of nightlife,* a narrative subgenre that would be sustained in works such as Eugène Sue's *Les mystères de Paris* (1843), which contributed to the modernity of Baudelaire's "poetry of apachedom" and, later, to Georges Bataille's often-obscene variant of Surrealism. Playing off the documentary aspect of the first generation of libertine novels (which might be described as the writing of spies), the forger/radical pressman William Dugdale published *Yokel's Preceptor* in the 1820s, "an underworld directory of smut shops, brothels, thieves' dens and gambling hells."[66] The full title of this work,

64. Worrall, *Radical Culture,* 153–154.

65. Wooler's *Black Dwarf* offers a tantalizing example of the material continuity, both practical and symbolic, of these Antinomian projects: Malcolm McClaren, the manager of the seminal punk band the Sex Pistols, claims to have in his possession a complete set of all the issues of *Black Dwarf,* passed down from generation to generation in his family. (This anecdote appears in an unpublished essay by Peter Wollen on the history of Situationism.)

66. McCalman, *Radical Underworld,* 218. Dugdale's scurrilous pamphlet probably follows the example of various guides to nightlife in London in the 1780s, such as *Harris' List of Covent Garden Ladies,*

which claims to reveal the secret life of London's "flash cribs," evokes the world of the canting crew.[67]

Although the incentive to publish obscene materials became increasingly mercenary during the 1820s—the infidel press was, in fact, the birthplace of the modern porn industry—the original impetus can be traced to the entanglement of Enlightenment rationalism and libertine philosophy, which called for a revolt against orthodox customs and morals. Thus, McCalman observes: "The body of Enlightenment ideas which spread to English artisan and lower middle-class circles in the latter part of the eighteenth century had always contained a libertinist or sexually libertarian aspect."[68] William Benbow, originally a shoemaker and ultraradical pressman, went on to become "the most prolific pornographer of the nineteenth century." The overlapping of political and sexual underworlds in Benbow's career was reflected in the heteroclite topos from which he ran his clandestine operation: a combination tavern-printshop, known as the "Byron's Head," in Leicester Square, the neighborhood where tradesmen in the smut industry were concentrated in London. Robert Southey, the British poet laureate (whose dramatic poem "Wat Tyler" shows sympathy for infidel causes), described Benbow's hybrid tavern-printshop as "one of those preparatory schools for the brothel and the gallows; where obscenity, sedition and blasphemy are retailed in drams for the vulgar."[69] As an emblem of the Romantic topology of nightlife, the Byron's Head adopted the name of a poet associated with revolutionary libertinism; yet the tavern also harbored the technical means to produce pirate editions of *Cain* and sections of *Don Juan,* thereby becoming a secret source of poetic populism. At the same time, the topos of the nightspot became a place where the politics of pleasure, radical dissent, and infidel culture intersected.

Among those active in the overlapping political and sexual underworlds of London in the first few decades of the nineteenth century was

an annual directory of prostitutes, with "a compendium of offerings, prices, and lyrical descriptions of anatomical precision." Cited in Palmer, *Cultures of Darkness,* 75.

67. The full title of Dugdale's pamphlet, published under the pseudonym H. Smith, is *Yokel's Preceptor: or More Sprees in London! Being a Regular and Curious Show-Up of All the Rigs and Doings of the Flash Cribs in this Great Metropolis* (n.d.).

68. McCalman, *Radical Underworld,* 208. The overlapping of political and sexual underworlds occurs most flamboyantly, according to McCalman, in the career of the Antinomian Methodist preacher John Church (an orphaned ex-ornament maker): "Church was accused in 1813 of preaching Antinomian libertinism of Commonwealth days in his Obelisk Chapel at St. George's Fields, and of putting his theology into practice by seducing young men and performing mock-marriage ceremonies amongst the transvestites at the Vere Street homosexual brothel" (59).

69. Robert Southey cited in McCalman, *Radical Underworld,* 205.

an illiterate mulatto seaman and Antinomian preacher named Robert Wedderburn. An obscure figure whose career integrated many of the disparate strands of the ultraradical underground, Wedderburn (a native of Jamaica and the son of a Scottish plantation owner and an African-born slave) first arrived in London in 1778 at the age of seventeen as a sailor in the British navy (a vocation historically predisposed, as a result of conscription, to political radicalism). Once in London, "like many discharged sailors, he drifted to the rookeries around St. Giles where a substantial community of his countrymen, including runaway slaves, congregated alongside other immigrant minorities, Jews, Lascars, and Irish. Here, he likely became part of a subculture of London 'blackbirds,' as they were known, who eked out a living by their own wit, strength, agility, and cunning—as musicians, entertainers, beggars, thieves, and labourers."[70] From this heterogeneous subculture, which sheds important light on the alien and racial components contributing to the radical/infidel community, Wedderburn first entered the netherworld of Jacobin sympathizers in the 1790s as a licensed and militant Methodist preacher: he established his own dissenting "chapel" in two back rooms of "a ruinous hay loft in Soho"—a millenarian revision of the topos of the nightspot.[71]

In his thrice-weekly sermons or lectures, "Wedderburn's emphasis on prophecy and dreams, talismanic attitude to the scriptures, and love of communal hymn-singing were typically West Indian." Thus, the manner in which Wedderburn combined the Methodist hymnody with radical politics and his lifelong fascination with magic and the supernatural contributed unique elements to Antinomian discourse in the early nineteenth century. In addition, Wedderburn's speeches were said to be "fraught with the beauties of Billingsgate slang"—an echo of the verbal demimonde in which he carried out his work.[72]

From his origins as "a dissident minister of enthusiastic disposition," Wedderburn went on to practice a secular doctrine of rationalism and libertinism, became a passionate advocate of the underground press, and emerged as "a ferocious infidel who quickly earned the nickname of 'the Devil's Engineer.'"[73] Wedderburn's libertine rationalism included working as an agent peddling obscene materials for the same printers who

70. McCalman, *Radical Underworld,* 54.

71. These biographical details about Wedderburn derive from McCalman's account of his career. McCalman, *Radical Underworld,* 132.

72. McCalman, *Radical Underworld,* 56, 137.

73. McCalman, *Radical Underworld,* 50.

published his seditious pamphlets, as well as several arrests for keeping a brothel.[74] Sharing in the public notoriety of persecution and illegality provided grounds, aside from common ideological goals, for libertinist and infidel writers to make the argument that blasphemy, obscenity, and political sedition were elements of a common cause.

Fairies and Infidels

The "cockney poets" of high Romanticism, Blake and Keats, sometimes found themselves caught up in these notorious circles. Following a bizarre incident with a soldier at his home in Felpham, Blake was indicted for sedition in 1803—a political crime with potentially grave consequences. He was, however, acquitted in 1804. Though the charges associated with this incident may have been largely fabricated, Blake's poetic language during this period ("I heard the Voice of Albion starting from his sleep") echoes, according to Worrall, the call to arms during the London Bread Riots of 1800.[75]

John Keats, as well, could be glimpsed on the periphery of ultraradical events: he was among the thousands, he records in a letter, witnessing the procession bringing Henry "Orator" Hunt into London to face trial for high treason in 1819.[76] Keats's sympathies were reciprocated, apparently, by ultraradical society: the *Endymion*'s "Hymn to Pan," which Wordsworth called "a very pretty piece of Paganism," represented "an infidelity in vogue in ultra-radical circles as much as with Keats's acquaintances."[77] Furthermore, according to Worrall, "Keats's 'To Autumn' is an apotheosis of contemporary Spencean articles of faith about natural English abundance and fertility, ideas circulated in postwar 'free-and-easies' and in the 1819 poems of E. J. Blandsford."[78]

Poetry of the dominant literary tradition was drawn into the ultraradical underworld as well by the extensive pirating of works by writers such as Southey, Byron, and Shelley, whose poems were seen as illustrating or otherwise advancing radical causes. The eroticism and anticlericalism of

74. McCalman notes the criminal aspects of Wedderburn's career. McCalman, *Radical Underworld,* 44, 205.

75. Worrall, *Radical Culture,* 67–68, 45–46.

76. Worrall, *Radical Culture,* 201.

77. Worrall, *Radical Culture,* 202. See also the biography in verse of Keats by the American poet Tom Clark, which includes several poems on Keats's familiarity with cant and infidel culture. Clark, *Junkets on a Sad Planet* (Santa Barbara, CA: Black Sparrow Press, 1994), 41.

78. Worrall, *Radical Culture,* 202.

Byron's *Don Juan,* for example, made it a favorite target of pirating by radical pressmen and pornographers such as William Benbow, whose underground printshop and tavern (Byron's Head) invoked Byron's revolutionary spirit (and his anatomy). Indeed, the practice of pirating itself raised broader issues of freedom of the press and could therefore be aligned with other subversive practices.

Some of Shelley's works, though perhaps less salable, were more overtly committed to radical causes. These writings from the earliest stage of Shelley's career reflect his reading (with Mary Shelley) of philosophical works associated with radicalism and his contact with certain figures in the infidel/radical underworld. McCalman writes that "snippets of information in the Home Office show that Shelley was implicated in clandestine radical and infidel activities during the years 1811–1815."[79] During this period, Shelley developed the peculiar habit—perhaps a measure of the extreme secrecy called for under the circumstances—of depositing his unsigned radical writings in bottles and setting them adrift (whole cartons of bottles, apparently) in the sea. Correspondence from an informant in August 1812 describes Shelley's suspicious behavior: "Mr. Shelley has been seen frequently to go out in a Boat a short distance from Land and drop some Bottles into the Sea, and that at one time he was observed to wade into the Water and drop a Bottle which afterwards drifting ashore was picked up, and on being broken was found to contain a seditious Paper."[80] The haphazard and anonymous means of Shelley's dissemination of radical materials calls to mind a nautical variation of the canting crew—or a naughty diversion for the yachting crowd—and a premonition of Shelley's death by drowning. In fact, the "seditious Paper" found in the bottle was a poem, "The Devil's Walk," a broadside based on a political ballad originally composed and published by Coleridge and Southey in the *Morning Chronicle* in 1799. In Shelley's version of the poem, England is envisioned as a farm owned and managed by the devil (a conceit familiar from the ultraradical discourse of Davenport and Blandsford).

Excerpts from Shelley's first major poem, "Queen Mab" (composed in 1812, the same year he bottled "The Devil's Walk"), appeared in the first issue (in 1815) of what would become the most influential journal of infidel thought and letters, the *Theological Inquirer*, edited by Joseph Cannon (Robert Wedderburn's principal sponsor and sometimes ghostwriter). Shelley's involvement in the ultraradical underground helps to

79. McCalman, *Radical Underworld,* 80.

80. Letter cited in Kenneth Neill Cameron, *The Young Shelley: Genesis of a Radical* (New York: Collier Books, 1962), 197.

explain why his poems, more than those by any other Romantic writer, made a direct impact on some of the artisan poets and thinkers in the world of infidel/radical letters. Excerpts from "Queen Mab" published in the *Theological Inquirer* were accompanied by commentary written by the shoemaker-poet Robert Fair. More significantly, Wedderburn adapted the title for his short-lived but influential journal *Axe Laid to the Root* (1817) from a phrase in "Queen Mab": "Let the axe / Strike at the root, the poison-tree will fall" (a passage alluding perhaps to Blake's poem "The Poison Tree").[81]

These all-but-invisible exchanges between Shelley, an aristocratic poet-philosopher associated with literary Romanticism, and Wedderburn, a mulatto, ultraradical propagandist and pornographer operating in the lower depths of infidel society, raise intriguing questions about the reciprocity of influence between these incommensurable worlds. Clearly, the radicalism of an aristocratic figure like Shelley would not have been possible without the revolutionary fervor, ingenuity, and industriousness of a figure like Wedderburn. The vehement tone of Shelley's politics was fortified no doubt by his exposure to the writing of ultraradicals in the pages of the *Theological Inquirer* (where Wedderburn published some of his work).[82] At the same time, the Romantic sensibility of a poem like "Queen Mab" (which first appeared in the *Theological Inquirer*) held special appeal for the infidel writer and activist. Commenting on the popularity of "Queen Mab" (and of C. F. Volney's *Ruins of Empires*) among readers of the *Theological Inquirer,* McCalman writes: "One of the reasons that *Ruins* and *Queen Mab* went on to become popular radical texts was their shared Romantic-Gothic sensibility."[83]

Confronted with the evidence of these nearly inscrutable transactions between the most elevated and the most volatile sensibilities of the Romantic era—transactions issuing from the anomalous topos of a printshop disguised as a tavern—one can hardly ignore the prospect of a sensibility that might be described as *working-class gothic,* a variation of the infidel sublime: a sensibility that converts the clandestine forces of insur-

81. Percy Bysshe Shelley, *The Poetical Works of Percy Bysshe Shelley,* ed. Edward Dowden (London: Macmillan, 1924), 14. The full title of Wedderburn's infidel journal was *The Axe Laid to the Root, Or, a Fatal Blow to the Oppressors, Being an Address to the Planters and Negroes of the Island of Jamaica.*

82. It is important not to exaggerate the extent of Shelley's direct contact with members of the radical underground or to endow him with liberal views he did not actually possess. Despite his radical sympathies, Shelley harbored—to an alarming and offensive degree—the prejudices of his class. For example, he referred to Joseph Cannon (who, like most members of the radical underworld, suffered the stigma of inferior social origins) as a "vile beast" and asserted that "it is disgusting to see such a person talk philosophy. Let refinement and benevolence convey these ideas." McCalman, *Radical Underworld,* 85.

83. McCalman, *Radical Underworld,* 81.

rection into delicate monsters (such as Mary Shelley's *Frankenstein*).[84] This evidence does not fully explain, however, why a "ferocious infidel" like Wedderburn would be attracted to the sensibility of a poem about the queen of the fairies, nor why he would name an organ of the "dangerous classes," *Axe Laid to the Root*, after a line in a poem suffused with language that is at once trifling and rhapsodic:

Her dewy eyes are closed,
And on their lids, whose texture fine
Scarce hides the dark blue orbs beneath,
The baby sleep is pillowed:
Her golden tresses shade
The bosom's stainless pride,
Curling like tendrils of the parasite
Around a marble column.[85]

Because "Queen Mab" circulated in the radical underworld in numerous pirated and adulterated editions, one must consider the possibility that it was not simply the radical politics but the precious and sometimes-lurid sensibility of Shelley's poem—a prototype of kitsch—that appealed to infidel tastes. Accordingly, one would want to emphasize the fact that the violent and didactic political vision of the poem, which consumes its lengthy middle section, issues from the mouth of a glittering fairy:

From her celestial car
The Fairy Queen descended,
And thrice she waved her wand
Circled with wreaths of amaranth:
Her thin and misty form
Moved with the morning air,
And the clean silver tones
As thus she spoke, were such
As are unheard by all but gifted ear. (3)

From the perspective of the infidel community, the "Fairy Queen" delivers her radical vision of world history ("a lesson not to be unlearned" and "a warning for the future") to those possessing a "gifted ear," to those

84. Bryan Palmer devotes a chapter, "Monsters of the Night," to the correlation between the threat of proletarian uprising and the creation of monsters in the gothic sensibility. Palmer, *Cultures of Darkness*, 116–136.

85. P. B. Shelley, "Queen Mab," in *Poetical Works of Percy Bysshe Shelley*, 3.

visionaries and initiates prepared to destroy the prevailing social and religious orders.

In Shelley's violent and "sparkly" poem, the see-through body of Queen Mab ("The broad and yellow moon / Shone dimly through her form") somehow spells an end to the sovereign who "smiles / At the deep curses which the destitute / Mutter in secret"—a figure targeted as well in "The Devil's Walk":

Fat as that Prince's maudlin brain,
Which, addled by some gilded toy,
Tired, gives his sweetmeet, and again
Cries for it, like a humoured boy.[86]

Queen Mab's appeal to the dangerous classes derives then not only from the poem's seditious "philosophy" but from its dialectical nature: the poem is at once a curse muttered in secret by the destitute and a "gilded toy" addling the "maudlin brain." This compound of base and epicurean elements recalls the dialectic of the "fancy" in the songs of the canting crew and the rogue's incubation of the dandy: the curious amalgam of the infidel sublime. The gilded and subversive toy—a delicate monster—of Shelley's poem sublimates the "ferocious" sensibility of the gothic infidel, a flowering of the enigma of sentimentality which remains, in its essence, a symptom of the topology of nightlife. More remotely, the gothic features of this tiny metropolitan underworld helped to shape the sensibilities of figures such as Thomas Wainewright, the nineteenth-century dandy, forger, and poisoner, as well as bohemian, middle-class literati like Wilde, Swinburne, and Beardsley.

Noctambulism

The hermeticism of the nightspot was first breached from within, I have argued, by inscription: by songs written in the jargon of thieves and by shorthand (the writing of spies). As such, public knowledge of the topology of underground nightlife was, from the start, intrinsically lyrical and unavoidably sentimental—because it was caught, unalterably, in the ambiguity of verbal reflection. Thus, insofar as the siren song of nightlife (a kind of beggar's chant) reached the ears of those outside the secret society of the demimonde, then the jargon of nightlife became increasingly

86. "The Devil's Walk," cited in Cameron, *Young Shelley,* 135.

audible—a demonstration of the enigma of sentimentality. Yet the scale and effect of this irremediable disclosure underwent a transformation, I have argued, when the topos of the nightspot incorporated the technical medium of print and when the substance of nightlife—its codes and desperate measures—became overtly politicized. At that point, the dissemination of the lyric substance of the demimonde began to occur on a massive scale, which marked the beginning of modern nightlife.

In 1814, a new technology appeared which dramatically altered and accelerated the reformation of nightlife already initiated by the revolutionary coupling of tavern life and print culture: the installation of the first gas lamps in the streets of London.[87] The use of gaslight in public places, which was widespread in Paris and London by the 1840s, expanded from street lamps to the illumination of shops and taverns. The spectacle of entire cities illuminated at night by artificial light drew crowds into the streets after dark, initiating what Walter Benjamin has called "the great era of *noctambulisme*."[88] Large numbers of people, dazzled by the effects of artificial light flooding the city at night, wandered the streets for hours—like zombies—penetrating for the first time the "dangerous quarters" of the city after dark. Contemporary descriptions frequently characterized the nocturnal spectacle in reference to some sense of *interiority:* one observer in 1854 described the scene as "always festively illuminated, golden cafés, a stylish and elegant throng, dandies, literati, financiers. The whole thing resembles a drawing room."[89] Another observer, in 1861, commented on the "glittering shops everywhere, splendid displays, cafés covered in gilt, and permanent lighting. . . . The shops put out so much light that one can read the paper as one strolls."[90] Interestingly, the aspects of interiority evoked in these passages (including the double retirement of reading) should not be associated necessarily with the space of the domestic interior, since gas lighting in domestic spaces lagged well behind its appearance in public places. In fact, interiority in this context has little to do, really, with the insides of buildings in any conventional sense. Rather, it is a new form of interiority—a form of inwardness, properly speaking—which combines a startling element of publicity with the sense of closure intrinsic to the topos of the nightspot. In the era of mod-

87. Schivelbusch, *Disenchanted Night,* 111.

88. Walter Benjamin, "The Paris of the Second Empire in Baudelaire," in *Charles Baudelaire: A Lyric Poet in the Era of High Capitalism,* by Walter Benjamin, trans. Harry Zohn (London: Verso Books, 1983), 50.

89. Emma von Niendorf cited in Schivelbusch, *Disenchanted Night,* 148–149.

90. Julien Lemer cited in Schivelbusch, *Disenchanted Night,* 152.

ern nightlife, the veil of secrecy and the aura of publicity are one and the same.

Though ostensibly unrelated to the philosophical and representational engines of the Enlightenment (libertine rationalism and the printing press) that were revising the topology of nightlife, the installation of streetlamps in fact hastened the social transactions precipitated by revolutionary means—that is, by forms of rationalization that were more overtly politicized than the ostensibly neutral medium of gaslight. For the increased public security afforded by streetlights made it possible for the middle and upper classes to safely visit the realms of the demimonde, to haunt the topology of the "dangerous classes": conditions advancing the development of a sociological sublime. The influx of so-called lawful society into the queer sites of the demimonde reversed, or reciprocated, the transfusions of social (and literary) capital from the underworld to society at large. Now, the topology of nightlife (the realm of infidel society) was breached not from within but from without.

Setting in motion these topographical exchanges, the sudden illumination of nightlife prompted as well certain temporal reconfigurations that were played out, like their spatial counterparts, in terms of class conflict: "Court society had underlined the distance separating it from the bourgeoisie by ostentatiously keeping late hours, day and night. Now the middle classes tried to distance themselves from the petty bourgeoisie and the artisan class in the same way. The later one began the day, the higher one's social rank. Consequently, everything began to happen later and later."[91] By producing an artificial regime of belatedness in public leisure, and by dispersing the literal darkness of quarters that had always harbored certain criminal elements of society, the industrialization of light (amounting, quite literally, to the industrialization of *Enlightenment*) advanced and elaborated, irresistibly, the rationalization of nightlife.[92]

It was no accident that the term "slang" (a cant word) came into general usage during the "era of *noctambulisme,*" as cant was evolving from a

91. Schivelbusch, *Disenchanted Night,* 140.

92. With the advance of lighting technology and the introduction of electric illumination in the 1880s, gaslight came to be viewed nostalgically by some observers, such as Robert Louis Stevenson, who described electric arc lighting as "a lamp for a nightmare! Such a light as this should shine only on murders and public crime, or along the corridors of lunatic asylums, a horror to heighten horror." R. L. Stevenson, "A Plea for Gas Lamps," in *The Biographical Edition of the Works of Robert Louis Stevenson* (New York: Charles Scribner, 1917), 13:168. Comments such as these make it clear that one should not think of artificial lighting as undifferentiated, either physically or ideologically. On the contrary, the material features of gaslight or electrical light would affect the topology of nightlife in diverse ways and therefore acquire distinctive ideological properties.

restricted verbal practice (the secret jargon of a closed community) into a more widespread phenomenon of illegitimate speech supplementing, and sometimes eroding, standard linguistic usage. Thus, the alien tongue of the underworld lost some of its insularity and obscurity—its queer identity—as the industrialization of light permitted the middle classes to penetrate (as pleasure-seekers) the secret topography of the demimonde.

The Nightspot and the New Chanson

The first truly modern nightclub, the Chat Noir, opened in Paris (in Montmartre) in 1881. The habitués of the club were known as *les apaches,* figures inspired by Baudelaire's "poetry of apachedom," of which examples (from *Spleen de Paris*) were recited, or set to music, at the Chat Noir.[93] Indeed, the literary inspirations for the Chat Noir encompassed its basic orientation and milieu: the club presented itself as a *cabaret artistique,* a new kind of public meeting place—at least in the initial stages of its operation—for writers and artists. The Chat Noir evolved from an earlier and more loosely structured group of poets and performers called the Club des Hydropathes, who met informally starting in 1878 at the Café de Rive-Gauche in the Latin Quarter.[94] Founded by Emile Goudeau, author of a book of poems entitled *Fleurs de bitumes* (Asphalt Flowers), the club became the focal point for a revival of antinomian spleen known as *fumisterie:* "a kind of disdain for everything, an inner spite against creatures and things, which translated itself on the outside by innumerable acts of aggression, farces, and practical jokes."[95]

At the core of the Hydropathe experiment was a group of poet-performers (or *chansonniers*) who gave new life to the traditional French *chanson*—a revival coinciding with the emergence of modern nightlife in the improvised space of cabaret.[96] Among the *chansonniers* of the Hydro-

93. Armond Fields, *Le Chat Noir: A Montmartre Cabaret and Its Artists in Turn-of-the-Century Paris* (Santa Barbara, CA: Santa Barbara Museum of Art, 1993), 15–16. For the broader context and insights into the European legacy of the Chat Noir, see Peter Jelavich, *Berlin Cabaret* (Cambridge, MA: Harvard University Press, 1993), 26–27, 45–46.

94. For a more detailed account of the origin of the Club des Hydropathes (and their peculiar name), see Harold B. Segel, *Turn-of-the-Century Cabaret* (New York: Columbia University Press, 1987), 5–7.

95. Emile Goudeau, *Ten Years of Bohemia,* cited in Jerrold Siegel, *Bohemian Paris* (Baltimore, MD: Johns Hopkins University Press, 1986), 221.

96. On the *chanson* in turn-of-the-century France, see Horace Valbel, *Les chansonniers et les cabarets artistiques* (Paris: E. Dentu, 1897); and Michel Herbert, *La chanson à Monmartre* (Paris: La Table Ronde, 1967).

pathes were Jean Richepin, Jules Jouy, Maurice Mac-Nab, and Charles Cros (close friend of Baudelaire and Verlaine, practitioner of marginal *métiers inconnus,* including the invention of a phonograph prior to Edison's version).[97] In the hands of these poets, the traditional *chanson,* a genre reaching back to the Middle Ages, incorporated elements of popular culture (from Mother Goose to scandal sheets to stereoscopes) in fin-de-siècle Paris, even as it betrayed an atavistic resemblance to the canting lyric. The new *chansonniers,* according to Harold Segel, "spurned a traditional repertoire in favor of songs of deep social concern, often antiauthoritarian and antibourgeois in character."[98] At the same time, the language of these poems is thick with Parisian *argot,* or slang, a residue of songs written in thieves' latin. Drinking songs, for example, were immensely popular—as might be expected in a tavern—as were militant variations of the beggar's chant.[99] Jean Richepin's most famous collection was entitled *La chanson des gueux* (The Beggars' Song), while Jean Jouy (whose dark songs of homelessness and vengeance are dedicated to Richepin) painted a more menacing portrait in "Le réveillon des gueux" (The Christmas Eve Revel of the Beggars):

We who are dying of hunger will rouse ourselves
Alongside a bright hearth, without a cent or a stitch,
We shall come one day to eat those chestnuts!
Yes, the vagabond without bread and without coats
Will come to destroy your Christmases and your gods![100]

The apocalyptic tone of this beggars' chant echoes (with the *digue digue digue* of bells in the song's refrain) the *fumisterie* of the canting crew.

In 1881, Rodolphe Salis (the future proprietor of the Chat Noir) approached Goudeau to establish a new home for the activities of the Hydropathes: a nightclub in Montmartre. Almost immediately, the new establishment, the Chat Noir, became what one critic called *une école chansonnière,* "a school for the new chanson," grafting the populist and anarchist sensibility of the Hydropathes—their *fumisterie*—on to the evolv-

97. On the technological premonitions of Charles Cros, see Charles Grivel, "The Phonograph's Horned Mouth," trans. Stephen Sartarelli, in *Wireless Imagination: Sound, Radio, and the Avant-Garde,* ed. Douglas Kahn and Gregory Whitehead (Cambridge, MA: MIT Press, 1992), 44.

98. Segel, *Turn-of-the-Century Cabaret,* 36.

99. Among the drinking songs performed by the Hydropathes, Segel cites Gaston Senéchal's "Chanson à boire" (Drinking Song) and Maurice Bouchor's "Beuverie flamande" (Flemish Drinking Party), among others. Segel, *Turn-of-the-Century Cabaret,* 11.

100. Segel, *Turn-of-the Century Cabaret,* 38–39.

ing topos of the *cabaret artistique*.[101] In essence, the Chat Noir staged in a deliberately flamboyant manner the integration of the artist (as a social outcast) into the gallery of criminals, revolutionaries, and libertines long associated with the underworld of taverns and secret clubs. Though criminal and political elements were peripheral to the operation of the Chat Noir (and though it was hardly a clandestine operation), the new topos of the nightspot cultivated an alluring, if deceptive, alliance between the "artist" and infidel society. The commercial and aesthetic appropriation of infidel culture thus became not only one of the distinguishing features of modern nightlife but a prototype for the evolving ideology of the avant-garde.

It is essential to bear in mind that the first modern nightclub, the *cabaret artistique,* was simultaneously the culmination of an evolving apparatus of sentimentality, which had been mapped on to the topology of nightlife during the nineteenth century, and an authentic locus of adversarial culture. Publicity became an integral part of the various registers of obscurity (literary, sociological, topographical, even architectural) associated with the modernism of nightlife. Almost as soon as the Chat Noir opened in 1881, Salis turned the club into a commercial venture, in part to advance the careers of writers and artists associated with the club. Following the precedent established by the ultraradical underworlds of Paris and London (though with entirely different objectives), the Chat Noir quickly exploited the medium of print to disseminate its brand of bohemianism and the ephemeral productions of its stable of artists and poets. Only a month after it opened, the club began publishing its own weekly journal (in tabloid format), with a print run that grew from 300 to 20,000 copies per week in seven years. A quarter of the four-page tabloid was given over (on its back page) to advertisements for local merchants and theaters, but also for the Eiffel Tower and various international expositions. Resembling a modern publishing enterprise, the stable of Chat Noir publications quickly grew to include the *Chat Noir guide* (a brochure for the club listing the artworks on view—for sale—at the club), the *Album du Chat Noir* (a portfolio of drawings to be sold by subscription), song sheets of lyrics recited or sung at the club, *Contes du Chat Noir* (stories and illustrations by club favorites), and theater programs for the famous shadow plays performed at the club.[102]

The success of the Chat Noir prompted it to move to three successively

101. The phrase "*école chansonnière*" is Maurice Donnay's, cited in Segel, *Turn-of-the-Century Cabaret,* 36.

102. Fields, *Chat Noir,* 23, 28.

larger venues in the course of its operation. Exploiting the new nocturnal mobility made possible by the installation of streetlamps, the publicity generated by the club's print apparatus drew large numbers of the bourgeoisie to its marginal location in Montmartre, to what was essentially a commodification of infidel society, a calculated spectacle of bohemianism. The practice of "slumming"—of middle-class city dwellers visiting self-consciously seedy clubs in marginal neighborhoods—became a powerful ingredient in the allure of modern nightlife, in advancing the modern culture of the sociological sublime. Walter Benjamin called his frequenting of clubs and cafés a "daily need" and "a vice"—perhaps acknowledging the false consciousness that had come to occupy the topology of nightlife.[103]

Tingeltangel

The appeal of a fraudulent underworld was especially strong in clubs that cultivated a deliberately coarse and promiscuous atmosphere. In Berlin, disreputable "joints" of this kind were known as *Tingeltangel* clubs—a nonsense word (similar to the American "honky-tonk") evoking lewd or rowdy behavior but also, perhaps, the sound of coins dropping into a collection plate passed around (along with dirty postcards for sale) between sets at a cabaret. The seedy atmosphere of the *Tingeltangel* club (including the latter two customs) is memorialized in the tavern scenes of Josef von Sternberg's film *The Blue Angel* (1931).[104] The tawdry club in the film, as well as Marlene Dietrich's performance as a smutty chanteuse, was modeled on historical *Tingeltangel* clubs such as the Hungry Pegasus (opened in Berlin in 1901), where one could see, for example, performances by a poet (under the pseudonym "Dolorosa") "who recited erotic and sadomasochistic verses" or by artists performing what reviewers invariably referred to as "niggersongs" (evidence of the contemporary infatuation with African American music).[105] With an audience, according to one observer, consisting of "artists and scholars, writers and financiers, ladies of the best society and piquant bohemiennes," the Hungry Pegasus was

103. Benjamin, "A Berlin Chronicle," 21.

104. Friedrich Hollaender, who wrote the songs performed by Marlene Dietrich in *The Blue Angel,* founded the Tingel-Tangel cabaret in Berlin in 1931 (shortly after the film opened). Joining the German expatriate community in Los Angeles after fleeing Germany in the mid-1930s, Hollaender, one of the most gifted of the Weimar cabaret artists, tried to revive the Tingel-Tangel club in a location on Santa Monica Boulevard (in Los Angeles), a venture that quickly failed. Jelavich, *Berlin Cabaret,* 2, 207, 258.

105. Jelavich, *Berlin Cabaret,* 86.

essentially "a place where middle-class citizens could observe, and even pretend to be, bohemians."[106]

Slumming—in many forms and permutations—in modern nightlife can be regarded as a ritualization of the enigma of sentimentality operating at the very core of the relation between nightlife and poetry. As the performative and emblematic properties of the word *Tingeltangel* suggest, the discourse of slumming in modern nightlife often has a verbal component. That is to say, in regard to the problematic of sentimentality, one may be lured back into an underworld that no longer possesses distinct physical limits by certain verbal resonances—by poetry. Evidence of the orphic (or perhaps Ariadnean) aspect of poetry's relation to modern nightlife can be detected in the configuration of the *speakeasy*—a secret club unlocked by a secret word. Yet evidence of the modern Opensesame! principle can also be found, more graphically, in clubs evoking elements of infidel society which had shunned the new publicity of the underworld.

These sorts of clubs, atavistic in nature, occupied an important niche (related to the *Tingeltangel*) in Berlin. Police records (we are once again back in the realm of spies and informants) monitored closely the performances of Hans Hyan, the owner of the Silver Punchbowl (which opened in Berlin in 1901)—not to mention the performances of "Dolorosa," who had taken her sadomasochistic act (including "The Song of Songs of Pain and Torture") to the Silver Punchbowl. In any case, Hyan, who had a rather-extensive criminal record (robbery, aggravated burglary), lured audiences with songs composed in the underworld jargon of Berlin: "he possessed an exceptional ability to imitate the speech of various social groups in Berlin, in particular the slang of the downtrodden and criminal classes. . . . at the moment [one reviewer wrote] there is probably no other author who has such a masterful command of the Berlin dialect and of the argot of the criminal underworld." Whether or not Hyan's renditions of Berliner canting speech were "imitations" or not, he certainly convinced the police of their authenticity: they shut down his club for good in 1904.[107] The very question of whether his canting songs were imitations or not underscores the problem of sentimentality in modern nightlife, though it does not detract from poetry's role in conveying the modes of obscurity (including the inauthentic) making up the partial world of the demimonde.

The new chanson of the demimonde found its most potent blend of obscurity and sentimentality (a condition pertinent to any dialect or

106. Jelavich, *Berlin Cabaret,* 87.
107. Jelavich, *Berlin Cabaret,* 89, 90.

slang "consumed" by literature) in the poetry and career of Aristide Bruant, whose club, the Mirliton (a term referring to doggerel verse or to a primitive flute), opened in 1885 in the original premises of the Chat Noir (after it had moved to a bigger location). Memorialized by painters and poets ranging from Toulouse-Lautrec (who created his first lithograph poster for Bruant) and Mallarmé (whose poem "Autour d'un Mirliton" confirms the club's notoriety), the Mirliton became the setting for Bruant's nightly impersonation of types from the Parisian underworld: "Instead of singing *about* the wretched and the criminal, Bruant assumed the personae of the whores, pimps, apaches, petty criminals, murderers, unemployed laborers, and other social outcasts who crowded the stark canvas of this other Paris."[108] As this description indicates, the subject matter of Bruant's lyrics was concerned less with the working class than with a social underworld, the milieu of the canting crew: "Bruant's usual subjects were not workers as such but the *miséreux,* the tattered, homeless, and degenerate who exploited each other, got in trouble with the police, and did not know where they would sleep the next night."[109]

A poem of Bruant's such as "Marche des dos" (March of the Pimps) draws back the curtain—for the bourgeois listener—on the unknown quarters of the "dangerous classes" of Paris: Batignolles, Villette, Belleville. In lines slashed or crumpled by elision ("L'soir, su' l' boul'vard, e j'la r'file"), Bruant strikes a defiant note familiar from the lyrics of the canting tradition:

Le riche a ses titres en caisse,
Nous avons nos valeurs en jupon,
Et malgré la hausse ou la baisse.
Chaque jour on touche un coupon.

[The rich keep their securities in vaults,
While we have our assets in petticoats,
And whether the market goes up or down
Each night you can touch the goods.][110]

The coherence of class identity—produced in part by the verbal effects of cant—reveals itself fully in the execution scene:

108. Segel, *Turn-of-the-Century Cabaret,* 56. Bruant's canting serenade did not, however, go as far as the Cabaret des Truands, where "customers were confronted by costumed bandits and criminals." Siegel, *Bohemian Paris,* 240.

109. Siegel, *Bohemian Paris,* 237.

110. Bruant cited in Segel, *Turn-of-the-Century Cabaret,* 60, 59.

Pourtant, les jours de guillotine,
Quand la loi raccourcit un marlou,
Nous allons lui chanter matine,
Pendant qu'on lui coup le cou.

[All the same, on guillotine days,
When the law is about to cut short a pimp,
We all sing matins for him
While they cut off his head.][111]

Depicting the final moment in which a pimp finds solidarity with his fellow crooks, these stanzas recall the prison scenes common to cant poetry. In addition, it becomes evident that the "matins" sung for the condemned pimp in Latin (a dead language) is actually the cant ballad "March of the Pimps."

Bruant, who was called "the modern François Villon" (the author, we should recall, of *Ballades en jargon*), drew audiences intrigued by his use of slang: "Bruant was as grim, caustic, and roughhewn as any singer of his time. But what he brought to his chansons that was different from those of his fellow *chansonniers* was an intimate knowledge of the mores and speech of petty criminals with whom so many of his songs deal, an even more striking realism of setting, character, and idiom."[112] Following the appearance of his first collection of poetry, *Dans la rue* (In the Street), whose chansons, including "March of the Pimps," were thick with slang, Bruant published a two-volume dictionary of Parisian argot.[113]

Smash Palace

Slumming, as the use of slang in Bruant's chansons reveals, can affect a pungent lyrical accent, yet these social migrations also leave legible traces in the architectural configuration of early modern nightclubs and in their interior design and furnishings, which played such an important role in establishing the atmosphere of a vanished underworld. One should therefore pay closer attention to the "interior design" of early modernism—including what appears to be a dangerous concoction of kitsch and

111. Bruant cited in Segel, *Turn-of-the-Century Cabaret*, 60.
112. Segal, *Turn-of-the-Century Cabaret*, 54.
113. Segel discusses Bruant's various publications in *Turn-of-the-Century Cabaret*, 54.

avant-garde props—especially in places, like nightclubs, that have been overlooked by architectural historians.

Seeking to establish the broadest possible perspective on such matters, historian Peter Jelavich develops an interesting argument concerning the formal correspondences between the eclecticism of cabaret and the modernist ideologies of collage or assemblage.[114] He calls cabaret a form of "metropolitan montage," though he misses a more seductive and philosophically informed genealogy of fragmentation: Weimar songwriter Friedrich Hollaender identified the "*aphoristic novel*" as "the secret of cabaret," alluding to Friedrich Schlegel's conception of the ideal—and therefore unattainable—form of poetic-philosophical discourse.[115] The link between cabaret and the Jena Circle is not as far-fetched as it might seem, since Nietzsche's critical philosophy was touted as one of the inspirations for the "literary vaudeville" of cabaret. The very first cabaret in Berlin, the Motley Theater (opened in 1901), had a bust of Nietzsche in its foyer and was often referred to as the *Überbrettl,* a neologism combining *Übermensch* and *Brettl* (stage boards).[116] In another example of cabaret's infatuation with Nietzsche, Mary Wigman (the pioneering Expressionist dancer) performed a dance piece to a recitation of Nietzsche's *Thus Spake Zarathustra* at the Dada Cabaret Voltaire in Zurich in 1917.[117]

Yoking together Nietzsche and vaudeville (or Expressionist dance) exemplifies the collision of high and low cultures in the experimental milieu of modern nightlife. The social bric-a-brac characteristic of the after-hours scene (a modern invention) insists on reproducing itself as well in the layout and furnishings of the modern nightclub. In terms of interior design, slumming does not preclude the importation of certain luxuries into the typically degraded environment of the tavern. Luxury in this context expropriates the category of portable or nomadic furnishings—regardless of stylistic gravities. Space in the Chat Noir (which had three floors, like many of today's more luxurious clubs) unfolded with a kind of institutional eccentricity: a tavern-like space on the ground floor; a theater for the famous shadow plays on the second floor; and

114. Jelavich, *Berlin Cabaret,* 19.

115. Friedrich Hollaender, "Cabaret" (1932), in *The Weimar Republic Sourcebook,* ed. Anton Kaes, Martin Jay, and Edward Dimendberg (Berkeley and Los Angeles: University of California Press, 1994), 566. Friedrich Schlegel's theory of "fragments," which led to the aphoristic composition of his novel *Lucinda* (1799), is developed in the *Athenaeum Fragments* (1798). The most concise statement of his doctrine of poetry, fragmentation, and the novel (*Roman/romantisch*) appears in the famous Athenaeum fragment 116. *Friedrich Schlegel's "Lucinde" and the Fragments,* ed. Peter Firchow (Minneapolis: University of Minnesota Press, 1971), 175–176.

116. Jelavich, *Berlin Cabaret,* 29.

117. Susan Manning, *Ecstasy and the Demon: Feminism and Nationalism in the Dances of Mary Wigman* (Berkeley and Los Angeles: University of California Press, 1994), 68–69.

"L'institut" (or VIP room) on the third floor, where the Chat Noir regulars planned the night's activities and prepared materials for the cabaret's journal.[118] A stricter segregation of vulgar and ethereal environments could be found at other clubs, such as the Café Guerbois, which had "two rooms: a white and gold outside room, described as a terrace, and an inside room, described as a 'crypt,' with a low ceiling."[119] The designation of the "white and gold outside room," which recalls references to "golden cafés" and "cafés covered with gilt" in the first, infatuated decades of gaslight, records for posterity the newly sublimated substance of nightlife.

Though it would be tempting to pursue the architectural figures of the "crypt" and the "gold room" into a full-blown differentiation between high life and low life in nocturnal culture—as does later occur in modern nightlife—and to discover (in the age of cinema) the luminous half-life of the nightspot glittering in the shadows of film noir, I want to linger a bit longer over the interior-decorating skills of the incipient avant-garde. Who would have guessed that their taste in wall coverings, light fixtures, and linens could tell us something about the underside of modernism? The ground-floor interior of the Chat Noir eddied about a large-scale painting entitled *Parce Domine* (God Have Mercy), produced expressly for the club by Adolphe Willette in 1885. It depicted a crowd scene in Montmartre resembling James Ensor's masterpiece *Christ's Entry into Brussels in 1889.* According to Emile Goudeau, Willette's painting represented "the life, gay and murderous at the same time, of the poetic troubadours and eccentrics" who formed the club's nucleus.[120]

Armond Fields offers a more detailed description of the "metropolitan montage" of the Chat Noir:

> The interior of the Chat Noir was decorated seemingly at random. In reality, the cabaret's environment had been carefully planned by Salis and his colleagues. It featured furniture and artifacts of the Louis XIII period but in such humorously grotesque settings as to make them incongruous. Walls were covered with green wallpaper or green drapes. Paneling was made with glazed doors of Louis XIII design. On all available wall space were hung paintings, drawings, and prints created by the cabaret's resident artists. Crowds of pots, plates, medieval armor, and other assorted bric–a-brac hung from the ceiling or were stacked on any available flat surface.[121]

118. Fields, *Chat Noir*, 18–19.
119. Fields, *Chat Noir*, 9.
120. Goudeau cited in Siegel, *Bohemian Paris*, 231.
121. Fields, *Chat Noir*, 12.

The rooms were lit—or half-lit—anachronistically, it should be noted, with candelabra and wrought-iron chandeliers casting shadows on fashionable Japanese screens. Aside from the new practice of "resident artists" decorating the club, one notes in the overall design a horror of empty space and surfaces, a superabundance of what Walter Benjamin would call the "trash of history" (from which one composes "dialectical images"), and the heavily ironized condition of certain pieces such as the Second Empire furnishings competing for space with the "resident" art. All in all, the haphazardness of object relations in the first modern nightclub appears to have been fueled by a kind of sadism. And one should not overlook the fact that the green drapes (resembling, perhaps, the green billiard-cloth trousers favored by bohemian dandies of the period) were hung to cover the rough limestone walls of a former post office.[122]

Shades of the Avant-Garde

Just as the first period of the Chat Noir (before it moved to larger quarters) was closely associated with the new chanson of the demimonde, so the second period (after 1885) became known for its elaborate presentations of shadow plays (known in French as *ombres chinoises*)—spectacular forms influenced by the shadow theaters of the Swiss pastor Johann Kaspar Lavater (1741–1801) and the Frenchman François-Dominique Séraphin (1747–1800).[123] Although canting lyrics and shadow plays may, from a formal perspective, seem to have little to do with one another, Segel's understanding of the shadow plays suggests a common impetus for the revival of the two forms at the Chat Noir: "The renewed interest in shadow shows during the fin-de-siecle can be best understood if seen within the context of the enthusiasm of the avant-garde for minor, or marginal, theatrical forms. Among these were puppet and marionette plays, pantomime, and the shadow show"—a vogue that would explain, for example, Mallarmé's fascination with mime.[124] In relation to the avant-garde's taste for the vernacular, one might describe both the canting lyric and the shadow show, quite literally, as *spectacles of obscurity*. As such, the production, material context, and reception of the shadow theater help to model the *sentimen-*

122. Fields, *Chat Noir*, 12.

123. On the history of the shadow theater in France, see Denis Bordat and Francis Boucrot, *Les théâtres d'ombres: Histoire et techniques* (Paris: L'Arche, 1956).

124. Segel, *Turn-of-the-Century Cabaret*, 66–67.

tality of the new canting lyric, as well as the role of sentimentality in the formation of an incipient avant-garde.

The shadow plays at the Chat Noir, which involved music, spoken word, and even commentary (usually by Rodolphe Salis), grew out of puppet shows staged at the earlier venue of the club. *Tableaux* and "mystery plays" by numerous artists—many of which contained a significant element of religious kitsch—were produced between 1885 and 1895, but the overall look and technical innovations associated with the shadow theater of the Chat Noir developed under the influence of the painter Henri Rivière. His first production was a silhouette performance of Jules Jouy's canting lyric "Sergots" (Cops), a mingling of underworld jargon and shadow theater which Rivière continued to elaborate throughout his career, at least visually, in his stage settings.

The most noteworthy innovations and special effects in Rivière's shadow productions occurred in the visual rendering of *crowds*—a commitment to mass culture (and to representation of the masses) which sustained an expressive relation with the "lower depths" of the new chanson (and, more directly, to the bohemian crowds depicted in Willette's painting *Parce Domine*). "Rivière," Segel explains, "discovered that he could achieve more dynamic effects, especially with crowd scenes, not by following the old practice of moving his figures along the base of the screen one at a time, but by attaching the figures to each other so that a large number of them could be paraded across the screen in a broad band."[125] Significantly, the kinds of crowds which became visible in Rivière's spectacles betrayed a fundamental correspondence to the demimonde of the new chanson. The critic Jules Lemaitre described a sequence of "hosts" animating Rivière's "mystery play" *The Procession to the Star:* "It was as if a painting by Millet were moving by. Afterward, the army of the wretched, of lepers, and of cripples, their incomplete silhouettes, bizarre and tormented, standing out against the clear sky, their bodies deformed, their outlines sharp, the intersection of their crutches and the jagged edges of their tatters. Later on, a crowd of slaves appears dragging their worn chains behind them."[126] The religious kitsch depicting Christ's nativity in this shadow play contains, one could argue, a deeper social concern that one associates more commonly with the canting songs performed at the Chat Noir.

By displacing and incorporating the vogue for the new chanson of the Parisian underworld, the shadow plays revised the enigma of senti-

125. Segel, *Turn-of-the-Century Cabaret,* 68.
126. Lemaitre cited in Segel, *Turn-of-the-Century Cabaret,* 73.

mentality associated with these lyrics. As the most popular and widely celebrated production of the incipient avant-garde (one of the Chat Noir shadow plays was staged at the Chicago World's Fair Exposition in 1893), an anachronistic medium (a toy medium) became a platform for technical innovations that replicated the effects of early cinema and for collaborations leaving significant traces in all of the arts. The young Erik Satie, for example, worked as a pianist accompanying the shadow plays, including Amédée Vignola's *The Sphinx* (which portrayed the dreams of the Sphinx, from antiquity to Napoleon's Egyptian campaign). When Satie published his first musical composition, *Ogives*, in 1889, he advertised it in the Chat Noir magazine and described the composer (himself) as a "sphinx-man."[127] Indeed, the spare, ambient quality of Satie's earliest compositions (the *Gymnopédies*, most notably) may owe something to the musical requirements of his work as an accompanist at the Chat Noir. Satie's modernist compositions took root in the orientalist kitsch of productions such as Vignola's *Sphinx,* just as Rivière's toy medium gave rise to images of crowds and collective experience (a development that calls to mind Walter Benjamin's thesis about the role of aerial photography in modern consciousness).[128]

The critic Jules Lemaitre viewed the shadow theater's formulation of sentimentality as a fusion of kitsch and philosophy. Reviewing the spectacles of Rivière and Caran d'Ache, he writes: "They have made of the 'Chinese shadows' the generalizing and philosophical art par excellence. . . . The shadows of Rivière or Caran d'Ache are truly the shadows of Plato's cave. That is because the outlines and appearances of things are the things themselves. All reality is nothing but a reflection."[129] Lemaitre wants to assimilate the trifling figures of the *ombres chinoises* to the fashionable and provocative phenomenalism of Nietzsche and Ernst Mach—a move that invites us to understand the new canting lyrics of modern nightlife as mere shadows or reflections, as examples of kitsch, impersonation, forgery. A surprising way—if these are indeed the productions of an incipient avant-garde—to start a revolution!

The popularity of the Chat Noir in Paris turned into a kind of franchise operation, with imitations of the club, sometimes including the name itself, sprouting across Europe for more than a decade after the demise of the Parisian club in 1897. Norway, for example, opened its Chat Noir in Kristiania before London christened its own version of the club

127. Segal, *Turn-of-The-Century Cabaret,* 79, 161.

128. Walter Benjamin, "The Work of Art in the Age of Mechanical Reproducibility," in *Illuminations,* by Walter Benjamin, trans. Harry Zohn (New York: Schocken, 1969).

129. Lemaitre cited in Segel, *Turn-of-the-Century Cabaret,* 71.

in 1912, the Cave of the Golden Calf (named after one of the rooms in the Parisian Chat Noir).[130] Founded by Frida Strindberg (the former wife of the playwright August Strindberg), the Cave of the Golden Calf served as the after-hours headquarters for what would become London's first avant-garde movement, Vorticism, which offered a new and more militant platform for the Imagist group of poets (the first organized expression of Anglo-American poetic modernism). Thus, one could plausibly argue that the avant-garde in London (in the form of the Vorticist movement) was housed in a nightclub. In addition, the Cave of the Golden Calf (which was founded the same year as the Imagist movement in poetry) furnished a dialectical space—its secrecy was a form of publicity—for the first attempts at modernist experimentation in poetry. Thus, the evolving topology of nightlife was providing, as it had so often in the past, a clandestine space (now dialectically publicized) for illegitimate or provocative forms of lyric expression and for social and cultural experimentation. Orpheus was once again revisiting and making songs about (and thereby making public) a floating "party" in the underworld.

But what kind of underworld was this space, defined by its late hours and by its belatedness, in London in 1912? What can we learn about the infidel aesthetic of Vorticism by examining the interior design of this improvised club (it stayed open only eighteen months) housed in a large basement below a warehouse off Regent Street? Strindberg complained: "It was naked and cold with no tables or chairs, with mortar and limestone dust everywhere. It looked like a construction site or a ruin"—a look still in vogue to this day in the design of contemporary nightclubs.[131] To decorate the place and provide entertainment, Strindberg gathered around her a stable of "resident" artists and writers, including Wyndham Lewis, Jacob Epstein, and Ezra Pound; Pound remembered the Cave of the Golden Calf as "the only night club (one of the first in London) which impoverished artists cd/get into."[132] The "Preliminary Prospectus" for the club (illustrated with woodcuts by Wyndham Lewis) claimed the cabaret would "do away with the necessity of crossing the channel to laugh freely and sit up after nursery hours"—an allusion to the success of the

130. Reference to a stained-glass window in the Chat Noir depicting the biblical narrative of the Golden Calf can be found in Fields, *Chat Noir,* 18. The relation between the Chat Noir and the Cave of the Golden Calf receives attention in Monica Strauss, *Cruel Banquet: The Life and Loves of Frida Strindberg* (New York: Harcourt, 2000), 178. Much of the information I present in this chapter concerning the Cave of the Golden Calf derives from Strauss's biography of Strindberg.

131. Strauss, *Cruel Banquet,* 179.

132. Ezra Pound, letter to Eustace Mullins, 6 April 1959, in Eustace Mullins, *This Difficult Individual Ezra Pound* (New York: Fleet, 1961), 99.

Chat Noir in Paris.[133] In addition, the Cave of the Golden Calf opened only three months after F. T. Marinetti's first visit to London, which gave added impetus (and a Futurist slant) to Strindberg's plans for the club.

The presentation of the Cave of the Golden Calf included a full range of printed ephemera: from the "Preliminary Prospectus" to programs, announcements, and menus—all designed in the latest Cubist/Expressionist style by Wyndham Lewis (who also created murals for the walls). The sculptor Jacob Epstein transformed "the cellar's structural columns into the painted plaster totem poles described by Ford Madox Ford in his novel *The Marsden Case* as 'white caryatids with heads of hawks, cats, and camels picked out in red.'" Opening night saw performances of shadow plays by Wyndham Lewis, an actor reciting Oscar Wilde's fairy tale for adults, "The Happy Prince," and "a young man with a cockney accent" abusing the audience—in true cabaret fashion. Sir Osbert Sitwell remembered "a super-heated garden of gesticulating figures, dancing and talking, while the rhythm of the primitive forms of Ragtime throbbed through the great room."[134]

The club was known, according to the "Prospectus," to offer an "artist's meal" and reduced admission to "the youngest and best of our contemporaries and Futurists."[135] (Yet one could also order cold lobster salad—a dish for nonartists, perhaps—at the first modern nightclub in London.) As a kind of soup kitchen (and showcase) for the avant-garde, the Cave of the Golden Calf presented an amalgam of dated Symbolist cartoons and cutting-edge material associated with various infidel causes—not to mention the fact that, according to Pound, the club "was probably an outpost for espionage"—good for public relations![136]

In the end, the Cave of the Golden Calf offered a distinctive example of the "metropolitan montage" of modern nightlife, possessing qualities which Ford Madox Ford captured superbly in an apology for Strindberg's ephemeral project: "Poor Madame S.—try to bear with her. She is trying to build up a Palace of all the Arts with three oyster shells and stale patchouli and sawdust and crème, the buttons off waiter's waistcoats, champaign corks and vers libre—which is what—including typewriters which go wrong and produce palimpsests—we are all of us trying to do in one field or the other."[137] The performative and aesthetic "palimpsest" described

133. Strauss, *Cruel Banquet,* 175.
134. Strauss, *Cruel Banquet,* 177–178, 179, 180.
135. Strauss, *Cruel Banquet,* 175, 179.
136. Pound cited in Mullins, *This Difficult Individual,* 99.
137. Ford cited in Strauss, *Cruel Banquet,* 182.

here by Ford captures the basic sociology of nocturnal culture: transient (and transitive) exchanges between disparate classes, races, genders, and sexualities. In this regard, I have emphasized nightlife's effect on the erosion of class identities and the practice of slumming: the descent of the middle classes—for purposes of recreation—into the milieu of a criminal and indigent underworld (a milieu appropriated and aestheticized by various artistic movements). Unlike the rationale for the hermetic sites of the criminal or political underworlds, the verbal, cultural, and topographical transgressions associated with class difference promised a night of "fancy milling" in a secret place (one of the invariable features of nightlife): the prospect of mixing with people—with *strangers*—of different persuasions.

My emphasis on class has come, unfortunately, at the expense of discussion about certain kinds of contact between races, or among individuals of various sexual persuasions, which could occur only in the clandestine and socially unrestricted milieu of the nightclub. I have neglected, for example, the history of "black and tan" clubs (places where blacks and whites could mingle freely), not to mention the "white pilgrims" of the Harlem Renaissance—phenomena that would reveal an important racial dimension to the topology of nightlife.[138] In addition, I have not been able to attend carefully to what may be the most distinctive social feature of modern nightlife: the opportunities for women, single or married, to circulate without male chaperones or companionship in complex and often unrestricted social environments. The liberality of these conditions for women led to often-hysterical responses on the part of public officials and patriarchal society. A public campaign against "tango pirates," "social gangsters," and "white slavers" developed in response to the imagined dangers (especially the specter of lower-class, nonwhite males) threatening white women in the unsupervised space of nightlife.[139]

In the many covert forms of social exchange and migration I have examined in this chapter, lyric poetry played an essential role in modeling and disclosing the configurations of obscurity essential to the clandestine—and heterogeneous—community of nightlife. In the most radical sense, the pockets of social integration made possible by the secrecy of the nightspot (which functions simultaneously as a mode of publicity in modern nightlife) led to new formations of anonymity recalling the hermeticism intrinsic to the origins of nightlife—to phenomena such as the Cabaret of the Nameless (Kabarett der Namenlosen), a club opened in Berlin in 1928.

138. On the racial components of modern nightlife, see Lewis A. Erenberg, *Steppin' Out: New York Nightlife and the Transformation of American Culture, 1890–1930* (Westport, CT: Greenwood Press, 1981), 23, 73–74, 255–257.

139. Erenberg, *Steppin' Out,* 83–86.

In a format resembling the *The Gong Show* or the more lurid talk shows on television today, the Cabaret of the Nameless offered a platform for private citizens (most without talent or training of any kind) to perform acts and recount stories of "helpless imbecility."[140] The namelessness of the performers, who were indistinguishable from the patrons of the club, became the focal point of public attention, thereby wrenching to its most extreme point what I have called the enigma of sentimentality. This dialectic of anonymity and publicity, of inwardness and exposure, became evident as well in contemporary reactions to the club, which was described as "a padded cell for the metropolis" (in which people "subject themselves to a psychoanalytic cure") and as a modern version of the Roman Coliseum: "The arena has become a cabaret. Armed conflict has turned into recitations."[141]

Though the exhibition of namelessness may appear to be a specifically modern formation of sentimentality, it subscribes in many ways to the logic of the open secret which has characterized the topology of nightlife since its historical inception. Siegfried Kracauer understood Josef von Sternberg's film *The Blue Angel* to be an instance of what he calls "the appearance of lost inwardness"—a phrase that may be applied as well to nightlife itself.[142] Strictly speaking, the appearance of "inwardness" in the external world—that is, the appearance of phenomena at odds with the ideologies of the visible world—is an impossible event, a contradiction that produces the intrinsic obscurity of nightlife (its location, its language, its social composition). As a show of inwardness, the nightspot appears in the world, though it seeks to erase, or obscure, any trace of that manifestation: it is an open secret, a queer place, a productive paradox. And the dialectic of obscurity in underground culture is precisely what aligns nightlife historically and conceptually with lyric poetry. For poetry as well may be described as "the appearance of lost inwardness"—an impossible event yielding unmappable places in language and queer combinations of social being. From the very beginning, we have known that Orpheus could not turn his back on the underworld and that by turning back he drew the gaze of those living in the upper world to the lyrical topos of the underworld. We have not sufficiently understood, however, that the underworld is at once the domain of metaphysical substance and a historical place, even if the ambiguity of its material conditions cannot be isolated from the substance of poetry.

140. Erich Kastner, "The Cabaret of the Nameless" (1929), reprinted in Kaes, Jay, and Dimendberg, *Weimar Republic Sourcebook,* 562.

141. Kastner, "Cabaret of the Nameless," 563.

142. Siegfried Kracauer, "The Blue Angel" (1930), reprinted in Kaes, Jay, and Dimendberg, *Weimar Republic Sourcebook,* 631.

SEVEN

Mother Goose and Mallarmé

Destruction was my Beatrice. STÉPHANE MALLARMÉ

The visible underworld of infidel culture, like the naked, slumbering existence of monadic substance, makes darkness visible, I have argued, in a manner resembling the open secrecy of the riddle or the canting song. Poetry, nightlife, and being itself are innately obscure, according to this model, yet each makes a spectacle of incomprehension and inscrutability. At the same time, the dialectical nature of obscurity under these particular conditions defines itself through its polarized relations to its contrary element, through unreported transactions between underground and normative cultures, between substance and phenomenon, between vernacular and literary poetries. In addition, extending the *analogon* of obscurity, a map of so-called lawful society from the perspective of the historical underworld would resemble a map of literary poetry from the perspective of the canting crew, or a reading of Stéphane Mallarmé's verse through the spectacles of Mother Goose.

Between 1879 and 1881, Mallarmé composed a sequence of brief writings in prose that, although they could arguably be described as the largest ensemble of prose poems he ever wrote, did not see light of publication until 1964. Many of these pieces resemble in tone, and sometimes in subject matter, the occasional verse (*vers de cironstance*) that Mallarmé was writing at about the same time, which range in topic from Parisian nightclubs (including the Mirliton), pitchers of Calvados, and ladies' fans to Easter eggs and gifts of candied fruit for the New Year.[1] Here is one of the curious rhapsodies from that long-lost book:

> I like candies, but I like toys too; and more than anything, I like little live animals, and sharing my sweet treats with them—I will tell you then that the sailors lined up on the deck were white mice.—Oh, how pretty it is! How many of them were there? Twenty-four.—If I had them, they would run away.—But no, the song goes on to say, they all had chains around their necks.[2]

Mallarmé's prose piece, like the other texts in this sequence, functions as an element in a pedagogical work—a collection of nursery rhymes—consisting of 141 lessons, most comprising a passage from an English nursery rhyme and a *thème* (the occasion for Mallarmé's lyrical prose) revising the English song. Although Mallarmé's little prose poems cannot escape their pedagogical context, many reverberations can be found between these vernacular sketches and canonical works by Mallarmé often regarded as the *non plus ultra* of literary artifice.

Since the publication in 1998 of the new edition of Mallarmé's *Oeuvres complètes* (edited by Bertrand Marchal), a revisionary approach to Mallarmé has begun to emerge in which his work is seen "less in terms of the absent 'Livre' than of an escape into the ludic ephemera of the *Vers de circonstance*"—a thesis first introduced by the poet Yves Bonnefoy in his 1996 preface to Marchal's edition of the *Vers de circonstance*.[3] Thus, Marian Sugano sees Mallarmé as "the poet of a civil, public language, a discourse at once domestic and obscure."[4] Further, she explains, "The later works [after 1873] evidence a ceaseless gesturing toward the world, staging a democratic, desolemnizing free circulation of poetry, and yet the bulk of this writing is precisely his most difficult, the most intractably obscure."[5]

1. One should also note, with regard to Mallarmé's love of frivolity, the fashion magazine *La dernière mode*, which he wrote and produced entirely by himself in 1874. For an English edition of this little-known project, see P. M. Furbank and A. M. Cain, eds., *Mallarmé on Fashion* (Oxford: Berg, 2004).

2. John Ashbery has translated a small selection of Mallarmé's nursery rhymes (including this one, with minor changes on my part) in "Secret Lives of Children," ed. Bradford Morrow, special issue, *Conjunctions* 54 (2005): 376. Stéphane Mallarmé, *Recueil de nursery rhymes*, ed. Carl Paul Barbier (Paris: Gallimard, 1964), 41–42.

3. Roger Pearson, *Mallarmé and Circumstance*: *The Translation of Silence* (Oxford: Oxford University Press, 2004), 4. See also Yves Bonnefoy, "L'or du futile," preface to Mallarmé, *Vers de circonstance*, ed. Bertrand Marchal (Paris: Gallimard, 1996), 7–52.

4. Marian Zwerling Sugano, *The Poetics of Circumstance* (Stanford, CA: Stanford University Press, 1992), 17.

5. Sugano, *Poetics of Circumstance*, 15.

From this perspective, the correspondences between Mallarmé's formidable poems and his nursery rhymes offer a striking illustration of the hypothesis that obscurity in literary poetry owes a general and sometimes quite specific debt to vernacular forms and idioms. Yet it is precisely the vernacular and pedagogical orientation of these writings which inhibited not only their publication but closer examination of their relation to Mallarmé's poetry.

One of Mallarmé's most famous lines of verse refers to the poet as "*l'ange / Donner un sens plus pur aux mots de la tribu*" (the angel / Giving a purer sense to the words of tribe).[6] These lines have been interpreted, especially by Anglo-American modernists (such as T. S. Eliot), as advancing a poetics of verbal sublimation, or rarefaction, which yields a substance of lyric purity—a substance in contrast to the unrefined "words of the tribe."[7] A poetic doctrine pitting lyric substance against "the words of the tribe" accords easily with what one might call the "proverbial" Mallarmé: the image of a poet appalled by what he calls "that universal *journalistic style* which elsewhere characterizes all kinds of contemporary writing."[8] Mallarmé elsewhere calls the journalistic style a "pestilence" threatening the "mystery" calculated by poetry—that is, by syntax whose function, according to Valéry, may be compared to "algebra cultivated for its own ends."[9] The proverbial Mallarmé looms, then, as a poet of almost mathematical refinement, scorning what he calls "language in the hands of the mob."[10]

I do not mean to suggest that Mallarmé does not contribute to a lively polemic pitting the esoteric "laboratory" of the prose poem against the interests of "the masses." One must take great care, however, in determining the precise configuration of this antithesis. Mallarmé, as I indicated earlier, builds his defense of "mystery in literature" specifically in opposition to the "pedestrian clarity" of the *newspaper*.[11] A variation of this antithesis, contrasting "self-interested" and "disinterested" par-

6. Stéphane Mallarmé, "Le tombeau d'Edgar Poe," in *Oeuvres complètes,* by Stéphane Mallarmé, ed. Bertrand Marchal (Paris: Gallimard, 1998), 1:380. Translations are my own unless otherwise noted.

7. In "Little Gidding" of the *Four Quartets,* T. S. Eliot writes, "Since our concern was speech and speech impelled us / To purify the dialect of the tribe." Eliot, *Complete Poems and Plays* (New York: Harcourt Brace, 1971), 141.

8. Stéphane Mallarmé, "Crise de vers," in *Oeuvres complètes,* ed. Marchal, 2:204–213. For an English translation, see "Crisis in Verse," in *Mallarmé: Selected Prose Poems, Essays, and Letters,* trans. Bradford Cook (Baltimore, MD: Johns Hopkins University Press, 1956), 42 (emphasis in original).

9. Stéphane Mallarmé, "Le mystère dans les letters," in *Oeuvres completes,* 2:229–234. For an English translation, see "Mystery in Literature," in *Mallarmé: Selected Prose Poems, Essays, and Letters,* 42. Paul Valéry, "Sorte de préface," in *Thèmes anglais,* by Stéphane Mallarmé (Paris: Gallimard, 1935), 15.

10. Mallarmé, "Crisis in Verse," 42.

11. Mallarmé, "Mystery in Literature," 33.

ties, appears as well in Mallarmé's essay on music and literature (two arts linked by their common claim on "mystery"): "Whenever the masses are being herded indiscriminately toward self-interest, amusement, or convenience, it is essential that a very few disinterested persons should adopt an attitude of respectful indifference toward those common motivations."[12] One might presume that Mallarmé's attacks on the masses and the "unceasing immobility" of the journalistic style would imply a wholesale injunction against vernacular expression. Yet he seeks to explain—and perhaps deliberately obscures—the antithesis a few paragraphs later in the essay by declaring that "the disinterested poet, eschewing all virtuosity and bravado, must project his vision of the world and use the language of the school, home, and market place, which seems most fitting to that purpose. Then poetry will be lifted to some frightening, wavering, ecstatic pitch. . . . Wherever you find it, you must deny the ineffable; for somehow it will speak."[13] In conjunction with the earlier passage pitting the self-interested masses against a "disinterested" minority, these statements demonstrate that Mallarmé's polemic against the "journalistic style" (and against the masses) does not extend to the demotic sources of language, or to the use of particular idioms (e.g., those of the kitchen, the classroom, or commerce). Indeed, the "purifying storm" he associates with poetry appears to issue from—instead of annihilating—the words of the tribe.[14] One therefore confronts in Mallarmé's statements a conception of poetry that is at once domestic and obscure, colloquial and arcane.

The figure of "the Mob" in Mallarmé's polemic—a term he never defines—is especially unstable in its vexed relation to the "mystery" of poetry. The iconic reference to "the words of the tribe" appears in an elegy to Edgar Allan Poe, whose famous story "The Man of the Crowd" compares the unfathomable "secret" of urban crowds to the paradox of an unreadable book: "It was well said of a certain German book *'er lässt sich nicht lesen'*—it does not permit itself to be read. There are some secrets which do not permit themselves to be told."[15] In addition, the narrator of Poe's story identifies the anonymous "man of the crowd" as "the type and genius of deep crime"—a description evoking another language which

12. Stéphane Mallarmé, "La musique et les lettres," in *Oeuvres complètes,* ed. Marchal, 2:62–77. For an English translation, see "Music and Literature," in *Mallarmé: Selected Prose Poems, Essays, and Letters,* 54.

13. Mallarmé, "Music and Literature," 55.

14. Mallarmé, "Music and Literature," 45.

15. Edgar Allan Poe, "The Man of the Crowd," in *Collected Tales and Poems of Edgar Allan Poe* (New York: Modern Library, 1992), 475.

"does not permit itself to be read": the jargon of the criminal underworld. Bearing in mind these correspondences in Poe's story, it becomes evident that Mallarmé's phrase "the words of the tribe" reveals a concern with the verbal affinities of the crowd, perhaps even evoking a *secret* language of the mob. In any case, the correspondence in Poe's story between the "secret" of the mob and an unreadable book makes it impossible to simply *contrast* the words of the tribe with a purified lyric substance. On the contrary, we are faced with the prospect that Mallarmé sees these two elements as reciprocal in some way.

The possibility that the words of the tribe may be the matrix of poetic mystery rather than its antithesis follows directly from Mallarmé's discussion of the "the Mob" in his essay "Mystery in Literature." Though ostensibly inimical to poetic mystery, the Mob is directly implicated in the phenomenon the essay seeks to defend: poetic obscurity. (Mallarmé's essay, published in *La revue blanche*, was written in direct response to Proust's essay "Contre l'obscurité," which appeared six weeks earlier in the same publication.)[16] Alluding to Matthew Arnold's poem "The Buried Life," which finds in "the world's most crowded streets" an intimation of "nameless" things, including "the mystery of this heart," Mallarmé writes:

> There is certainly something occult in men's hearts; I am convinced that there is something abstruse, something closed and hidden in the Mob. For whenever She sniffs out the idea that obscurity may be a *reality*; that it may exist, for example, on a piece of paper, in a piece of writing (heaven forbid, of course, that it should exist within itself!), She . . . blames the darkness on anything but herself.[17]

Although the mob refuses to acknowledge its genetic relation to obscurity in writing (a version of obscurity-in-itself), Mallarmé insists that what is "closed and hidden in the Mob" is *identical* to the obscurity that the Mob ceaselessly projects outside itself. For Mallarmé ultimately claims of the Mob that "She Herself is the enigma": instead of being antithetical to poetry, as appears to be the case elsewhere in this essay, the Mob betrays the economy of a poetic form—the riddle—that serves as the oldest and most enduring model of poetic obscurity. Hence, the enigma of poetry finds expression in the Mob, and the Mob functions like an enigma.

Mallarmé's reference to "the language of the school" (*les mots, les aptes*

16. Mallarmé's polemical essay "Le mystère dans les lettres" first appeared in the 1 September 1896 issue of *La revue blanche*.

17. Matthew Arnold, "The Buried Life," in *Poetry and Criticism of Matthew Arnold* (Boston: Houghton Mifflin, 1961), 78; Mallarmé, "Mystery in Literature," 30 (emphasis in original).

mots, de l'école) as one of the principal sources of "the ineffable" (*l'indicible*) indicates an unlikely source for what he calls "the reciprocal elements of Mystery"—that is, the transactions between the obscurity of modern poetry (which he defends at length) and the obscurity of the words of the tribe.[18] During a brief period of Mallarmé's career as an English teacher, he was obliged to produce several pedagogical works—including a collection of English nursery rhymes—in order to keep his job at the lycée Fontanes and to supplement his meager income. Although these works (only one of which, *Les mots anglais,* was published during his lifetime) were clearly designed for practical use by students of English at various levels, and although they treat idiomatic and vernacular materials exclusively, it has not entirely escaped Mallarmé's closest readers that these works may be consistent—in their ideas about language and poetry—with Mallarmé's own poetic principles. Henri Mondor, for example, commenting on the unexpected revelations to be found in *Les mots anglais,* writes:

> Some of his most cherished ideas and intentions, along with his loftiest concerns, are revealed in these modest works. . . . It's as if, thanks to a moment of exquisite surrender, an artist consented to examine his box of tools under our very eyes, to prepare his palette with complete candor; or, as if a great scientist modestly gave us a peek into his luminous laboratory.[19]

Similarly, Paul Valéry, in his introduction to one of Mallarmé's unpublished pedagogical works, *Thèmes anglais,* writes:

> It would perhaps be useful to recall briefly the constant theme of his thinking about poetry, by no means absent from this didactic work. . . . He believed from the very start that the Poetic Act [*le Fait Poétique*] in its essence is no different from language itself, which merges with poetry and sustains all possible poems, and of which the individual elements forming it suppose a kind of creation.[20]

By implication, therefore, Mallarmé's selection and annotation of English idioms address indirectly *le Fait Poétique* and, more specifically, Mallarmé's own poetic production. Valéry, like Mondor, suggests that these neglected pedagogical works offer invaluable, if eccentric, glimpses into Mallarmé's poetic reflections. Concerning Mallarmé's treatment of English, Valéry observes that "he attempted to apply to the study of that

18. Mallarmé: "Music and Literature," 50.

19. Henri Mondor, commenting in Stéphane Mallarmé, *Oeuvres complètes,* ed. Henri Mondor (Paris: Gallimard, 1945), 886.

20. Valéry, "Sorte de préface," 13.

language the infinitely expansive feeling he possessed for the musical delicacies of our own. Is not the book *Les mots anglais* perhaps the most revealing document we possess of Mallarmé's most intimate labors?"[21]

Evidence that Mallarmé's pedagogical works (whose materials he used in the classroom) display a close, if unexpected, rapport with his own poetic discourse can be gleaned as well from an entirely different perspective—from the brutal teaching evaluations he endured at the hands of his peers at the lycée Fontanes. After citing verbatim Mallarmé's rather-free translation of the nursery rhyme "Liar, liar lick spit," in the classroom, one reviewer advised him not to "dictate" to his pupils such "inane verses" and concluded the report on his classroom visit by remarking, "One is tempted to ask oneself whether one is in the presence of a madman."[22] Another *inspecteur* condemned more pointedly the tension between Mallarmé's pedagogy and his career as a poet: "This teacher is preoccupied with things other than his teaching and his students. He seeks notoriety, and no doubt a certain profit, in . . . senseless productions, in prose and in verse. Those who read these strange lucubrations of Monsieur Mallarmé's brain must be surprised that he holds a teaching position at the lycée Fontanes."[23] It appears, however, to have escaped the notice of either reviewer that there might be an instructive correspondence between the "stupidities" Mallarmé dictated to his class from Mother Goose and the "senseless productions" of his own poetry.

Although Valéry contrasts the sordid *usefulness* of the work to which Mallarmé turned his hand as a teacher and the exalted nature of Mallarmé's poetry (which Valéry extols as "a purely useless production"), the idea that Mallarmé's pedagogical writings were somehow useful would have found little support, as I've indicated, among his peers at the lycée.[24] Likewise, his publisher rejected the manuscripts of *Thèmes anglais* and *Recueil de nursery rhymes* after having published *Les mots anglais* in 1878. In their judgments, Mallarmé's most pragmatic endeavors were not merely useless, from a professional or commercial standpoint, but "senseless." Thus, Mallarmé appears to have contributed to a generic innovation: works intended for practical use but possessing no utilitarian value, works in which, for example, proverbs used to teach grammar are subsumed by their own "hermetic system," in which proverbs become "veritable enigmas."[25]

21. Valéry, "Sorte de préface," 17.

22. Documents cited in Henri Mondor, *Vie de Mallarmé* (Paris: Gallimard, 1943), 414.

23. Documents cited in Mondor, *Vie de Mallarmé*, 371.

24. Valéry, "Sorte de préface," 8.

25. Comments by Carl Paul Barbier on Mallarmé's *Thèmes anglais* in his introduction to Mallarmé, *Recueil de nursery rhymes*, 19.

Unlike *Les mots anglais,* which aims to provide a comprehensive, if eccentric, history of the English language, the two pedagogical works that remained unpublished during Mallarmé's lifetime (*Thèmes anglais* and *Recueil de nursery rhymes*) share a narrower set of philological and methodological principles, which contributed to, or even anticipated, certain developments and ideas in Mallarmé's poetic production. The shared principles—and poetic affinities—of these two pedagogical works find expression as well in a curious, linguistic toy which Mallarmé designed in 1880 (and proposed for manufacture) as a device to supplement his textbooks. Called the *Boîte pour apprendre l'anglais en jouant et seul* (Box for Learning English While Playing Alone), it was "composed of twelve panels bearing complex mechanisms which present students with an automated sequence of questions, answers, and colored pictures illustrating them."[26] The marvelous aspects of this device—its mechanical ability to divulge, or to withhold, the inscrutable laws of English; its ability to converse with its interlocutor—conform to the rhetoric and methods of Mallarmé's curious textbooks. (One would also want to suggest that the "English Box," by virtue of its properties as an illusionistic device, is also a *poetry machine*—a toy medium revealing an undiscovered grammar of ordinary language.)

Mallarmé's principal thesis concerning the poetic value of the vernacular (examples of which he catalogues—by the thousands—in his textbooks) is that "proverbs and idiomatic expression . . . contain the very soul of English," as do, by implication, the proverbial elements of *any* language. Further, in his prefatory remarks to *Thèmes anglais,* one discovers a matrix of ideas which clarify the exact meaning of the phrase "the words of the tribe"—along with their significance for poetry. He claims, for example, to have collected phrases "sprung from the instinct of the race and polished by centuries of use," all of which constitute a "repository of national genius." Elsewhere in the same preface, he refers to phrases "drawn from the very depths of language" (the domain, one might add, of "mystery in letters") in geological terms: he follows the "seam" or "vein" of the vernacular, mining "one of the most precious deposits, a treasure of well-turned phrases, proverbs, sayings, and idiomatic expressions."[27] Evidently, the poet seeks the "very soul" of language in precious verbal substances that must, however, be recovered from the depths: "the angel giving a purer sense to the words of the tribe."

The learning toy, the English Box, with its pop-up questions, answers,

26. Documents cited in Mondor, *Vie de Mallarmé,* 411–412.
27. Mallarmé, *Thèmes anglais,* 229, 26, 230.

and illustrations, provides an automated (and perhaps enchanted) model of the instructional methods employed in *Thèmes anglais* and *Recueil de nursery rhymes*. As the former title indicates, this method is built around the pedagogical device of the *thème*—a term meaning, in French, "topic," "subject," or "theme" but also "composition" or, simply, "prose." Preceded by a particular rule (*règle*) or concept of English grammar, the themes in *Thèmes anglais* take the form of a set of English proverbs illustrating, by their grammatical structure, a given rule. "Each phrase," Mallarmé explains, "turns out to bear the obvious imprint, almost exclusively, of a particular rule"—hence the tendency of the vernacular to bear traces, like a fossil, of the "buried life" of English: a grammatical record of the "very soul" of language.[28]

Significantly (for the impact of the *thème* on Mallarmé's production as a poet), the order of *règle* and *thème* is inverted in his collection of nursery rhymes: a passage from an English nursery rhyme is followed by a "*thème*" translating, transforming, and reflecting upon the example. Indeed, as a result of the mutability of the *thème,* Mallarmé's collection of nursery rhymes offers fertile ground for exploring the correlations between his interest in vernacular expression, the development of his ideas about poetry, and his own poetic practice.

Mallarmé's eccentric redaction of Mother Goose reflects the vogue for collections of nursery rhymes that reached France from England in the 1870s. He selected the examples in his own collection, as Carl Paul Barbier has shown, from various British editions of Mother Goose, including James O. Hallwell's *Nursery Rhymes of England* (1846), Walter Crane's *Baby's Bouquet* (1879), and other books illustrated by Randolph Caldecott and Kate Greenaway.[29] In addition to drawing upon these books for his source materials, Mallarmé modeled his presentation of the rhymes (and the attendant themes) on the example supplied by these British anthologies—a model that may help to explain, in part, the literary aspect of Mallarmé's ostensibly pedagogical text. Many of these British editions replicated (and sumptuously enhanced) the fanciful models of antiquarian scholarship and moral instruction characterizing the earliest anthologies of children's rhymes in English, which were published in the latter part of the eighteenth century. One of the first English editions of Mother Goose, for example, called *Mother Goose's Melody, or Sonnets for the Cradle,* was published in 1780 and contained "the most celebrated Songs and Lullabies of the old British Nurses, calculated to amuse Children and to excite

28. Mallarmé, *Thèmes anglais*, 26.

29. Barbier, introduction to Mallarmé, *Recueil de nursery rhymes,* 11–12.

them to Sleep."[30] Yet these rhymes also served another function—a didactic purpose—for the title page indicates that they are "Embellished with Cuts and Illustrated with Notes and Maxims, Historical, Philosophical, and Critical." Each of the rhymes is thus supplemented by epigraphs, illustrations, and moral maxims, not to mention the sagacious introduction to the anthology by an anonymous editor (all this in a book—a toy book—that measures only two and a half by four inches). This is the model followed by the late-nineteenth-century editions from which Mallarmé derived his materials and his format.

It would appear, then, that the template for collections of nursery rhymes offers a lively example of didactic, or homiletic, literature—hence its pedagogical appeal. Yet the very first edition of Mother Goose turns out to have been a literary hoax (produced, it seems, by Oliver Goldsmith): a collection of rhymes amplified and deflected by an apparatus consisting of a mock introduction, facetious maxims, invented notes, and incoherent illustrations. This apparatus, which reveals itself to be a masterful and beguiling literary contrivance, underlies the function of the *thème* in Mallarmé's collection of nursery rhymes. The counterfeit—that is to say, lyrical—nature of the original apparatus survives in the highly unstable element of Mallarmé's themes and in each theme's uncertain relation to the rhyme itself.

Concerning the range of effects to be found in Mallarmé's themes, Barbier observes: "Some of them offer commentary on the songs, while others are little more than amplified translations; and still others turn out to be veritable prose poems."[31] The most eccentric "themes" are sometimes lyrical, but their principal effect often depends on drawing out the most provocative elements of the nursery rhyme, as in the case of the verses witnessed by the *inspecteur* who compared Mallarmé to a "madman":

Liar, liar lick spit; your tongue shall
Be slit, And all the dogs in town
Shall have a little bit.[32]

And here is Mallarmé's robust "imitation" of the song (translated back into English), which the *inspecteur* recalls being recited by students in class:

30. A superb (and inexpensive) facsimile of this edition has recently become available: *Mother Goose's Melody, or Sonnets for the Cradle* (1780), introduced by Nigel Tattersfield (Oxford: Bodleian Library, 2003).

31. Barbier, introduction to Mallarmé, *Recueil de nursery rhymes,* 13.

32. Mallarmé, *Recueil de nursery rhymes,* 70.

"Liar, swallow your spit," says the song known to all children; and the liar has more to swallow than any other because of all the words he has to throw around to avoid telling the truth! Although his tongue may already be split like a viper's—as he often speaks ill of others—it will be cut up in still smaller bits, so that every dog in town may have a little piece.[33]

Mallarmé breaks the verses into a dialogue, corrupting and leavening the punitive tone of the original, in order to produce a bizarre portrait of the liar (and perhaps of the poet himself in the classroom) condemned for his deceitful words.

As Mallarmé's "themes" convert the metrical verse of the original songs into prose, he often forsakes instances of repetition or nonsense, especially the "burden"—the refrain—of the song. Yet he manages to capture the *charm* of the nursery rhyme—its incantatory effect—and its disconcerting tone by trimming it, breaking it up into an implied dialogue, or, most often, amplifying it by explaining an elliptical line or inserting a moral "maxim" (familiar from the eighteenth-century British model). More broadly, Barbier explains:

He sometimes is content to espouse the spirit of the original by recalling each of its elements; other times, he finds a formula or framework of his own invention which permits him to convey the charm and the naivete of the song; still other times, he departs from the song to follow his own fantasy, turning idioms into moral maxims or slapstick, even going so far as to adopt a point of view which makes the reader wonder whether Mallarmé has grasped the basic sense of the poem.

In the end, however, Barbier concludes that "the majority of the themes clearly bear the imprint of Mallarmé; indeed, they are truly little poems in prose, combining the exigencies of the artist with the aims of the teacher."[34]

In one of Mallarmé's nursery rhymes, a variation on the familiar "Hey! Diddle diddle, / The cat and the fiddle," the interpolated voice of the poet speaks to the influence of these fantastic scenes on his train of thought: "And then it seemed to me, as I contemplated this spectacle, that my ideas ran away with themselves, one after another, just as—in the words of the song—the dish runs after the spoon. Hey! diddle, diddle."[35] Indeed, Barbier contends that Mallarmé's exposure to Mother Goose, following on

33. Mallarmé, *Recueil de nursery rhymes*, 70–71.

34. Barbier, introduction to Mallarmé, *Recueil de nursery rhymes*, 22.

35. Mallarmé, *Recueil de nursery rhymes*, 99.

the heels of his engagement with Poe's writing, granted the poet significant license—a turning point—in his pursuit and manipulation of poetic materials: "Thanks to his contact with these nursery rhymes, the translator of Poe opens afresh, if only in the imagination, a window giving onto a forbidden sky, where anything is possible."[36] From this perspective, it appears that Mallarmé's attraction to nursery rhymes coincides not only, as I indicated earlier, with the vernacular menagerie of occasional verse (a world of nightclubs, toys, fashion, and candied fruits) but with the macabre—the "forbidden"—tableaux of Poe's tales: a combination of elements conspiring to marvelous effect in the violent cartoon of the nursery rhyme.

The convergence of Edgar Allan Poe and Mother Goose in Mallarmé's poetic development is more than a coincidence, since the reference to "the words of the tribe"—which we now realize alludes, in part, to the vernacular palette of the nursery rhyme—occurs in the lyrical "tomb" Mallarmé constructs for Poe. Indeed, it appears that some of Mallarmé's nursery rhyme poems supplement, or perhaps anticipate, the model of the poetic *tombeau* that he will revisit following his affair with Mother Goose. For the very first sequence (indeed, the longest sequence) of verses and themes in Mallarmé's collection of nursery rhymes pertains to a series of songbirds—Cock Sparrow, Tom Titmouse—and ultimately to the murder (at the hands of the Sparrow) and elaborate funeral of Cock Robin.

The ten poems in this sequence assemble a veritable congress of birds to fill the many roles necessary for the elaborate funeral of Cock Robin: the Rook (parson), the Lark (clerk), the Kite (undertaker), the Dove (chief mourner), the Wren (pallbearer), the Thrush (psalmist).[37] What's more, the funeral cortege follows a Linnet carrying a "link" (a torch)—a yellow primrose, it turns out—indicating that the ceremony takes place under the burning brand of a *link-bird,* an archaic emblem of the nocturnal underworld of the demimonde.[38] Indeed, all of the birds are continually singing or, as Mallarmé puts it, *gazouiller,* a verb meaning "to chirp," "to babble," which recalls the dual meaning of the word "jargon" (birdsong and slang). Hence, the confusion between song and slang signals a correspondence between the congress of birds and a canting crew of thieves and rogues.[39] Indeed, the group of songbirds appears to anticipate the gallery of Parisian street figures assembled in Mallarmé's *Chansons Bas* (Street

36. Barbier, introduction to Mallarmé, *Recueil de nursery rhymes,* 23.

37. Mallarmé, *Recueil de nursery rhymes,* 36–39.

38. Mallarmé, *Recueil de nursery rhymes,* 37–38.

39. Several forms of the verb *gazouiller* appear in the first two segments of Cock Robin's *tombeau.* Mallarmé, *Recueil de nursery rhymes,* 31–32.

Songs): "The Newspaper Vendor," "The Seller of Garlic and Onions," "The Road Mender," and others.[40]

In the final verses of the avian *tombeau* (or at least in Mallarmé's rendering of these verses), the psalm warbled by the Thrush mingles with the sighing of animals and, finally, with the dead language of the bell tolling for Cock Robin: "This bell says: 'And so, Cock Robin, farewell.' All the birds of the field and the woods gathered round as they heard these words understood by them alone; a thousand other creatures joined in and those holding back their sobs were sighing."[41] Thus, the weeping of the songbirds seems to answer, and perhaps even echo, the resounding "words" of the bell.

Earlier in the songbird sequence, Mallarmé depicts the bell-house as being stocked with books. He also reveals that a book of particular interest lies concealed in the *tombeau* of Cock Robin, tucked under the wing of the Rook (*petit livre sous l'aile*). For some of these songbirds are readers, whose books are lost—nibbled by scavengers—in their sleep. Here is poor Tom Titmouse as he appears in the verse presented by Mallarmé in "Leçon no. 4":

Little Tom Titmouse,
Lived in a bell-house,
The bell-house broke,
And Tom Titmouse woke.

The English text of this nursery rhyme contains no books, yet Mallarmé's theme turns the bell-house into a library visited by scoundrels at night: "How soundly you sleep; a rat gnaws at your clothes and your books, without even waking you."[42]

The mystery of the disappearing books reappears later in Mallarmé's collection of nursery rhymes as an enigma, as part of a famous riddle:

I had four brothers over the sea,
And they each sent a present to me.
The first sent a goose without a bone,
The second sent a cherry without a stone,

40. Mallarmé's *Chansons Bas* were written in 1889 to accompany the illustrations of Jean-François Raffaëlli's *Les types de Paris*. The *Chansons Bas* were set to music by Darius Milhaud in 1917. Mallarmé, *Oeuvres complètes*, ed. Marchal, 1:33–35.

41. Mallarmé, *Recueil de nursery rhymes*, 39–40.

42. Mallarmé, *Recueil de nursery rhymes*, 37, 34.

The third sent a blanket without a thread,
The fourth sent a book that no man could read.[43]

Though I won't reveal the identities of these riddle creatures (Mallarmé provides the solutions in the next lesson), I do want to suggest that the "book that no man could read" calls to mind several real—and unreal—books in Mallarmé's poetic career. First, it alludes to the literal book in which this riddle appears, to the lost book which lay unread for over eighty years—that is, to Mallarmé's collection of nursery rhymes. In this respect, the "book that no man could read" also describes the innate obscurity and crippled logic of nursery rhymes in general—a counterpart of the fabled obscurity of Mallarmé's canonical poems. Second, and more perversely (in the antic spirit of the rhymes themselves), the "book that no man could read" can be viewed as the earliest incarnation of Mallarmé's grandiose figure of *Le Livre*, "reverberating and useless," calling for "a total expansion of the letter": "Not personalized," Mallarmé explains, "the volume, from which one is separated as the author, does not demand that any reader approach it. You should know that it happens, as such, all alone, without human accessories."[44] Further, the infinite scope of *Le Livre* requires that "all earthly existence must ultimately be contained in a book."[45] Yet this metaphysical and, indeed, monadological "book" (recalling Schlegel's doctrine of infinite poetry) first makes its appearance in Mallarmé's work as a tiny bird book in a nursery rhyme, a readerless book in a riddle: a toy book in a world of animals, "without human accessories."

It is no mere coincidence—or perhaps it is—that Mallarmé first renders the readerless "book" as the object of a riddle, since riddles occur quite frequently in his collection of nursery rhymes, including a riddle that appears in the *tombeau* of Cock Robin:

Elizabeth, Elspeth, Betsy and Bess,
They all went together to see a bird's nest.
They found a bird's nest with five eggs in,
They all took one and left four in.[46]

43. Mallarmé, *Recueil de nursery rhymes,* 60–61. Immediately following these lines, Mallarmé begins his theme by declaring, "All this seems to be an enigma."

44. Mallarmé, "Quant au livre," in *Oeuvres complètes*, ed. Marchal, 2:214–225. For an English translation, see "As for the Book," in *Selected Poetry and Prose*, by Stéphane Mallarmé, ed. Mary Ann Caws (New York: New Directions, 1982), 78, 82, 80.

45. Mallarmé, "As for the Book," 80.

46. Mallarmé, *Recueil de nursery rhymes*, 33.

Here, the obscurity of the riddle—a model for all poetry, in Mallarmé's view—cannot be separated from the variable signatures of a single thief, a phantom crew snatching a single egg from the dead Cock Robin's nest—a crime imagined by Mallarmé in his rewriting of the riddle, a fault in the otherwise-elegiac context of the *tombeau*.[47]

The themes of fraud and larceny—crimes of writing which bind the riddle's obscurity until it is solved—recur in another riddle about a songbird in Mallarmé's collection of nursery rhymes:

The winds they did blow,
The leaves they did wag;
Along came a beggar boy
And put me in his bag.

He took me up to London.
A Lady did me buy.
Put me in a silver cage,
And hung me up on high.[48]

In Mallarmé's rewriting of these verses (whose narrative bears a striking resemblance to Baudelaire's essay on toys), the leaves "wagging" like tongues expose what Mallarmé calls "the hidden birds" (*les oiseaux cachés*).[49] A beggar steals one of the "hidden birds" from its gossip tree—a tree of idle talk and hearsay—takes it to London, and sells "the little singer" (*le petit chanteur*) to a Lady, who keeps it in a silver cage for its song. The "hidden bird" appears to be a figure for the riddle itself, which links the obscurity of the literary poem (in a silver cage) to the obscurity of birdsong, jargon, and the rhymes of Mother Goose. Indeed, since the hidden bird and its song are sold into elite society by a *beggar*—a figure from the demimonde—one suspects that the native song of the hidden bird may bear some correlation to the troubling and alluring chant of the beggar, to a canting song.

47. In his revision of the English verse, Mallarmé inserts the following question about the eggs in the nest: "*Ce sont des rouge-gorges?—Oui, il y a juste cinq oeufs*." Mallarmé, *Recueil de nursery rhymes*, 33.

48. Mallarmé, *Recueil de nursery rhymes*, 72.

49. Mallarmé, *Recueil de nursery rhymes*, 72.

Afterword: Social Inversion, Kitsch, and the Art of Disappearing

Λάθε βιώσας EPICURUS

The prospect that the exalted obscurity of Mallarmé's canonical verse may be genetically related to the nonsense of Mother Goose is perhaps no more surprising than Leibniz's assertion that the artificial language (the *charactéristique*) underlying his invention of a logical calculus—the structural foundation of his metaphysic—resembles the *Rotwelsch,* or canting speech, of the demimonde.[1] The resemblance between cant and the *charactéristique* is based, according to Leibniz, not in the complete arbitrariness of these languages, ostensibly so far removed from one another, but in the fact that they both "involve a mixture of chosen features and natural and chance features of the languages upon which they are built."[2] That is to say, the "chosen" features of both languages conform to the logic of the natural languages forming their matrix. Thus, the obscurity of the "jargon" of the logical calculus, like the jargon of cant, is in accord with the expressive configurations of natural language—with forms of language familiar to all.

In a similar fashion, the "algebraic syntax" of Mallarmé's

1. G. W. Leibniz, *New Essays on Human Understanding,* trans. Peter Remnant and Jonathan Bennett (Cambridge: Cambridge University Press, 1996), 3.2.1.

2. Leibniz, *New Essays on Human Understanding,* 3.2.1.

canonical verse—one source of its vaunted obscurity—takes its cue, as he himself asserts, from "the language of the school, home, and market place," thereby producing a poetic medium that is at once domestic and obscure, colloquial and arcane.[3] When lyric obscurity, or even logical obscurity, is understood to be consistent with the expressive powers of ordinary language, then expression guarantees the radiant properties of obscurity: the coherence of any verbal code (whether shadowy jargon or national language) coincides, like the Janusian aspect of a riddle, with the obscurity of its medium. Communicability and referentiality must be viewed as specialized functions within a broader spectrum of linguistic expression. In addition, acknowledging the priority of expression redraws the map of obscurity, expanding its territorial reach beyond the literary sites of virtuosity and experimentation, thereby blurring divisions (based solely on the criterion of obscurity) between literary and vernacular poetries.

To argue that lyric obscurity clings historically to the netherworld of the vernacular (an occupation without memory), even as demotic speech continues to function as little more than an accessory to literary poetry, suggests that certain kinds of vernacular poetry may be described as *uncanny* in their relation to traditional lyric. Vernacular speech is subject to expulsion from literature precisely because one cannot distinguish effectively, on the basis of obscurity alone, between vernacular and literary poetries. Hermann Broch makes a similar argument about the threat posed by kitsch to the integrity of fine art (and to the avant-garde), declaring that kitsch is "lodged like a foreign body in the overall system of art" and acknowledging further: "The danger is all the greater when at first glance the system and the anti-system appear to be identical."[4] Precisely because kitsch is able to pass for "true" art—hence its uncanny nature—Broch goes so far as to claim: "Kitsch is the element of evil in the system of art."[5] The appearance of the "element of evil" in this context suggests that the uncanny properties of kitsch coincide with the threat of the infidel.

A similar polarity, rooted in the substance of obscurity, obtains between literary poetry and canting verse, for example, except that the relation between them, unlike the one Broch identifies between art and kitsch, is more than a matter of appearances. Infidel poetry, like kitsch,

3. Stéphane Mallarmé, "Music and Literature," in *Mallarmé: Selected Prose Poems, Essays, and Letters*, trans. Bradford Cook (Baltimore, MD: Johns Hopkins University Press, 1956), 55.

4. Hermann Broch, "Notes on the Problem of Kitsch," in *Kitsch: The World of Bad Taste,* ed. Gillo Dorfles (New York: Bell Publishing, 1969), 62.

5. Broch, "Notes on the Problem of Kitsch," 63.

is anathema to literature because of its vulgarity and sentimentality (because of its "crimes" against literature). In fact, no aesthetic category is judged to be more alien to literary poetry than kitsch: the anathematic properties of kitsch explain why it hovers like an enigma on the horizon of literary poetry, synthesizing the dangers of vulgarity, sentimentality, and enchantment. As such, kitsch, like the kinds of vernacular poetry I have discussed in this book, preserves (in opposition to the rationalized avant-garde) the magical dimension of art—including its enigmatic relation to terror—which must be suppressed to establish the dominant features of literary poetry.

Revising the coordinates of lyric obscurity in these ways exposes the social function of secrecy, even if all secret societies (and the secret dimensions of society itself) stem from a kind of negative sociability. If the aesthetic effect of lyric obscurity may be described as the magical simulation of an object's partial disappearance—a way of making things disappear with words—then the sociological dimension of obscurity approximates a kind of internal exile or social death, a disappearance from society. Although social obscurity may in many circumstances be a function of external oppression, the formation of infidel culture and the canting tradition demonstrates that social obscurity can also be a historical condition that is deliberately produced and sustained by those who inhabit marginal, or unknown, communities.

The conditions of social disappearance are reflected, I have argued, in the lyric formation of anonymity, in the historical figure of Anon. E. M. Forster, who shared with Virginia Woolf an interest in literary anonymity (and its bearing on modern social experience), declares, "all literature tends toward the condition of anonymity" and, more precisely, "literature wants not to be signed."[6] The conditions of literary anonymity coincide, in Forster's view, with a "queer" domain of oblivion—"Literature does not want to remember"—which can overtake even a signed text by a known author, as "it becomes anonymous."[7] The possibility of *becoming* anonymous thus offers a key to the practice of lyric subversion.

Forster's emphasis on the dynamics of literary anonymity—on becoming anonymous—identifies anonymity not only as a historical event but also as a social and political strategy that borrows its repertoire of obscurity effects from the nameless apparition of poetry. The lyric formation of Anon therefore offers a productive model of negative sociability that

6. E. M. Forster, *Anonymity: An Enquiry* (London: Hogarth Press, 1925), 24, 22.

7. Forster, *Anonymity*, 15, 14. On the submerged domain of anonymity, Forster writes that "each human has two personalities, one on the surface, one deeper down. . . . The lower personality is a very queer affair. . . . There is something general about it" (16).

poetry must reclaim for itself (a blow against the commodification of art and its equation with unthinking) but that also activates "in dark times," according to Hannah Arendt, a "flight from the world to concealment, from public life to anonymity."[8] Borrowing a phrase from a poem by Bertolt Brecht, which pointedly addresses poetry's possible response to—or collusion with—the trauma of "dark times," Arendt observes in "dark times" the phenomenon of "inner emigration," which is a "form of exile, a withdrawal from the world into an interior realm."[9] At the same time, Arendt insists, "flight from the world in dark times of impotence can always be justified as long as reality is not ignored, but is constantly acknowledged as the thing that must be escaped."[10] Although "inner emigration" may be equated with silence, one must also emphasize, with Paul Mann, that the lyric equation of obscurity and disappearance relies on the exercise of craft and technique, on *practice:* "What one must imagine is an unprecedented silence, exile, and cunning; samizdat networks, amnesiac and subhistorical; a moratorium, a boycott, an invisible *grève* that pretends to neither Parnassian nor critical autonomy, that makes no pretense whatsoever, that is fully committed to its anonymity."[11] By promoting such measures, the nameless identity of the lyric Anon becomes a general model of social and political resistance, synthesizing agency and obscurity, defiance and inscrutability.

The basic premises of anonymity may appear to restrict social and aesthetic resistance to the conditions of privacy, solipsism, and discontinuity. Yet for the "inner emigrants" of infidel society—for whom all times are dark times—"the world's reality is expressed by their escape."[12] Advocating a model of lyric subversion inherent in the two-way mirror of exile, I have sought to demonstrate throughout this book that the conditions of solipsism and connectedness, of secrecy and expressiveness, are not necessarily exclusive or antithetical. Indeed, the phenomenology of lyric obscurity, which is innately solipsistic, sustains a variety of expressive correspondences which operate beyond the threshold of causality or cognition. The seeming paradox of solipsistic expression in riddles finds corroboration, I have argued, in the fugitive lyric of the canting crew and

8. Hannah Arendt, "On Humanity in Dark Times," in *Men in Dark Times,* by Hannah Arendt, trans. Clara Winston and Richard Winston (New York: Harcourt, Brace, and World, 1968), 22.

9. Arendt, "On Humanity in Dark Times," 19. Arendt claims to borrow the phrase "dark times" from Brecht's famous poem "To Posterity" (1938), though the phrase appears even earlier, in his poem "In Dark Times" ("In finsteren Zeiten"), of 1934.

10. Arendt, "On Humanity in Dark Times," 22.

11. Paul Mann, *The Theory-Death of the Avant-Garde* (Bloomington: Indiana University Press, 1991), 144.

12. Arendt, "On Humanity in Dark Times," 22.

in the coincidence of discontinuity and connectedness that is essential to modern conceptions of metaphysical substance. Leibniz's theory of monads, in particular, offers a rigorous explanation of the "solipsistic perception" of windowless entities, of the infinite expressive correspondences among discontinuous substances. The lyrical terms of monadic substance bear directly on the conditions of anonymity and the prospect of social inversion. Just as the phenomenological *epoché* of the riddle condemns real things to verbal annihilation—a verbal apocalypse—in order that they may be revealed by words, so must individuals craft the inaction of social death to produce a society of inverts, to find new substance in the spectacle of counterfeit relations.

Index